PSYCHOLOGISTS AND EDUCATORS PRAISE
YOU CAN DO IT!

"Useful. . . . An extremely valuable resource for parents. The content is clearly communicated, and the information will help parents. . . . This book 'cuts to the core.'"
—**Ann Vernon, Ph.D., professor and coordinator of counseling, University of Northern Iowa, and director, Midwest Center for Rational-Emotive Behavior Therapy**

"Parents and educators are today focusing on the necessity of a value-based education. . . . The You Can Do It! program is an excellent vehicle particularly for achieving such positive outcomes for students."
—**Pat Lynch, executive director, New Zealand Catholic Education**

"Filled with practical information. . . . I strongly recommend You Can Do It! Education."
—**Gilbert Losier, Ministry of Education, New Brunswick, Canada**

"Goes straight to the heart of parents' concerns. . . . Empowering and very heartening at a time when so many of them feel overwhelmed."
—**Marie R. Joyce, Ph.D., associate professor, head of social sciences, Department of Psychology, Australia Catholic University**

"An excellent guide. . . . I strongly recommend this book. . . . I have personally used many of these ideas with my own children."
—**Raymond DiGiuseppe, Ph.D., professor of psychology, St. John's University, director of the Graduate Program in School Psychology**

"YOU CAN DO IT! is an unusually effective program for young people who want to do well in school, in their social relations, and in other important aspects of their life.…I highly recommend it!"
—**Albert Ellis, Ph.D.**

"YOU CAN DO IT! presents an alternative to parents yelling at their children and counselors reviewing failure warnings.…Dr. Bernard's creative approach is an essential purchase."
—**Stephen G. Weinrach, Ph.D., professor of counseling and human relations, Villanova University**

"This is one of those rare books that is filled with timely, valuable, and common-sense approaches to what is sometimes a very difficult job in the modern world. Bernard provides all of us who are engaged in the school and child improvement business with many practical tips on how to work better as parents and with parents—tips that will pay off, no doubt, in students who achieve more at higher levels."
—**Carl A. Cohn, superintendent of schools, Long Beach Unified School District**

"Dr. Michael Bernard's thinking and his program are eminently sensible and based on sound principles of child development and psychology."
—*The London Times*

You Can Do It!

How to Boost Your Child's Achievement in School

Michael E. Bernard, Ph.D.

Illustrations by Roger Roberts

WARNER BOOKS

A Time Warner Company

If you purchase this book without a cover you should be aware that this book may have been stolen property and reported as "unsold and destroyed" to the publisher. In such case neither the author nor the publisher has received any payment for this "stripped book."

Copyright © 1997 by Michael E. Bernard
All rights reserved.

Warner Books, Inc. 1271 Avenue of the Americas, New York, NY 10020

Visit our Web site at http://warnerbooks.com

A Time Warner Company

Printed in the United States of America
First Printing: August 1997
10 9 8 7 6 5 4 3

Library of Congress Cataloging-in-Publication Data
Bernard, Michael Edwin
  You can do it : how to boost your child's achievement in school /
Michael E. Bernard
    p. cm.
  Includes bibliographical references.
  ISBN 0-446-67193-2
  1. Education—Parent participation. 2. Home and school.
3. Academic achievement. I. Title
LB1048.5.B47 1997
371.3'028'1—dc21   96-48245
                                           CIP

Book design and text composition by Spinning Egg Design Group, Inc.
Illustrations by Roger Roberts
Cover design by Andy Newman

ATTENTION: SCHOOLS AND CORPORATIONS
WARNER books are available at quantity discounts with bulk purchase for educational, business, or sales promotional use. For information, please write to: SPECIAL SALES DEPARTMENT, WARNER BOOKS, 1271 AVENUE OF THE AMERICAS, NEW YORK, N.Y. 10020

To the memory of my father-in-law, Danilo Rebula, whom we all miss very much.

Acknowledgments

This book would not have been possible without the contributions of the following people:

Colleen Kapklein, my editor at Warner Books, for her support of the book.

Roger Roberts, the extremely talented illustrator responsible for all the drawings in this book.

The many professionals whose names appear in the References at the back of this book and who have written about children and parents and about the importance of school-home partnerships.

Albert Ellis, founder of Rational-Emotive Behavior Therapy, for his inspirational theory and for identifying many of the Habits of the Mind that block achievement.

Marie Joyce, colleague and long-time friend, for our many hours of discussion concerning best practices in parenting.

Terry O'Connell and **Harry Tyler,** of the Australian Scholarships Group, for their support of You Can Do It! Education in Australia, New Zealand, and the United Kingdom.

Debbie Taylor, who as Program Director of You Can Do It! Education in Australia has spent many years in helping me promote my message to parents, teachers, and students.

Alan Merrie, for his efforts in helping to set up the You Can Do It! Education organization in Australia and New Zealand.

Paul and **Martha Hindle,** for their help in supporting the dissemination of You Can Do It! Education material and training programs throughout Canada.

Alexandra Bernard, who provides me with so much sunshine, laughter, and love.

Jonathon Bernard, for his love, fun, and sense of humor.

And **Patricia Bernard,** who in so many ways provided not only invaluable professional advice during the writing of this book, including its final editing but, in addition, unwavering love and support of myself and our family.

Table of Contents

Introduction	Parents Make the Difference	xi
Chapter One	Parent Update: Educational Underachievement	1
Chapter Two	Parent-Child SOS: Immediate Solutions for the Underachieving Child	26
Chapter Three	Not-So-Good Parenting Styles	46
Chapter Four	Best Parenting Practices for Achievement	62
Chapter Five	How Today's Teacher Helps Your Child Achieve	100
Chapter Six	Habits of the Mind for Achievement: Getting to Know Your Child's Habits	126
Chapter Seven	Destination Achievement: Helping Your Child Take the Right Bus	146
Chapter Eight	How Your Child's Interests Drive Motivation and Ambition	210
Chapter Nine	How Your Child's Traits of Personality May Contribute to Underachievement	230
Chapter Ten	How the Way Your Child's Brain Operates May Contribute to Underachievement	264
Chapter Eleven	Getting Homework Right	291
Chapter Twelve	Tutoring Boosts Achievement	313
Chapter Thirteen	Helping Your Child to Put Off Putting Off Schoolwork	331
References		349
Additional Resources		354
About the Author		357

Introduction

Parents Make the Difference

This book is written for the parents of children of all ages, and it contains a very simple message that I convey with many words and pictures. The message is this: Parents make a tremendous difference to their children's achievement. This book is all about knowing what you need to know about parenting, about your child's needs, and about educational achievement in order for you to do the things that make the difference.

If you have a child who has fallen off the academic tracks, or if you want your child to excel at school, what you do makes a big difference. This point needs to be stated repeatedly because sometimes, especially when our children reach adolescence, it feels as though we are not very important. This perception is wrong. Throughout your child's educational career, what you do and do not do has a big impact on the extent to which your child realizes his potential in school and in other extracurricular activities.

Many parents today still have the belief that it is the school's responsibility to educate their children, not their own. However, as we enter the twenty-first century, it is becoming recognized that the education of children is enhanced when there is a partnership between school and home. This book is about how parents can maximize their contribution to the education of their children.

In helping your child to be successful, it is good to begin relatively early in life. Laying the foundations with good parenting practice is a good insurance policy that can be cashed in when problems arise.

In working with many parents and children over the past twenty years, in reading the work of other parenting experts, and in my own experience parenting my two children, I have discovered some key ideas I believe you need to know in order to be able to encourage your children to achieve. I present these ideas in some detail throughout this book.

For example, you will want to keep an eye on your child's effort at schoolwork. Without a doubt, the more you can do to encourage your child to spend time studying and doing homework, the greater will be his achievement. Early on in my own professional career, I came to understand that in order to achieve in different areas of schoolwork, children need to be able to do work that they find boring, difficult, and frustrating. In this book, I refer to this capability as High Frustration Tolerance. I discuss why your child might not be putting in optimum effort on his schoolwork, and I provide you with many ways to motivate and encourage your child to do work he or she doesn't feel like doing (chapters 4, 7, and 13).

This book combines understanding with good practice. In order for you to optimize your child's achievement, you will need to be aware of different signs that your child might be underachieving at school (chapter 1).

One of the most interesting things I discovered from my own research is that achieving children think in ways that are different from children who underachieve. I acquaint you with ways to evaluate your child's Habits of the Mind (chapter 6), and I discuss ways in which you can directly influence your child's patterns of thinking (chapter 7). By teaching your child Habits of the Mind, you lay the foundations for achievement and emotional well-being.

You need to be guided by your child's unique characteristics in deciding how to go about encouraging his or her achievement. I present up-to-date information on how different personality traits influence achievement (chapter 9), and I describe how children's brains operate (chapter 10). I discuss how your child's developing interests need to be taken into account in planning educational and leisure-time experiences (chapter 8). I provide you with many new ways to look at your child, which will help you to be more precise in the way you go about helping your child.

Teaching today is no picnic. It is much more difficult to be an effective teacher today than it was years ago. I believe it is important for you to know something about good teachers and to know how you can recognize teachers who will maximize your child's success at school (chapter 5).

I also spend several chapters discussing what we have learned about how different styles of parenting influence children's motivation and achievement (chapters 3 and 4). This will help you to take a good look at your own parenting methods. I discuss the five key parenting practices that contribute to children's achievement: calmness, affection, firmness, involvement in education, and using motivational methods. I devote chapters to techniques that will help you manage your child's homework (chapter 11) and will help you get him to do schoolwork he doesn't feel like doing (chapter 13). A chapter on tutoring describes additional methods you can use to boost your child's achievement (chapter 12).

If you have a child who at this very moment is causing you significant concern about schoolwork, you can find solutions that you can use immediately (chapter 2). You might also like to turn to the last section of the chapter dealing with best practices in parenting (chapter 4) for a summary of some ideas of how you can boost your child's achievement.

The ideas in this book come from my extensive reading in the area and more than twenty years of experience in working with children and their parents. During this time I have founded You Can Do It! Education, an approach to parenting and teaching children that is designed to help all children achieve to the best of their ability. Currently, You Can Do It! Education materials (books, videotape, and audiocassette learning programs), which I designed for students, teachers, and parents, are being used in the United States, Canada, and England as well as in over 40 percent of high schools in Australia and New Zealand. (For a listing of available material, see the References and the Additional Resources sections of this book.)

The evidence is accumulating from studies that have examined the effectiveness of You Can Do It! Education: By changing the way we teach, parent, and motivate children, we can dramatically influence their enthusiasm and effort in school and help them to achieve to the best of their ability.

I have elected to use the word "child" to refer to school-age children enrolled in kindergarten through final year of secondary school. I also have tried to balance my use of the pronouns "he" and "she" in describing children who are either underachieving or who could excel even further in schoolwork.

I encourage you not to sit back and wait for achievement to happen, or to hope that any current problems will mysteriously disappear with the passage of time. Achievement is too important in your child's life for you to be only a spectator.

It is never too late to help a child who has a problem. You will be able to locate solutions in this book to help restore your child's motivation and hope.

If you take away at least one idea from this book that will help you help your child achieve in school and in life outside school, I will have been well rewarded. There is nothing more special for me than knowing I have had a positive influence on the achievement and happiness of children.

— Michael E. Bernard

YOU CAN DO IT!

CHAPTER

1

Parent Update: Educational Underachievement

All children are born to achieve. All have unique talents and extraordinary potential. All children have brains with tremendous capacities for achievement; the sky is their limit. And all children begin life with an unbridled enthusiasm for learning. I know that under the right circumstances, all will achieve. I am a strong believer that home and school and the community have the ability to discover the circumstances that will unleash the potential of each individual child. I know that with the will, we can provide the way.

Unfortunately, many students today are not achieving the results and success in school of which they are capable. Casting our eye into the urban and rural classrooms in the Western world, when we visit the schools of New York City; Davenport, Iowa; suburban Toronto, Canada; Birmingham, England; Paris, France; Melbourne, Australia; and Auckland, New Zealand, we see many students who have lost the motivation to succeed they had when they first arrived at school. Despite the best efforts of teachers, we see frustration, lack of interest, hopelessness, resistance, and boredom written on the faces of too many of our children.

Within a very brief period of our lifetime, as a result of the rapid changes in the family structure, the acceleration of technology, reduced employment opportunities, increased economic disadvantage, immigration, and other social, cultural, and political forces, we see that some very significant changes in our children call for changes in teaching and parenting that will help them not only to achieve to their capabilities, but also to enjoy sound emotional health and interpersonal adjustment.

One fact that is not widely recognized is that in education, there has been an incredible explosion of the knowledge base: what we know and what we expect children to learn. It has been estimated that the knowledge base of biology has expanded 60 to 80 percent over the past half century, yet the time for instruction in biology remains the same. I believe that many schools today, because of the increasing sophistication of the curriculum, are demanding more and more of children at an earlier and earlier age.

A CAUSE FOR CONCERN

Large numbers of children today arrive at school unprepared to cope with the pressures of the curriculum and unprepared to cope with the pressures of growing up. In addition, the emotional and learning needs of children are far greater and more complex than ever before. As a consequence, underachievement may well be on its way to becoming the norm rather than the exception.

Underachievement is a condition that knows no economic or cultural boundaries. Children from all socioeconomic strata and cultural backgrounds are failing to develop their potential. While it is true that economic disadvantage, limited proficiency in English, and cultural diversity place children at great risk for poor achievement in school, there is also a sizable proportion of children who, while not at risk due to poverty or language and cultural background, are not performing as well as they could.

Some children are very public in their underachievement. They rarely do homework, hang out with peers who show little interest in school, cut classes, have many absences from school, are a handful and a half to manage in class, fail many classes, and drop out of school. Other underachieving students are far less easy to observe. They easily blend in with other students. They bring their schoolbags to school, appear to listen in class, have fairly good attendance records, make some attempt to do their homework (frequently under pressure and conflict with their parents), and for the most part get passing grades. However, these quiet underachievers, the children who find it easier, more comfortable, and safer to set the high-jump bar low than to excel by setting it at a challenging height, occupy many seats in today's classrooms.

Update: What Is Educational Underachievement?

Educational underachievement means that your child's performance at school as seen in grades or test results is lower than what you would predict from your child's age, ability, and potential. Said another way, underachievement is a large discrepancy between what your child is capable of doing in school and what he is actually achieving.

Determining your child's scholastic capacities and potential in order to estimate the extent of her underperformance at school is not straightforward. Unless your child has received a test of scholastic aptitude resulting in a score comparing your child with other children of your child's age, your own observations, along with school reports, will form the basis for determining the extent to which your child is performing at a level inconsistent with his ability.

Children have different scholastic capacities to do schoolwork. Some are extraordinarily gifted in their capacities for the verbal and/or mathematical reasoning that make school learning a much easier experience than it is for children who have average scholastic abilities. Children with potential well above average are said to underachieve when their school grades and achievement test results fall in the average range. Children who receive grades of B and C when they are capable of getting As are considered to be underachievers. For other children who have average scholastic abilities, grades of B and C do not represent underachievement.

So in thinking about your child's achievement, you should consider his or her potential for academic learning. If your son or daughter is working hard and getting good but not outstanding results, your child is not underachieving.

Grades Don't Tell the Full Story

A good starting point for determining whether your child is underachieving is your child's grades, as commonly recorded in report cards. Generally speaking, there is cause for concern when low grades are combined with a high estimate of your child's scholastic capabilities.

Class grades are only one indication of your child's achievement. Another is her performance on local, state, or nationally standardized tests of achievement. For example, every year all students enrolled in Hillsborough County in Tampa, Florida, are administered the Stanford Achievement Test, a commercial test that evaluates student achievement in reading, math, and other school subjects. Throughout the country, some students take the Iowa Test of Basic Skills, while other students take the California Achievement Test. On these tests, your child's level of knowledge and skills acquired in different curriculum areas is compared with that of a large group of students from many different schools. It is quite possible that whereas your child's achievement as reflected in class grades is below the average for her own class, her performance on standardized tests of achievement may be above average for her grade level. She may also have a higher achievement test score than students in her class whose class grades are higher than hers.

So while your child can appear to be an underachiever when his class grades are used as a measure of achievement, when other measures of achievement are employed, he might appear to be an achiever. Children who do not like doing homework, but who still have learned the material taught in class, get penalized in their grades for their lack of application on homework.

What this all means is that you need to gather as much information as possible on your child's actual achievement rather than just relying on school grades. If your child's grades are low but performance on achievement tests is high, there is less cause for concern.

Is Your Child Underachieving? The Telltale Signs

For many different reasons, some of which I will discuss shortly, many children today set minimum goals for their schoolwork. They set the high-jump bar too low. They have figured out that by setting low goals, with minimum effort they can clear the bar and achieve their goals. By setting the bar a lot higher and by putting in a lot more effort to achieve their goals, they would receive better results.

A smaller number of children underachieve because their expectations for their school results are unrealistic; they set the high-jump bar too high. Under these circumstances, children come to realize that they will rarely achieve their goals, and, as a consequence, they stop trying. Children who have unrealistically high expectations may or may not have parents who have excessive expectations. Some children who are perfectionistic by nature appear to decide on their own, with very little parental prodding, that they must do things perfectly.

One of the most common signs of underachievement is the failure of a child to put in enough time and effort on his schoolwork. Research conducted at universities by many different scholars reveals the following: When students are actively engaged in academic activities at which they achieve accuracy or success at an 80 percent rate or higher, their level of achievement tends to be more consistent with their abilities. In other words, if your child is spending sufficient time engaged in schoolwork in which he is achieving lots of success, he will be an achiever. If your child is spending too much time socializing, is involved in too many extracurricular activities, is being assigned material that is too dif-

> **SIGNS THAT SUGGEST YOUR CHILD MIGHT BE UNDERACHIEVING**
>
> - performs much better on a test of scholastic ability than in school
> - performs well at one time and then does poorly at another
> - performs well in some subjects at school, such as English, but not in other related subjects, such as history
> - occasionally reveals in what he says or does good academic or creative ability relative to his usual performance
> - reveals poor self-image, chronic feelings of inferiority, and helplessness
> - fears mistakes and failure
> - rebels against limits, especially having to do homework
> - manages time poorly
> - sets goals that are too high or too low

ficult (or easy), or is not spending enough time in class actively studying her academic subjects, she will likely be an underachiever.

Further, what I have learned from working with countless children of all ages is simply this: For children to be successful, they must do work they find difficult and frustrating. It's not just effort and time on a task that's important. The effort must be put toward the things that a student finds tough if his level of achievement is to improve. I learned about the importance of High Frustration Tolerance many years ago from a boy named Andrew.

The Cutting Edge of Underachievement: Low Frustration Tolerance

Andrew came to me as a result of underachievement in math. His scholastic aptitude test results indicated that he wasn't reaching his potential, and his mother and teachers doubted whether Andrew would graduate from ninth grade.

In our first session, Andrew and I worked on his organizational skills. We cleaned out his locker and discovered several month-old, half-eaten sandwiches. We organized his notebook into sections and wrote out lists of items Andrew needed to bring to and from school daily to be better prepared for homework and class work. Within two weeks, Andrew was approaching his schoolwork in a more organized manner.

On the Monday following our first meeting, Andrew came to me with a glum look on his face; he had scored only 60 out of 100 points on his biweekly math quiz. We both knew he could do better.

This called for immediate and dramatic action. I assigned Andrew the task of increasing his effort on his math homework 20 percent over the next two weeks.

When I suggested this, Andrew replied, "Won't work. Tried that with Miss Smith last year."

"Andrew, this year it will work. In fact, I'll make you a bet. If your grade on your next math quiz doesn't go up after you put in twenty percent more effort, I will pay you two dollars; if it does go up, you pay me two dollars."

"Okay. I hate to take your money, but you've got a bet."

For the next two weeks, Andrew increased his homework effort so much that at the end of the first week, his mother called me and raved about my motivational talents. She said she had never seen Andrew work so hard on his math; he was even timing himself with a stopwatch!

I suggested that we wait for his next math quiz results before I collected the Nobel Prize for Motivation.

Two weeks after we made our bet, Andrew came into my office with an ambivalent smile on his face, his hand open ready for payment, and a score of 59 on his math quiz.

I was dumbfounded. How on earth could more effort not produce better results? I was ready to resign from the Nobel Academy.

"Andrew," I implored, "tell me how this happened."

Andrew, who wanted to win the bet but wanted to please his mother with better grades even more, launched into his explanation: "Well, before this silly bet, I would do the ten math problems I had to review each night. I would finish the first and second problems easily. The third and fourth were tougher, and the fifth problem was usually so hard that I'd give up. In the past two weeks, I would have my ten math problems to do. I'd do the first and second problems easily; the third and the fourth were a little bit harder, but I'd get through them. I'd start the fifth, but that was too hard, and I'd give up. But then I remembered: 'Twenty percent more effort.' So I went back and checked the first problem, the second problem, and the third."

What I discovered from my work with countless Andrews (and Ellens) is that underachievers successfully dodge work they do not feel like doing. The Parent Reflection Sheet "Achievement and Your Child," presented at the end of this chapter, will help you determine whether your child is underachieving.

Oh Those Boys

Underachievement appears to be much more prevalent in boys than in girls. In one sense, this should not be a total surprise, given the much higher incidence in males of reading difficulties, attention deficit hyperactivity disorders, and conduct disorders. What does rattle my sensibilities and challenge my curiosity is that in the regular classroom of students who do not have any discernible learning or behavioral disorder, boys are underperforming to a greater extent than are girls.

It is easy to offer different though equally plausible explanations for the apparent maleness of the problem. It has been argued that boys are born with more feisty biological temperaments that resist the best efforts of school and home to instill the self-discipline required for seatwork and concentrated study. It has been argued that girls, as a result of different early socialization experiences geared toward pleasing others and, perhaps, different brain chemistry, bring to their schoolwork a greater desire to please the teacher and a greater capacity for self-discipline than do boys.

Other experts have proposed theories that deal with a mismatch between the sex-role-related characteristics of male students and their largely female teachers. The argument goes that due to their socialization and, in particular, their relationship with their mothers, boys are more antagonistic to the efforts of their female teachers directed at control, management, and discipline than are girls.

At the upper grade levels, where essays and written examinations are more in evidence, it has been suggested that girls may outshine boys due to their advanced capacity to display in written form what they have learned in school.

Of course, many girls, especially when they reach adolescence, demonstrate underachievement. Some attribute underachievement in teenage girls to their socialization; looking pretty and deferring to boys is the norm. There is plentiful research that indicates that girls in postelementary grades are less active in their academic participation in class, including asking questions of the teacher. If they ask questions and are seen by their peers to be "smart," girls may receive considerable hostility and ridicule from other classmates, boys and girls alike. In order to protect their daughters from pernicious sex-role social and peer influences, some parents are enrolling their daughters in single-sex private high schools.

Relatively Few Underachieving Students Are Learning Disabled

In some states such as California, students are identified as having learning disabilities when a significant discrepancy is observed between their scholastic ability and their achievement. However, over the years, learning disability has been typically defined as a disorder in one or more of the basic learning processes that students need to learn to read, write, and do arithmetic, including short-term memory problems as well as auditory and visual deficits.

The criteria used to identify students with learning disabilities are precisely the same criteria that are used to identify underachievement. At first glance, it would appear, then, that every child who underachieves has a delay or disorder in one or more basic processes of learning. However, fewer than 10 percent of students have delays of inhibitions in basic learning processes, whereas more than 40 percent of students are evaluated by their teachers as underachieving. What this means is that most underachievement is influenced by student characteristics other than learning disabilities. These are made up of a host of personality factors, including those that have a direct impact on student motivation.

The Antiachieving Peer Group

A recent study of twenty thousand high school students has revealed that the peer group your child hangs out with has a tremendous influence on your child's academic achievement. If your child hangs out with peers who believe that getting by is good enough, and if there is substantial pressure to underachieve, this is not good news for you or your child. In fact, some peer groups of minority students dismiss academic achievement altogether as "thinking white."

Not all peer groups are bad. If your child has academically oriented friends, it is likely that he will do better than if he spends his time with peers who get into trouble.

WHEN IT COMES TO STUDYING, CHILDREN TAKE THEIR CUE FROM THEIR FRIENDS

"At least by high school, the influence of friends on school performance and drug use is more substantial than the influence of parents."

—L. Steinberg, S. Dornbusch, & B. Brown, *Beyond the Classroom*

As much as you can influence your child's choice of friends, you will want to encourage him to join an academically focused peer group who spend time studying together and who encourage each other to get good grades. While this is easier said than done, we know that this is one of the important ways that you can help gently steer your child toward achievement.

The Statistics

It is somewhat difficult to arrive at an accurate estimate of the total percentage of students who are failing to realize their potential at school. The Office of Economic Development in France, which analyzes international trends, places the number of students who are achieving poorly at 40 percent of the total student population. Poor achievement and underachievement are somewhat different. Underachieving students may receive poor grades in school. Some may receive pretty good grades in school, but they could be doing a lot better.

> **EDUCATIONAL UNDERACHIEVEMENT:**
> **AN INTERNATIONAL EPIDEMIC**
>
> 30–40 percent of all students are underachieving
>
> 70 percent of underachieving students are boys
>
> 30 percent of underachieving students are girls
>
> These findings are based on questionnaires administered to principals/head teachers, teachers, mental health practitioners of students in grades 1–12 in different parts of the United States, England, Australia, and New Zealand.

In my professional workshops and lectures, I have asked teachers to provide me with their own estimates of the numbers of students in their class who are underperforming. As you can imagine, their estimates vary greatly and depend a lot on the type of school and specific characteristics of the student population. In schools in more financially well-to-do areas, where many parents are professionals, the estimates of underachieving students tend to be between 20 and 30 percent. Teachers who work in schools in economically disadvantaged areas and in schools with large numbers of students from diverse language and cultural backgrounds estimate that as many as 80 percent of their students are underachievers.

It is my view that these estimates of underachievers tend to be on the conservative side. It is sometimes very hard to know if a child could be doing better in her schoolwork than her current performance indicates. The quiet underachiever is difficult to detect.

The Up- and Downsides of Achievement

Achievement is the act of accomplishing or finishing something successfully especially by means of exertion, skill, practice or perseverance.

There is a difference of opinion heard in professional circles, as well as in more informal discussions among parents, as to whether our society places too much importance on achievement and whether we are pushing our kids too hard or not hard enough. You may well have heard of the horror story of a mother hiring a hit man to rub out a high school cheerleader to ensure her daughter's place on the squad. In my own professional practice, I have worked with adolescents suffering under unrelenting pressure from parents and schools to excel. At the other extreme, there are far too many parents who show insufficient interest in their child's education, and, as a consequence, their child's motivation to learn is lower than it might otherwise be.

There are distinct pleasures and satisfactions for children that accompany the process of acquiring skills and knowledge, both in school and beyond, that once mastered come to represent achievement. The process of achieving, while not always pleasurable, accompanies the process that Abraham Maslow calls self-actualization. Achieving is a part of being human and growing. Feelings of confidence, efficacy, and optimism accompany achievement. Accomplishments and their lack also provide children with information about what their abilities are. They can use this information to decide on the direction to take in their lives, to pinpoint areas for self-improvement, and to judge where to commit their time and resources.

I love to see my own children achieving things great and small. Achievement is healthy and leads to happiness, to a sense of well-being and being alive.

There is a downside to achievement. When children use their own or others' achievements as a yardstick to measure their self-worth, when their achievement in comparison with that of their peers is used as a basis for self-evaluation and a source of ego gratification, then

> **CHILDREN LOVE TO ACHIEVE**
>
> In a recent survey, almost 50 percent of children chose "being smart" (school success, achievement) over athletic ability, having money, or beauty.

achievement is loud, noisy, and can be harmful to the development of their human spirit. When children develop the fear of not achieving good grades in school because adults have failed to help them focus on the pleasures of trying and have graded them on ability rather than effort, curiosity, and involvement in learning, their quest for achievement can cause harm.

We have to be both proactive and reactive in providing the optimum environments for children, to encourage them to continue learning and achieving and not to turn off. When we do not, children begin to resist learning. Children turn off when they "take personally" their slower progress in school. In this book, I advocate teaching all children Self-Acceptance as a Habit of the Mind, to inoculate them against the sometimes extreme pressures of parents, teachers, and peers to do well and to deal with the times when they are struggling. Achievement requires as much struggle in overcoming the obstacles along the way to success as it does pleasure in getting there.

Of more practical importance, achievement provides greater opportunities for children. It opens the doors of our society to job opportunity and financial reward.

"At-Risk" Kids or "At-Risk" Environments?

The term "at risk" indicates that we have to take special notice of children with special needs; particularly, their economic, language, and cultural backgrounds. Unless we take steps to help address their particular needs, these children have a high probability of not doing as well in school as they could. A child at risk is a child whose unique needs are not sufficiently understood and catered to in the school and home environments. Indeed, it makes sense to use the term "at risk" to describe all classrooms and homes that are not attuned to unique individual student needs.

The children at greatest risk for underachievement are those who grow up in poverty. Severe economic disadvantage is associated with insufficient money for basic educational materials. Many children coming from this background receive little encouragement for achievement, are not read to when young, and do not often participate in after-school and other extracurricular activities such as trips to museums and libraries. Many children from these homes lack school readiness because of the lack of parental support that extends throughout their schooling. During the first few years in school, these children are likely to experience failure in reading. By third grade, these children become bored, discouraged, and resistant, and they begin to lose interest in school.

> **RESEARCH STUDY FINDS PARENTING PRACTICES MAKE A DIFFERENCE IN STUDENT ACHIEVEMENT**
>
> The findings from a research study indicate that high-achieving African-American children from low-income families had parents who stressed the value of education for their future, monitored their academic progress closely, and fostered an internal sense of control over and responsibility for academic outcomes.

Of course, many children from poor homes do well at school. These children have parents who commit themselves to their children's education and instill in them the value of studying hard. There is also a group of children, called resilient children, who, despite coming from economically disadvantaged homes, possess the personal qualities such as optimism and perseverance that are necessary for accomplishment at school. Resilient children tend to have someone who has taken an abiding interest in their welfare. The fact remains, however, that poverty takes its toll on children's achievement.

Both the language and cultural backgrounds of children can place them at a disadvantage. Some children in this country who come from homes where a language other than English is spoken face tremendous barriers at school due to not being able to understand the language of mainstream instruction. While bilingual education and other instructional methods designed for children from different language backgrounds are meeting the needs of some of these children, other children from families with limited English proficiency are finding schooling hard going.

Children from culturally diverse backgrounds (e.g., Native American, Mexican American) may bring with them traditions of social communication, styles of communicating, and distinct motivational needs (e.g., cooperative group work, listening and writing rather than orally responding to teachers' questions, group assessment and reinforcement rather than individual), which unless catered to by their school and teachers will make it much more difficult for them to achieve their potential.

The good news is that solutions abound for helping all children achieve; we know what we need to do to help. Unfortunately, the resources and time needed to implement some of the solutions are a bit tricky to find.

News from Asia

Of interest is the recent research of scholars who compared the levels of achievement of students in the United States with those of students in Japan and China. Harold Stevenson and James Stigler, in their book *The Learning Gap*, reported on five major studies, funded by the National Institutes of Health and the National Science Foundation, that indicate that our children are lagging behind in achievement compared with students in Japan and China, and that we may be losing ground. This appears true for different age levels and different academic subjects. After studying and rejecting the explanation that large class sizes and television are the major cultural differences that might explain the differences in achievement (there are large class sizes in China; Japanese children watch the same amount of television or more than their U.S. counterparts), these investigators cited child-rearing practices that seemed to explain differences in achievement.

> **PARENTS MAKE THE DIFFERENCE**
>
> No matter what the age of the child, parents are the most important influences over a child's achievement in school—even more important than peer group or teachers! Parent involvement in education and their encouragement of their child directly influences the extent to which their child excels at school. Parents also play a vital role in helping an underachieving child get back on the academic playing field.

In studying the influence of child-raising patterns on achievement, Stevenson and Stigler noted the Chinese conception of childhood as a time that is divided into two periods. The first, the Age of Innocence, is the period from birth through the age of six. During this period, children are thought to lack the cognitive maturity to learn academic skills, are indulged by their parents, and are encouraged to develop social and exploration skills. When their children enter elementary school and the Age of Reason, Chinese parents' expectations for their children change. At this age, children are taught by their parents that education is their number one priority. Home becomes a place for study and learning rather than playing. The child-rearing practices of both Chinese and Japanese families change as their children enter the Age of Reason and begin formal schooling. Asian families mobilize themselves to provide their children with the environment and lessons that will help children grow up. They believe that it is too much to expect teachers to be able to handle this learning process, and that if their children are to learn the skills necessary for them to succeed in school and life, parents must have a great deal of involvement.

In contrast, many Anglo-American parents do not distinguish between these two periods of child development. Rather, a child's entrance into school represents a time for a significant change in the parent-child relationship. Whereas many Anglo-American families go to great lengths to prepare their children to be cognitively ready to meet the academic challenges they will encounter on the first day of school, they withdraw much of the time and energy they devoted to preparing their child for school, hoping that the foundations for learning have been laid. Almost breathing a sigh of relief, they back off the educational role with their children, handing the children over to the school. Unlike their Japanese and Chinese counterparts, elementary-age Anglo-American children do not experience strong parental demands for homework completion and academic accomplishment.

The important point that Stevenson and Stigler make in their analysis and review is not that we should adopt Asian child-rearing practices. Rather, their analysis highlights the important role that parents play in the socialization of their children and, in particular, the development of an orientation to education that promotes motivation and achievement.

Your concern, of course, is probably the same concern as mine. Is your child doing as well in school as he could? You may have clear indications from his teachers that he is not doing his work. Or you may have a parent's intuition that your child's creative abilities are not being adequately tapped at school.

> **FOOD FOR THOUGHT**
>
> John Wilmot, Earl of Rochester, wrote in the late 1600s, "Before I got married, I had six theories about bringing up children. Now I have six children and no theories."
>
> As John Wilmot discovered, one of the most challenging aspects of having children is figuring out how to parent effectively without a manual to guide parents through their children's various stages of development. Parents need help to solve problems unique to each child's character and disposition—especially problems in school. Parenting is a great test of our intestinal fortitude, as our children often provoke in us a variety of intense feelings.

Who Is to Blame?

It seems that when we have a problem that affects us, we humans have a natural instinct to seek someone or something to blame and punish. The epidemic of educational underachievement is no exception. If you ask teachers who is to blame, many blame parents. Upper-grade-level teachers blame lower-grade-level teachers. Parents often point their fingers at teachers. It is easy for parents and teachers to blame the government for insufficient resources, large class sizes, and politically driven and rapidly changing school policies. Parents and teachers can blame students for their lack of motivation and overall poor attitudes toward learning and school. Children who underachieve blame their teachers, parents, and sometimes, they even blame themselves.

My view is that no one is to blame for the problem. Children today are much more challenging and difficult to raise and educate than were children of my generation. We all have the responsibility for making a difference in reducing the problem. Since the early 1980s, schools have made efforts at renewal and reform to better educate children. Schools and teachers have great responsibility in developing a school culture and classroom learning environment that meets the diverse needs of all our children today. In addition, we parents have to be very active in helping our children deal with the pressures and demands of schooling today. The skills and knowledge necessary to help our children achieve in the twenty-first century are the substance of this book. Our children need to be more responsible for working in ways, and with the effort necessary, to be as successful as possible. Together, we will change the trend.

The Good News!

Sometimes you might think there is nothing else you can do for your child to help him perform better at school. You might feel like you are in a big black tunnel with no light at the end. Feelings of doom and gloom, frustration and anger, worry and panic may be preoccupying your own emotional life and, perhaps, clouding somewhat your ability to invent new solutions to help get your child on her way.

Many students re-cycle into achievement at various stages of their schooling. Some do so because of a favorite teacher who maintained an interest and faith in them over the years and whom students remember as making a big difference to them. Others re-cycle because their parents were sensible enough not to withdraw them from extracurricular activities as punishment for their poor performance at school. For some students, the confidence they receive from their sailing, surfing, computer skills, drama class, or horseback riding enables them to take the risk of trying once again in their schoolwork.

FACTORS THAT REVERSED UNDERACHIEVEMENT

1. child allowed to pursue out-of-school interest (computers, community theater, disc jockey)
2. parent attitude (never gives up on child, still loves and supports child, did not kick child out of home)
3. child takes a challenging class
4. child knows what long-term goals he wants to achieve (does what is required in the short term to reach goals)
5. a special teacher (past or present, whom child keeps visiting)
6. self-confidence (success in outside school activity leads child to think "If I can do that, I can achieve that")

The Search for Solutions: Your Child, the Individual

I have learned from many years of experience that children are different. What works for one child to help motivate, maintain interest, and promote achievement does not work for another. I've had many parents tell me "I treat all my children the same. It wouldn't be fair otherwise." I usually counter by stressing the importance of treating each child fairly, taking into account each one's own uniqueness and needs. Sometimes, by treating a second child the same as we treated the first, we are treating the second child unfairly. At different stages of their education, to overcome problems of poor motivation, some children require plentiful support and more reinforcement for successfully completing their work, while others require less reinforcement for its successful completion.

In talking with teachers, I introduce the idea of rotation, which best describes my general approach for helping the individual child. For many children, specific factors or circumstances need to be in place in order for them to feel motivated to achieve. By exposing an underachieving child to different types of curriculum and instructional methods, to tutors or mentors, to more or less intrusive parenting, to different peers, to different extracurricular activities, to cooperative parent-teacher efforts, each of which takes into account the unique needs and characteristics of your child, you will discover the individualized set of solutions that enables your child to unleash his potential. The word "rotation" emphasizes the need to change what you offer, to provide different sources of educational stimulation, until you notice your child's star starting to rise. Rotation is the key to unlocking the potential of all children.

In chapter 2, I present a road that will lead you to some immediate solutions for a child who could be doing better at school but is not.

**PARENT REFLECTION SHEET:
ACHIEVEMENT AND YOUR CHILD**

1. How many of these signs of underachievement does your child show?

Has your child ever performed better on a test of scholastic ability than in his schoolwork?	___ yes ___ no
Has your child's school results ever dropped off after having done well at an earlier time?	___ yes ___ no
Does your child do well in some subjects (e.g., English) but not in other related subjects (e.g., history)?	___ yes ___ no
Has your child ever revealed to you that she has more academic or creative ability than she shows in her schoolwork?	___ yes ___ no

2. Place a circle around the characteristics below that describe your child.

    lacks confidence   fears failure
    fears making mistakes   rebels
    poor time management   gives up easily
    sets goals too low   sets goals too high

3. Describe the attitude and behavior of your child's peer group toward achievement.

_____

_____

_____

_____

PARENT REFLECTION SHEET (continued)

4. Estimate your child's academic ability/potential (check one).

Ability/Potential

	Extremely High	High	Average	Below Average	Well Below Average
English (reading, spelling, writing)	___	___	___	___	___
Math	___	___	___	___	___

Provide your child's grades on his/her last school report. If your school doesn't provide letter grades, try to estimate (check one).

Grades/Achievement

	Extremely High (A)	High (B)	Average (C)	Below Average (D)	Fail (F)
English	___	___	___	___	___
Math	___	___	___	___	___

If there is a significant difference between your child's ability and achievement, your child may well be underachieving.

CHAPTER 2

PARENT-CHILD SOS: IMMEDIATE SOLUTIONS FOR THE UNDERACHIEVING CHILD

Over the past few years, you have probably tried many different things in an effort to help your child become more successful at school. What you tried depended on the nature of your child as well as your style of parenting. If you have a dependent or perfectionistic child, you may have tried to encourage your child to relax and not worry so much about mistakes or not doing things perfectly. If your adolescent is rebellious, you may have tried and possibly lost the battle of wills. For the easily frustrated child who appears to you to be bone lazy, you may have resorted to bribes and threats that didn't seem to be effective for very long.

As a parent, I know the pain of seeing children underperform at school. I know the worry of "What if he doesn't do well enough to compete in the competitive world of tomorrow?"; the anger of "Why doesn't she do more homework, and why is it so sloppy?"; and the guilt of "As the parent, I should be able to help my child." I know how incredibly frustrating it can be to try many different solutions without finding the key to unlocking the puzzle: why a child is not excited about learning, and is receiving poor grades. I also know how easy it is for your own frustration to produce negative effects on your relationship with your children, which, in turn, makes it much harder to be of any help to them when they need it.

This chapter will offer you some very practical and immediate steps to take to change the course of your child's efforts and achievements in school. They have been taken by many parents who have helped change their child's chronic pattern of underachievement. You may have taken some of the steps before. What is new is that the first step starts with you.

Mirror, Mirror on the Wall . . .

One of the most beautiful experiences for me is when one of my children is being successful in any area of endeavor, including schoolwork. I feel like a proud peacock, and whether I deserve it or not, I pat myself on the back for being a good "Pops." And when things are going well, I would be all too happy to look at myself in the mirror and take stock of my parenting. My inner glow from my child's success helps me to look and accept my parenting style, warts and all.

When things aren't going so well, when my kids get up to mischief or their schoolwork drops off, I feel like smashing the mirror. But I have learned not to. I have learned that I wasn't born with all the tools I need for parenting and that by looking at myself, however difficult it is to examine my reflection, I learn a whole lot.

In the section that follows, when you catch sight of an area of your parenting that needs work, remember, you are a member of a pretty big club. There is no need to hit yourself over the head. Accept yourself. No one is born the complete parent!

In order for your children to change their approach to and attitude toward their schoolwork, you may catch sight of something in the mirror that you may have to change. There is a very basic principle that applies to all sorts of interactions among people: We cannot really make anyone else do what we want. We can only change our behavior toward them and hope that if we do so, they will be motivated to change.

Alice, mother of Jane, had become increasingly exasperated with her daughter's lack of application to her schoolwork. Her last report card contained grades no better than C. "All she does is defy me. She refuses to do any homework. All I end up doing is yelling at her, and she slams her door and turns up her CD. Then I really explode." This is an all too common scenario in the homes of underachieving children and their parents.

Trapped in a cycle of child not doing work followed by parent getting upset followed by child getting upset and doing less work followed by more parent upset, many parents find it impossible to achieve success in taking the positive steps necessary for their child to change.

In order for Alice to be effective in helping Jane, she had to change herself first. She had to learn the specific tools of parenting that are vital in order to maintain an overall positive relationship with a child who is not doing as well in school as she could. Use the questions that follow for personal reflection. They will help you see yourself in the mirror. Your own self-examination will help you pinpoint changes you may need to make before you implement a plan for helping your child at school.

Do you express strong negative feelings toward your child concerning schoolwork or other aspects of his behavior? The beginning point for Alice is to calmly go about her efforts at problem solving without giving herself an additional emotional problem in response to the practical problem of Jane not doing her work. I will spend some time later in this book helping you de-stress yourself about your child's stressful behavior. In general, to remain calm, don't take your child's behavior personally. Focus on your child's behavior, not on your child. It is almost impossible for you to help your child in any way while you are extremely angry, anxious, or guilty. If you are, do whatever you have to do to tone down your own emotional temperature.

Do you focus too much on what your child cannot do and is not doing? Parent nature is such that we all tend to keep an eagle eye on our children's weaknesses and turn a slightly blind eye to their strengths. There is nothing more disheartening to a child already discouraged about schoolwork than to hear negative remarks from a parent. Attention to your child's weaknesses will result in your child closing the door to your problem-solving efforts. If you find that your child has closed the door, redirecting your eagle eye toward those things that are positive about your child and her schoolwork will help to pry it open.

Do you listen to your child without interrupting, offering advice, or being negative when your child talks about a problem? As children enter adolescence, they look less toward you for resolution of their problems than they do toward their peers. That is not to say they do not appreciate your support. It's just that they will be more private about their issues than they were in an earlier stage. At any age, listening to them offers them the opportunity to see the ball off the rebound. And they appreciate you for not telling them what to do. Listening is one of the most important things you can do for your child.

Do you show your child love on a regular basis? Children are extremely sensitive about the words their parents use when they are being disciplined or lectured to about not having done homework or doing poorly at school—especially around report card time. Boys in particular take their mothers' words to heart! For some children, a little criticism goes a long way and can result in your child's concluding that he or she isn't loved. Children who perceive the loss of their parents' love are not good candidates for self-improvement. Whether your child falls into this category or not, it is very important in building and maintaining a strong relationship with your child to show your child with your words and actions that despite any problems he or she has with schoolwork, your love is constant.

Do you provide your child with clear expectations concerning the importance of doing schoolwork to the best of her ability, including, if necessary, rules for homework? The one style of parenting that research cites as extremely harmful to a child's development of self-discipline and achievement is permissive parenting. By "permissive," I mean that the child grows up without very much structure and with few boundaries in evidence for what is and what isn't appropriate behavior. Most children, especially in their younger years, require guidelines that spell out their responsibilities for homework and schoolwork, including how much homework will be done, when the homework will be started, and its quality. Whereas some children may rebel against parents who are overcontrolling and restrictive in their rules, many children who are not living up to their potential require not only a climate at home that supports their learning but also structure, rules, and direction.

Do you consistently follow through with rewards or penalties previously discussed with your child in regard to when your child does not live up to his or her responsibilities? As I will discuss later on, the setting of rules and the use of rewards and penalties need to be done with care in order not to interfere with the development of your child's internal motivation. However, it is very clear that when parents are not firm in backing up their words with actions and are inconsistent in their enforcement, their children are more likely than not to underachieve. This is because most children have tendencies toward testing limits, avoiding homework, and having fun. Our rules at home concerning schoolwork provide us with the main means for teaching our children the self-discipline that is necessary for success at school. Consistency and persistence are the keys to ensuring that home rules for homework bring out the desired degree of self-discipline.

Do you encourage your child's curiosity, persistence, involvement, and pleasure in schoolwork? Sometimes you can achieve the wrong results with your children, even though for all intents and purposes everything would appear that you and they are on the achievement track. If you are a believer in the benefits of positive reinforcement for the behavior of your child, be careful. An overreliance on rewarding (or penalizing) your child for school achievements can take away from your child's internal motivation. As I'll discuss in chapter 4, in order for your child to become an internally motivated learner, your efforts sometimes need to be directed toward the process of their learning (curiosity, persistence) and not so much the outcome.

Do you show interest and become involved in your child's education? It is clear, especially with younger children, that the more you are involved at home and school, the more your child will value the importance of education. Older children's interest in school also requires your active interest. The more interest you show without actually doing the work for your child, the more interest your child will have. In chapter 12, I discuss ways in which you can tutor your child.

Do you hold realistic expectations for your child's educational achievement and future choice of college or job? It is vital that your expectations for your children are reasonably consistent with their abilities, interests, and personalities. Children of parents with excessive expectations can give up prematurely because they feel helpless and hopeless. Low expectations can produce an equally diabolical effect. Children who are capable of much more than is expected of them can drop the achievement ball due to lack of challenge or self-doubt. If you are uncertain how realistic your expectations are, seek the advice of a counselor or school psychologist who may, besides providing good advice, be able to assess your child's scholastic aptitude and interests.

Do you teach your child helpful ways to think about schoolwork and especially about work that is hard or boring and that he doesn't feel like doing? I have discovered that parents can help their children remain motivated, confident, organized, and committed to doing their best by teaching the Habits of the Mind using a variety of methods (outlined in chapter 7) that lay the foundations for achievement and enable children to fully realize their potential. Teaching your child the Habits of the Mind I call Self-Acceptance, Risk Taking, and Independence can help reduce any feelings your child may have of doom, helplessness, and anxiety about lack of school success and increases confidence. Optimism, High Frustration Tolerance, and Internal Locus of Control for Learning contribute to your child's persistence and to motivate himself to do work he does not feel like doing. Parents who teach Goal Setting, Time Management, and High Frustration Tolerance help their children become organized. Reflective Problem Solving, Tolerance of Others, and Tolerance of Limits establish a basis for your child in managing conflict and staying out of trouble. Many parents do not know how to work actively to instill in their children Habits of the Mind that can help when they are not around.

Jane is now getting Bs and As in her schoolwork, and her mother, Alice, is thrilled. While there is still the occasional difference of opinion about homework and curfew, they no longer fight the homework wars. Alice found it difficult to even look at herself in the mirror, and when she finally peeked, she really didn't like what she saw. What she saw was a mother who, while loving her child, was so exasperated and anxious about Jane's poor results in school and lack of application that she had ceased using the skills she had used with her other children. Upon seeing her reflection, she decided it wasn't all that great, and that before she could expect her daughter to change, she herself would make some changes.

Today, Alice is much happier with her reflection. She no longer flies off the handle so quickly with her daughter. She is much more patient, offering a listening ear rather than parent advice. Alice has decided to accentuate the positive, and she is helping Jane with her self-acceptance so that she doesn't take bad marks or mistakes so personally. Jane is reveling in the changes she is seeing in her mother and has decided to give her schoolwork another chance.

Problem Solving in Action

Once you have had a good look at ways in which you can change to help your child change, you can begin to focus more on solving the problem: Your child is not doing as well in school as you are pretty sure he or she can. If there is a discrepancy between what you think your child is capable of doing and what your child is actually achieving, it's time for action!

There is an eight-step method for increasing the time your child is actively engaged in schoolwork. As in any problem-solving activity, you will want to keep an eye on whether the method is working. Signs that the method is working include: more application and time that your child devotes to schoolwork; better grades on reports, quizzes, and other class evaluations; a more positive attitude toward going to school and doing homework; better attendance; fewer fights about homework; and more favorable reports from someone at school who is monitoring your child's progress in various classes or subjects.

Does this method help all children achieve to their potential? Definitely not! A lot depends on your child's characteristics and your parenting style. Younger children who have been raised in a home with not too many rules and expectations will tend to flourish if you take the steps.

If you have an older, very creative child who has grown up in a structured home with many rules and consequences in evidence, the recipe for change may be somewhat different. As I'll discuss in chapter 8, some children require less structure and more autonomy in order to develop more academic motivation. In addition, better matches between adolescent interest and curriculum often hold the key to unlocking these children's potential.

I'll also have a lot more to say in chapter 11 about a strategy that involves backing off and giving your child total responsibility for doing schoolwork, and bearing the natural consequences of not doing the work. If your child is a teenager, and if you have already tried and persisted with a structured program of interventions such as the one mentioned above, it may be that your child's difficulties stem from having too much support at home and not having to face the music. In my discussion of homework management, I will outline the reasons for handing the responsibility for schoolwork over to your child. For many parents, letting go of responsibility is extremely difficult.

If this method does not hold appeal for you, don't panic. This book is all about providing you with many different alternatives for helping your child. For the moment, I present a method that has been successfully used by countless parents in helping inspire their children to achieve to their capabilities.

Step 1. Call a family meeting. The interaction of your family may have to change, to remove any barriers that may interfere with your child's doing schoolwork and to provide your child with necessary structure and support. You will need the support of your husband, wife, or significant other to enlist the cooperation of all family members. Any existing conflict between other family members and your child needs to be discussed and resolved. This becomes uppermost in your family's list of priorities. Criticism, teasing, and fighting must cease. The right of your child to privacy for study needs to be observed. Extra adult time may be needed to help your child get organized. You may need to show increased interest in the specifics of your child's schoolwork. Schoolwork requirements may need to be clarified and enforced.

You may need to sweeten your own relationship with your child in order to remove any unhelpful tension between you, so that your child is prepared to work with you to solve his academic problems. Extra time, privileges, being more positive, and other changes may be necessary to start the program off on the right foot.

Step 2. Schedule a parent-teacher-child conference. Once you have your family ready, enlisting the cooperation and expertise of one or more of your child's teachers is the next step. Contact your child's teacher or the teacher in whose class your child is having the most difficulty. Over the telephone, explain that you'd like to have a meeting that includes your child. Indicate that the purpose of the conference is to help you solve a problem: Your child is not achieving as well as she could.

On the telephone, be sure to be calm and not aggressive or accusatory. Many teachers are extremely sensitive to the concerns of parents. Some will view your request as indicating that you think they are to blame. Even if you believe they are partly or fully responsible, you get nowhere by saying so. One approach is to say that you do not think your child is very happy at school. In this case, you may share your own genuine feelings of worry.

When you have a meeting, the first thing to do is to make sure that your child is actually underachieving and/or lacking in motivation. Simply because you believe your child is underperforming, it is not always the case that she is. Especially at older ages or because of your closeness to the problem, you may not be the best judge. For example, sometimes your expectations for your child can be unrealistically high. In these instances, the quality of your child's schoolwork may, in fact, be appropriate for her age, class, and capabilities. If this is the case, then it is you who has the problem, not the child! Keep an open mind when listening to the teacher's impressions of your child's work, and when the teacher tells you whether it could be improved. Be prepared to modify your judgment if the weight of evidence the teacher provides is that your child is performing up to scratch.

More often than not, however, you will be a pretty good judge of whether your child could be doing better, especially if he has not put in sufficient time on homework or if his work is careless. See if you can be as concrete as possible in describing your concerns about your child. Indicate, for example, that you believe the neatness of written assignments is less than the best your child can produce, or that your child's written work has not been edited for errors before being handed in.

Explore various alternatives with the teacher and your child about different ways schoolwork can be designed or assigned that would be more compatible with your child's interests, learning style, or motivational style. Your child's teacher has options to make the material being assigned more difficult or easy, to employ material that is in tune with your child's interests, to provide different peers with whom your child could work, or to offer alternative ways to assess your child from those typically used. Your child's teacher will normally have worked with other students who share similar characteristics with your child. She can use her experiences as a guide for redesigning instruction.

Sometimes, an incentive scheme may need to be put into place temporarily. This involves your child's receiving stars, marks, or tokens for performing at a certain level. Once a certain total has been reached, your child can "cash in" the tokens for a predetermined reward that your child would enjoy receiving for his hard work. For more specific information on setting up a contract with your child and the teacher, see the section in chapter 4 that deals with motivation.

Once a plan has been agreed to by all members of the conference, it will be important to establish a regular means of communication with your child's teacher to monitor progress and the effectiveness of the plan. At least once a week, there should be a two-way communication via telephone or note so that each of you communicates the extent to which your child is completing the work successfully.

Some parents will say to me "My child will not attend a meeting with his teacher and refuses to follow any plan." It is important to remember who should be calling the shots. It is you who is Head of State, not your child. Explain to your child that you have no choice but to take steps necessary to help her improve her schoolwork. That's what parents do. Children have a similar responsibility to maintain involvement in their schoolwork. Just as when they are sick, they have to visit the doctor and take medicine, so, too, when schoolwork drops, they have to temporarily take certain "medicines" that might not taste so good. Be confident and persistent. In the face of total disobedience and resistance, you may have to explain that you will be going on strike in the transportation department until you get some cooperation.

As my uncle Arnold is fond of saying, sometimes you have to treat your child like you would a horse: "lightly, politely, but firmly."

Over the next week or two, judge the effectiveness of the plan drawn up and see whether a different approach needs to be tried. Keep trying new solutions with your child's teacher until you find one that works.

Step 3. Help your child manage homework time. Depending on your child's degree of self-discipline for homework, you may well have to be not only the Head of State but the Field Marshal, ensuring that your child is using time effectively and completing homework. No matter what her age, your child will need to decide ahead of time when she is going to do her homework, the amount she will get done, and that it will be of a high standard. You can help your child get organized by reviewing together when all assignments and tests are due and scheduling the exact day and time she is going to do her work. Underachieving children who rush their work at the last minute frequently lack, or fail to use, time management skills. Many do not decide ahead of time when they will begin their homework and how long they will study. Rather, they wait until they are in the mood before they start to do their homework.

Help your child locate or design a semester or monthly calendar, a weekly timetable, and a daily schedule that she can use for this purpose. Volunteer to help your child break down long-term projects and assignments into simpler steps and to help her estimate how long each step will take. By scheduling each step ahead of time, she will become more focused and organized. More detailed information on how to teach your child time management as a habit is contained in chapter 7.

Step 4. Make sure that your child does work that he finds hard and/or boring. Most progress will be made when your child applies himself to the work that is least fun and that he usually avoids. It is time for your child to take the bull by the horns, and you need to follow through and persist in making sure that your child has not evaded the

work. It is okay for you to take charge and say to your child—no matter what his age or size—that it's his responsibility to do the work. Explain that the more effort he puts into the unpleasant work, the more pleasant his results will be in the long term.

Step 5. Find someone to take an interest in and/or tutor your child. One of the most powerful solutions to the problem of underachievement is individual attention. This is as true of a six-year-old in first grade as it is of the eighteen-year-old in the final year of school. This recommendation has two parts.

First, make sure that your child reports on a regular basis to someone who your child feels is interested in her overall welfare and progress in school. This special person is someone who provides general support and guidance for your child over the school year. If your relationship is strained with your child—or your partner has a strained relationship with the child—you should select someone else to take on this responsibility, such as a favorite uncle, grandmother, or neighborhood family friend. Sometimes, the business community sends mentors into schools to spend time with individual students.

Second, if your child has missed out on learning some basic skills in reading, math, or other subjects that are necessary for current or future study, he will profit enormously from tutoring. When my son was younger, I found that when his teacher introduced some new material in class, he really needed to go through it again at home with me in order for it to sink in. In addition, during his middle elementary years, I discovered that his performance greatly improved by my providing him with an intensive review and practice of basic math or reading skills just before the end-of-unit or end-of-semester test.

If your child is in secondary school and studying material beyond your grasp, an older sibling can sometimes provide tutorial assistance. Also, you may be able to locate in your school or local newspaper a low-cost college or high school tutor. Try to select a tutor with whom your child would enjoy working. I'll have much more to say on tutoring in chapter 12.

Step 6. Provide frequent reinforcement for your child's efforts. It will be very important for you to turn your attention away from what your child has not been doing and to focus on current and future progress. Put away any expectations you may have. Any forward progress made by your child needs to be encouraged. Down with negatives! Smile, be enthusiastic, and leave sarcasm in the closet.

How can you motivate your child to do work he doesn't feel like doing? In chapter 13, I will present several different techniques you can teach your child to overcome procrastination in the area of schoolwork. At this point, however, you need to know the power of the principle of reinforcement.

The principle is simple, but it communicates one of the most important cause-and-effect relationships discovered in the study of human behavior. Basically, if you want to increase a particular behavior, present the person with positive consequences (reinforcement) immediately after he has engaged in the behavior. The reinforcement you select should be some type of praise or activity that you know the person appreciates and values.

Alice knows that her daughter Jane appreciates verbal praise, so she praises Jane fairly often when she notices Jane putting in effort on work she finds boring or hard. Showing your child that you value persistence as much as the final product of the effort will help your child to value effort. When you see your child doing the right thing, offer praise.

Step 7. Monitor ongoing progress of your child for all to see. Sometimes, when change is occurring slowly, it is difficult to see. Without appropriate measuring instruments, we would have no knowledge of the minor increases in the average air temperature worldwide in the latter part of the twentieth century. In a similar fashion, you will need to be able to detect and communicate to your child the small increments in what your child is learning, as a result of the redesign or styling of work requirements and her renewed effort. During the parent-teacher-student conference, it will be important for you to ask this question: "How can we keep track of progress on a daily basis?" Sometimes your child's teacher will provide daily ratings, on a five-point scale, of your child's application to schoolwork or homework. She might also provide the results of regular quizzes that reflect current mastery of material in the curriculum unit under study.

It is important that all concerned parties (including your child!) can see any progress that is being made in schoolwork. The more concrete you and your child's teacher can be in helping your child actually see improvements in the quality and quantity of work, the better.

For certain subjects, designing a graph to represent visually the level of your child's work as she begins to improve is a good way of showing your child the extent of her improvement as a result of increased effort. Helping your child see progress helps challenge her idea that "It doesn't matter how hard I try, I'll never be successful."

Step 8. Pat yourself on the back for trying. Do not take your efforts for granted. The more you invest in your child—even if there is not a lot to show immediately—the better off your child will be. And in the long term, both you and your child will reap the benefit of trying hard to solve the current problem. No matter how difficult it seems and feels, you are the most important person in your child's life. Your help makes a huge difference in the future for your child. Persist, and give yourself credit.

CHAPTER 3

NOT-SO-GOOD PARENTING STYLES

You may not have given that much thought to the connection between your parenting style and your child's performance at school. After all, traditionally, home is where love, nurturance, socialization, and other basic needs of children are fulfilled. It is the institution of school that has the responsibility for the formal education of children. Many parents have the perception that because teachers are trained to teach, and they are not, there is little in the way of a positive contribution that they, the parents, can make to their child's achievement. Nothing could be further from the truth!

In fact, you are a most important influence on your child's educational aspirations and achievement. In chapter 4, I will bring to light five parenting practices that will aid you in the process of laying the foundation for your child's achievement. These practices can positively influence your child's level of achievement.

First, it is important to examine some parenting styles that are associated with underachievement and poor motivation. Most of us mortal parents can find something in the way we parent on our worst day that is unhelpful to our children. Sometimes, as we go about the most challenging and difficult job in the land—laying the foundations for achievement and happiness in our children—we can fall into bad habits. Our style of parenting may not produce the results we hope for. The practices described in chapter 4 work best when you've had a chance to become aware of and to change aspects of your parenting that are not so helpful.

Let's begin with a brief look at different parenting styles that are associated with children who underachieve. Once again, you'll have an opportunity to see your own style of parenting in the mirror. Many of us bring about the wrong results in our children, despite our best intentions! We often parent the way we were parented. Whenever I present this list of parenting styles, I am provided with glimpses of my own parenting style that need some polishing.

Overprotective Style

Some parents today, for different reasons, take a great deal of responsibility for the affairs of their children—too much responsibility. Whether it is sorting out fights between siblings, screening potential friends, or making sure their child's homework is done, they hover like a helicopter over their child. One of the main concerns of these well-meaning, overprotective parents is to make sure that nothing bad befalls their child. These parents may subconsciously believe that their child should never be frustrated, that it is always harmful and awful to her self-esteem when she experiences mistakes, failure, criticism, or does not know what to do. These parents rescue their child from frustration and difficulty. Overprotective parents can end up doing their child's assignments in order to ensure that he doesn't suffer the discomfort of handing in work that is not as good as it could be.

> **RESEARCH STUDY FINDS BEING TOO PROTECTIVE OF YOUR CHILD HAS NEGATIVE CONSEQUENCES**
>
> In a study of forty-three middle- to upper-middle-income Caucasian families, overprotective parenting behavior has been shown to be significantly related to children's low self-concept, provoking negative behaviors and poor school functioning.

Children of overprotective parents can become sensation sensitive, fear making mistakes, lack confidence in their own capacities, avoid challenging and competitive situations, and come to depend on their parents and teachers to rescue them from having to do difficult work. The more responsibility these parents take for their child's schoolwork, the less inclined their child is to assume such responsibility.

It is the overprotectiveness that is the problem. In order for children to develop the autonomy necessary for achievement, they need to be able to tolerate a fair amount of pressure, frustration, and mistakes. It is important to protect your child from situations in which there is a high likelihood of significant distress. However, your child may need you to take the schoolwork ball out of your court and throw it into his. Your child benefits from doing difficult schoolwork on his own, even if it's tough to do, and even if it is not at the level of other students' work.

Permissive Style

If you were raised by strict parents, or if you are member of the Woodstock generation, you may be reluctant to impose rules on your child. You may have the conviction that children shouldn't be frustrated. Rules frustrate children, of course. You may believe that rules inhibit creativity. Alternatively, while you may have communicated expectations to your child concerning homework requirements or what constitutes unacceptable behavior, you might not be firm in making sure that your child conforms to expectations.

I know that I do not always keep after my children when they have done unsatisfactory work at school. When I'm tired or too busy, I sometimes allow my children too much latitude.

Of all the parenting styles I will describe, permissiveness is the one that research clearly finds associated with educational underachievement. Children are born with no ability to put up with frustration and no self-discipline. They have to have what they want now and cannot delay gratification. Still, children need progressively greater amounts of frustration tolerance in order to achieve. Fortunately, for many children, maturity helps. With increased cognitive capacities, many children begin to be able to tolerate not getting what they want and having to do what they don't want to do. Some children, however, are not able to acquire on their own the self-discipline necessary to fulfill all of their parents' and teachers' expectations for work.

One of the most important influences on a child's self-discipline is a structure of rules at home that clearly spells out right and wrong and, specifically, expectations for schoolwork.

If you see yourself as being a bit permissive in your parenting, you may notice that at least one of your children appears to have an allergy to hard work. This is more likely to be the one that was born with a feisty, demanding, easily frustratable temperament—the one who as an infant was the most difficult to calm. This may not be the case with your other children.

Without structure and firmness, some children develop a frustration phobia. They do not have the Habits of the Mind that are required to do work they do not feel like doing. In addition, giving too much freedom and power for making decisions to young children may contribute to a rebelliousness later on. As these children become adolescents, they continue to exercise the right given to them by their parents to decide what they do with their time and money, and whether they do their work or not. Once you give up your power and authority, it is sometimes impossible to get it back when you notice your child abusing hers.

Not-So-Good Parenting Styles

Parenting children who are extremely frustratable by nature requires much more of parents than does parenting those who readily adapt to adult-imposed expectations for schoolwork. If you and your child fall into the first category, you will need to incorporate the art of being firm into your parenting practice. Firmness is discussed in chapter 4.

Powerless Style

Not too long ago, my wife told me of chatting with a neighbor as our young daughters were riding their bicycles together. My wife was surprised that while our daughter had her safety helmet on, our neighbor's daughter was not wearing hers. My wife told me she had asked her friend, "Why isn't Joan wearing her helmet?" Joan's mother turned to my wife and said, with a look of frustration and disappointment, "I can't get her to put it on."

My wife was surprised. She couldn't understand why, for the sake of safety, our neighbor, who was a very loving and caring parent, could not get her child to put on her helmet. I wasn't surprised; I was appalled. My children know that they never have access to their bikes unless they have helmets on. End of discussion.

For a variety of reasons, some parents today feel helpless to influence their children's behavior. Strong-willed children are especially adept at challenging and abusing the implicit authority of their parents. Unless we have a strong hand on the controls to begin with, they will quickly learn to take the controls themselves. When children are younger, some parents feel uncomfortable and anxious about exercising their authority because they know that if they do, their children will get upset and angry, and may reject them. With adolescents, unless we maintain our own authority, they can run out of control.

As a society, we are more tolerant of excess and less tolerant of authority than were previous generations. Fewer role models in the media and on family TV demonstrate that it is okay to say no to your kids and mean it. For many reasons, it is hard for many parents today to take a strong stand with their children.

Needless to say, a powerless parenting style results in a child's feeling that he has power to decide what he will do and what he will skip. If your child has natural scholastic aptitude, loves school, and aspires to high levels of achievement, then there is no problem. However, in school subjects in which your child anticipates boredom or failure, or when she has the option to do things that are enjoyable like socializing or playing on the computer, she will likely exercise her own authority to dodge schoolwork and have fun. Once again, firm parenting is a key in helping bring out the best in your child.

Authoritarian Style

Do you have many rules that you impose on your children without too much discussion? Do you see yourself as the boss at home and believe your children should do your bidding? Do you find yourself disciplining with anger? Do you find yourself saying humiliating things that you later regret when your children break rules? Do you withdraw your love as a punishment for disobedience? Is your nonverbal communication aggressive when you believe your children have done the wrong thing? Could you be described as being harsh at times?

If you are answering yes to many of these questions, you might come from the old school of parenting, in which parents ruled the roost and children were to be seen but not heard. While this style of parenting can result in children's getting their work done out of their fear of the consequences for substandard work, it often doesn't and it can have some undesirable side effects.

Children of authoritarian parents often feel inadequate and anxious, never sure of where they stand in the eyes of their parents, and doubting whether they can live up to their parents' expectations. Anxiety and feelings of self-doubt are not a good foundation for achievement. Another fallout from being too authoritarian is that your child may decide to get back at you for what she perceives as unfair treatment by underachieving at school. She might think "I'll pay you back for yelling at me. I won't work."

Sean was a sixth-grade boy who was referred to me because he was uncooperative around the house and was not handing in any homework. A fairly large child for his age, Sean was known as a bully. In a meeting with his parents, it wasn't difficult to determine that his father was an even bigger bully than his son. Sean's father thought that his family existed to do his bidding. He would yell and abuse all family members, including his wife, when they failed to perform.

In my private discussions with Sean, it became apparent that he believed that "No one can make me do anything I don't want to do." He had decided this at an early age. Because he didn't find reading easy, and his parents and teachers wanted him to read, he dug his heels in. I was curious about the origin of his belief. Was there a specific incident that stuck out in his mind? "I was in third grade," recounted Sean. "My father was hitting me because I didn't want to go with him somewhere. I made up my mind that no matter how hard he hit or yelled, I wasn't going to do it."

If you have evidence that you are a bit on the authoritarian side and that you are not producing the results you want, you are halfway to making changes. It took over six months of regular meetings with Sean's father for a change to begin. He began to see that while he got what he wanted in the short term, in the long term, problems with his son were continuing. It took another three months of Sean's seeing dramatic changes in his father's behavior before Sean started to consider the negative consequences for himself of not doing his schoolwork merely because he thought his father wanted him to do it.

Overemotional Style

Some of the strongest and most intense feelings we have concern our children. It is quite natural, normal, and human for us to feel upset when our children do not do their schoolwork, receive poor grades, or fail to

Not-So-Good Parenting Styles

excel in areas of their strength. However, I have learned an extremely important lesson concerning the inability of parents to influence their children: If you get too upset with your child on a regular basis, it is extremely difficult for you to modify her behavior. I'm talking about degrees of upset. Concern, disappointment, and annoyance are negative feelings that do not interrupt your thinking process and do not hold your child's problem in place.

However, when you are highly anxious, guilty, or furious with your child for what she has or has not done: a) it is very difficult for you to think creatively to solve the problem, b) you tend to do the same thing you have always done in the past even though it has not worked, and c) your upset can provide your child with secondary gain, making it harder for your child to give up her behavior.

Let's say your daughter decides to stop trying in algebra because it's boring and she doesn't like the teacher. Her lack of effort results in a primary gain; she is getting out of doing something she doesn't want to do. However, if she also receives a secondary gain of getting you upset, it will be harder for her to decide to change her behavior.

The principle to follow: Do not get *too* upset about your child's lack of progress in school. If you find yourself going over the deep end, either remove yourself from your child until you calm down, or put on a calm face. In the following chapter, I'll provide some strategies to manage stressful times, such as when your child brings home a bad report card.

Excessive Expectations Style

If you tend to nag your child a great deal about not doing better at school than he is ("Come on, you can do better than that!") and if your child perceives he can never please you, you will be placing your child under an unfair amount of stress. If you are seldom satisfied with what your child is accomplishing and find yourself pointing out to your child how much better other brothers, sisters, or friends are doing, you can be heading for trouble.

Recent research indicates that adolescents whose parents hold expectations that they cannot fulfill and who are subjected to extreme pressure to perform may come to believe in the futility of ever pleasing their parents. At this point, they give up trying hard at school.

You have to follow your child's lead. Why would a parent hold unrealistically high expectations of a child? It may be because the par-

> **RESEARCH FINDS ASSOCIATION BETWEEN MIDDLE-CLASS PARENTING AND ADOLESCENT UNDERACHIEVEMENT**
>
> In studying eighty-seven eleventh and twelfth graders enrolled in a large well-to-do suburban high school, researchers found that upward-striving patterns of parenting (parental pressure, nagging, criticism, expectation that child does well in all subjects) were significantly associated with underachievement. Apparently, the prodding and pressuring of these adolescents aroused reactions of anger, resentment, and rebellion.

ent has a false sense of a child's true capabilities. If you are unsure, you might consider having your child tested at school. Perhaps your child is at the end of a long line of achieving brothers and sisters, and you unthinkingly apply a standard of achievement because it holds for other members of your family. This might be quite inappropriate for you to do. I've known parents who live much of their lives through the accomplishments of their children. The better their children perform at school, the more accomplished the parents feel. High expectations that are realized by a child in school can lead to a parent's temporarily feeling good. However, worry about the child's not performing well the next time and the stress of trying to get him there make the pleasure extremely short-lived.

Whatever the reason for the excessive expectation, you need to know that it often produces an effect opposite from what was intended. Your child underachieves due to his despair or resentment about expectations set for him that are out of his sight.

Unsupportive of School Style

There isn't a parent I know (including myself) who cannot find fault with some aspect of his child's school or teacher. Sometimes we think we have a lot to complain about, and at times we do. There is too little or too much homework. The teacher doesn't show enough interest in your child. Assignments are not relevant to your child's interests and concerns. The teacher treats every child in her class the same way. The teacher is weak in discipline, or too harsh. The existence of problems, while undesirable, is, unfortunately, inevitable.

Many teachers have told me that when a parent criticizes the school or teachers on a regular basis in front of her child, the child begins to lose respect for school and for the authority of the teacher. Children whose parents knock school can stop taking school seriously and lose interest. My wife and I occasionally have to bite our tongues to stop ourselves from being critical of something at school in front of our children. If you have a concern or stronger objection, it is best to discuss the matter directly with your child's teacher or with someone in the school's administration.

It is my belief that parents have an obligation to show respect for teachers as a way of educating their children that teachers are profes-

Lack of Expectations Style

Some parents do not communicate to their children high enough expectations for achievement and the value of education. They demonstrate little interest and involvement in their child's education. Some parents believe it is up to the school to discharge these responsibilities. Some of these parents who fail to communicate to their child any expectations for their child to do well in school, and who fail to support and reinforce their child's educational efforts, may themselves not have much education. Some parents simply do not understand how important it is for their child to know that her parents expect her to work hard at school and to perform to the best of her ability.

Poverty appears to be a factor for some parents who do not encourage their child's education. There is little money at home for books and educational materials. When young children are not educationally enriched, they enter school not ready to cope with the curriculum. Expectations are often expressed in the different types of involvement and support parents provide. The lack of educational outings, discussions about schoolwork, or provision of a suitable study area can lead to a child's acquiring the belief that school is unimportant and that nothing of value is taught in school. Lack of educational interest and poor achievement are frequently due to parents who do not hold or communicate high expectations for school learning to their children.

Before moving on to what we know about how to parent for achievement, it is time to reflect upon aspects of your own parenting style that might need to be fine-tuned.

**PARENT REFLECTION SHEET:
KNOW YOUR PARENTING STYLE**

1. (a) Describe the type of parenting you received as a child.

   _____

   _____

   (b) What effect did it have on your attitude toward the value of education and the importance of achievement?

   _____

   _____

   (c) What effect did your parents' style have on your own parenting style?

   _____

   _____

2. Place a check next to the style(s) of parenting you see in the mirror on your bad days.

   _____ Overprotective   _____ Authoritarian   _____ Lack of Expectations

   _____ Permissive   _____ Overemotional   _____ Unsupportive of School

   _____ Powerless   _____ Excessive Expectations

3. What effect does this style(s) have on your children, including their level of motivation and attitudes toward school and homework?

   _____

   _____

4. What are some changes you can make in your parenting to eliminate the blemishes in your parenting style?

   _____

   _____

CHAPTER 4

BEST PARENTING PRACTICES FOR ACHIEVEMENT

For the most part, schools today cannot do it without you. In other words, they can do it better with you as an informed partner in the collaborative process of educating your child. I am not suggesting that you have to do the actual teaching. For the most part, this is the province of schools. However, there are a whole host of other things you can do to help your child to excel at school. If you have a child who is underachieving, much can be done to get her back on track.

> **RESEARCH STUDY FINDS HOME-SCHOOL PARTNERSHIPS WORK**
>
> Research has demonstrated that when teachers and educational administrators are strongly committed to drawing parents into their children's education, the academic outcomes for their children can be very positive.

I have spent many years discovering how parents can help their children achieve at school. My study of the experts' research findings has

BEST PARENTING PRACTICES

shed light on exemplary parenting practices that are associated with children's motivation and achievement. I have also spent many years working with individuals and with groups of parents, most of whom

---

A VIEW OF HEALTHY FAMILIES

Well-functioning families are groups of people who are able to accomplish the task of aiding the personality and social development of their offspring. In an effective family system, the parents comprise a cooperative working team that operates as the "executive" unit of the system, and the children are a subsystem of clearly secondary power and status. The tasks of the parental subsystem are to work cooperatively in socializing the children and to be able to modify rules and expectations as children grow older. The task of the sibling system is to offer its members the opportunity to learn how to negotiate, cooperate, share, compete and make friends with peers.

—N. Woulff, "Involving the Family"

were seeking solutions to the problem of their children's underachievement at school. In the parent education classes I developed in Australia, as well as in those classes we offer in our Educational Psychology Clinic at California State University, Long Beach, I continuously seek feedback from parents about the practices they find most beneficial in helping them to raise achieving children. Finally, I have over a decade of experience in parenting two children and have—along with my wife—tried out a whole host of ways to parent for achievement.

Below are five of the most important parenting practices that encourage children's achievement. I'm sure I haven't covered them all. I'm sure that there are some practices that you strongly believe make critical differences for children's achievement that are not on my list. Hold on to your favorites, and if you think I've missed something in my search that is critical, write me and let me know.

You will notice that the practices deal both with your relationship with your child and with your involvement in your child's education. I will provide some tips on how to incorporate each practice into your own style of parenting.

One final point: There are different roads to take to Rome. There are achieving and happy children whose parents do not use all of the following practices. Sort through the practices, and see which have greatest appeal to you. Some of the practices are common sense and some may already be incorporated into your parenting. There's nothing like a little confirmation that you're on the right track.

Best Practice 1: Calmness

I have already made the case, in discussing the Overemotional Parenting Style, that too much parental upset in the face of our children's problems is not, generally speaking, a good practice. Especially if you want your child to improve the effort and level of his schoolwork, before your child will change, you yourself will have to change. If you find your emotions running amok because of how passionate you are about your child and because of your anxieties about his future, it's time to rein them in.

I am not saying that you should be passive. Sometimes you have to take a strong, forceful stand with your child. However, when you do, it is important that you be calm, not furious.

How do you stay relatively calm when you see that your child isn't doing homework, isn't showing much interest in school, or has come home with an unsatisfactory report card? Most parents I have talked to do not find counting back from 10 all that helpful. Learning to relax using deep breathing and other physical techniques can be of great assistance. There are a variety of methods for reducing your overall level of stress, including recreation, exercise, and a healthy diet. When we are very stressed out, it is far harder to remain calm and patient with our children.

Many parents find the ABC method extremely valuable for remaining calm with their children. The ABC method requires you to have a clear idea about the cause of your emotional upsets.

Suppose there were ten parents sitting around the room discussing their children. If all were asked how they would feel about their child repeatedly not doing his homework, you would get quite a range of emotional reactions. A few parents might admit to being quite angry or even furious, while others would be merely annoyed. A few parents might be quite anxious, while others would feel more concerned. One or more of the parents might express various degrees of guilt. In summary, you would find a range of emotional reactions and upset about the same event—a child repeatedly not doing homework.

We normally think that our child's behavior makes us upset ("He makes me so angry or guilty or anxious"). If that were true, however, then every parent in the room of ten parents would feel exactly the same about a child who repeatedly did not do homework. This example shows that parents feel different amounts of emotional stress, which I'll label C (Consequences), in the presence of the same child behavior I'll label A (Activating Event).

Our children's behavior never directly causes our emotional upsets, because if it did then all parents would feel the same about their children's behavior.

The question I'd like you to consider at this point is: Why does the same child behavior (Activating Event) lead to so many different emotions (Consequences)? Why do parents feel differently about the same source of stress? When I've asked this of parents, the typical response is "Well, we're different from one another. We've had different histories and experiences." I then probe further and ask, "How does your unique past and personality influence you today in relation to your child?" After some thought, parents gradually begin to see that what makes them different is the way they perceive, evaluate, and think about their child's behavior. In the ABC model, the B stands for beliefs, your thoughts about, and attitudes toward your child's behavior, the A.

A = Activating Event (what happens)
B = Beliefs (thinking about what happens)
C = Consequences (how you feel and what you do about what happens)

What has been known for many years but is not often enough discussed is that our calmness or emotionality concerning our child's behavior has as much to do with our own way of thinking as it does with our child's behavior.

In the past forty years, Albert Ellis, a psychotherapist in New York City and founder of Rational-Emotive Behavior Therapy, has helped millions of people understand and manage their own emotional upsets, using a range of techniques for helping people detect, challenge, and change their own stress-creating thinking. It is a wonderful power to have—the power to control your own upsets with your children when they are not doing the right thing (homework) or doing the wrong thing (fooling around).

> **WAYS TO INCREASE YOUR EMOTIONAL STRESS**
>
> 1. Lack of emotional responsibility ("My child can really upset me by acting that way.")
> 2. Exaggerating the badness of your child's behavior ("My child's behavior is awful and terrible.")
> 3. Global rating of child ("My child is horrible/stupid.")
> 4. Low frustration tolerance ("I can't stand my child's behavior.")
> 5. Self-downing ("Because of my child's failing, I think I'm a failure.")
>
> —P. C. Bernard & M. E. Bernard,
> *The You Can Do It! Little Book for Parents*

I once asked a group of teachers how they stay calm when one or more of their students refuses to work. A school principal succinctly summarized what sometimes takes me four hours of talking or ten pages of writing to explain: "I tell my staff not to take the student's behavior personally and to focus on the child's behavior, not the child."

These Beliefs about Activating events will lead you to emotional Consequences of calmness.

A = child isn't doing homework; gets a poor grade in school
B = "Don't take it personally. His behavior is bad, but he is not his behavior."
C = calmness

Here's how we often subconsciously upset ourselves about our children and lose our calmness as parents:

Think of a time when you found yourself totally stressed out about what your child was doing or saying—or not doing or saying. Your child's behavior should be one that led you to being either furious, guilty, or panicked. At the time when you were really emotionally stressed, how bad was your child's behavior, on a scale of 1 to 100? Rate the degree of badness of the behavior on the following scale, where 100 is the "worst thing that could be happening," 50 is "medium bad," and 0 is "not bad."

0	10	20	30	40	50	60	70	80	90	100
not bad					medium bad					the worst

Now look at the Catastrophe Scale, below.

See if you can come up with other examples of events that could happen in the world or to you that you can add to the list of real catastrophes (90–100), things that would be bad or somewhat bad but no catastrophe (10–90), and things that are not really too bad (0–10).

Catastrophe Scale

real catastrophes	**100**	example: nuclear war, death of family member
	90	
	80	example: house fire, no one hurt
bad but not catastrophic	**70**	
	60	
	50	
somewhat bad	**40**	example: minor car accident
	30	
	20	
a little bad	**10**	example: flat tire
	0	

Using this scale of catastrophes, would you still give the same badness rating to your child's behavior as you had previously? Place a "Y" on the Catastrophe Scale where you would now rate your child's behavior. Place an "X" on the scale by the number where you rated it earlier. Is there any difference between your first and second set of ratings?

> **WISDOM OF THE AGES**
>
> Epictetus, a Roman philosopher in the second century A.D., wrote: "People are not affected by events but by the view they have taken of events."
>
> Shakespeare captured this essential message in his words: "Things are neither good nor bad but thinking makes them so."

Many parents who complete this activity see that when they are faced with problems with their children, they blow the problems out of proportion. This is a quite normal aspect of the way we think. The good news is that once you recognize any tendencies you might have to exaggerate the badness of your child's behavior, you can change your own perception. By not blowing things out of proportion, you stay calmer.

A related stress-creating thought pattern is "I can't stand it," which you can apply to any aspect of your child's behavior such as: "I can't stand it when he doesn't do his work"; "I can't stand it when he has a negative attitude"; or "I can't stand it when I hear he fools around in class." Your idea that "I can't stand it" serves to brainwash you. If you say it often enough to yourself, you believe it, without really questioning whether you can stand it or not. Telling yourself "I can't stand it" takes you from emotional calmness to emotional upset.

To challenge what Albert Ellis calls your "I-can't-stand-it-itis," which causes you to upset yourself about your child's behavior, you can ask yourself this question: "Can I stand things I do not like?" When my children show me assignments they have rushed through, I have to work hard at reminding myself that even though I do not like it when they rush their work and do not follow rules for neatness and doing the best they can, I indeed can stand it.

When I feel that I cannot stand my child's behavior, or that something terrible will happen to my child, I have learned not to trust the feeling. I use the Catastrophe Scale to help me keep things in perspective. At times when I feel my upset with my children starting to get the better of me, I remind myself "Even though I don't like it, I can put up with my child's not doing the right thing." If you take on the general belief that you can put up with things you do not like, you will have a Habit of the Mind that will help ensure calm parenting.

Another Habit of the Mind that can help inoculate you to the inevitable frustrating and difficult behavior of your child is called Self-Acceptance. Sometimes you can lose your calmness with your children when their behavior leads to this perception: "Because my child is failing in English, I have failed. I'm responsible. I should have done more. I'm hopeless."

WAYS TO DECREASE YOUR EMOTIONAL STRESS

1. Emotional responsibility ("I choose to upset myself about my child's problems or behavior.")

2. Keeping things in perspective ("While my child's behavior or problem is bad, it certainly isn't the worst thing that could happen.")

3. Focus on the behavior, not the child ("While I really don't like my child's behavior, that is only one part of my child. My child is still okay.")

4. High frustration tolerance ("While I don't like my child's behavior, I can stand it. I'm not going to faint.")

5. Self-acceptance ("It is impossible to rate my total self-worth on the basis of my child's behavior.")

—P. C. Bernard & M. E. Bernard,
The You Can Do It! Little Book for Parents

If you imagine yourself as a cube, made up of an unlimited set of smaller cubes, that grows with you as time goes on, and if each of the smaller cubes represents one aspect of your parenting at one point of time in your life, you can see that it never makes sense to rate yourself as a good or bad parent or person on the basis of that one small cube. It never makes sense to say that all of my cube is bad because I wasn't this way or that with my child at a certain point in my career as a parent, or because my child is having problems.

This line of thinking helps you to accept yourself with your imperfections as a parent and person and to tackle rather than deny or run away from those aspects of your behavior that require changing in order for you to meet your goals as a parent.

Learning to recognize and modify your own stress-creating thinking is tremendously powerful in helping you become a calmer parent. Knowing that the center of your emotions is you, not your child, is a real breakthrough. By staying calmer about your child, you will be in a great position to accept things about your child that are difficult or impossible to change, to have the courage to change those things that you can, and to have the wisdom to know the difference. Sound familiar? Serenity is synonymous with calm parenting.

Best Practice 2: Affection

One benefit of being or becoming a calm parent is that your child feels more loved and

> **IS LOVE THE ANSWER?**
>
> A few years ago I was chatting with a colleague who was an international expert on child rearing and parenting whose main message was that parental love was all that was necessary for young people to grow up happy and successful. As we were discussing his latest book, his two young children ran through the backyard, where concrete had just been poured to extend the patio. Catching sight of his children running through the concrete and leaving large footsteps, he yelled at the top of his voice, "Get out of here! Now look what you've done, you little rotten kids!"
>
> I looked up at John and said with some surprise, "John, what about love?"
>
> He looked at me and said, "I love my kids in the abstract, I just don't love them in the concrete."

is less likely to feel rejected. Children whose parents discipline with lots of anger can often experience depression, low self-esteem, and hostility. A good solid foundation for your child's achievement is unconditional parental love. It is important for your child to know that while you might dislike some parts of her behavior, you still love and respect her. A word I use to describe the feeling of tenderness, warmth, and love is affection.

Even the so-called experts make their mistakes. While it may be easy to know how to deal with our children, following through consistently is another case entirely.

How often you communicate love is important too. You may get so negative and so stressed out about your child that you may come across to your child as very unloving. Some children—especially young ones—require frequent shows of parental love. Parents express their love in different ways. Some are fairly constant in the area of physical affection, including hugs and kisses. Other parents communicate their love by spending time with their children and are not so public in their expression of caring. Affectionate parents share a few characteristics in common. Chief among these is treating their child as a person with the same rights as any other person. We call this respect. Treat your child as you would treat anyone else. Afford your child the same consideration and dignity. If you do not believe in slavery, do not treat your child like a slave. If you do not like to be bossed around, do not boss your child around. The same rules of social convention apply to one and all.

You communicate respect by offering your child limited options and choices in how he goes about his life. "Do you want to brush your teeth before or after the show is over?" gives your child some say. Children need to feel they have some say over their lives, including how they spend their time. Give them choices and options.

An important way for you to communicate affection is to be supportive of your child. When young adults were recently asked which aspects of their relationship with their parents they found most supportive and helpful, they mentioned four: a) physical affection, b) sustained physical contact (sitting on knee), c) companionship, including shared time together, and d) being available when needed. Just because your teenager isn't spending hours discussing what he did in school, this doesn't mean that he doesn't value your being around. While it may appear that his peer group occupies 99+ percent of his waking time, he still needs to have your support, especially during those difficult times.

When you listen to your child, you communicate affection. At times, when your child has a problem, he will need someone to listen and not offer advice. Many well-meaning parents are too quick to jump in with what they would or would not do rather than hearing their child out. Practice just reflecting back what you hear so that your child can see his own ball off the rebound and decide himself what to do.

Earlier this morning as I was thinking about the importance of listening as a way of communicating warmth to children, my daughter announced she hated P.E. Rather than jumping in and lecturing on the benefits of physical education, and telling her how she will never be a world champion soccer player if she doesn't exercise and stay in shape, I simply said, "So you hate P.E."

"Yeah, Dad, I really hate it."

Sensing I was on a roll, I continued, "So you *really* hate it."

"Well not all of it," she replied, as if she sensed that I was confused. "It's all those laps I hate. People don't do them right, and they do them sort of silly."

"Oh, it's not P.E., it's the silly way they do the laps," I answered, greatly relieved, knowing that she was still a chance for our Olympic team.

"Yeah, I like the games, especially kickball."

I smiled.

When you express affection toward your child through respect, support, communication, and physical closeness, you build a strong and positive emotional relationship with your child. Make sure, in your efforts to bring out the best in your child's schoolwork or behavior, that you do not neglect this very important practice of parenting. Without it, all your other parenting efforts will be diluted.

Best Practice 3: Firmness

Firmness in structure and follow-through is an important aspect of parenting. Current research indicates that when you set rules that are consistent with the needs and maturity of your child, provide rational explanations or reasons for the rules, do not overreact when your child breaks rules, and make sure there is consistency between parents in the enforcement of rules, your child is more likely to be an achiever.

Achieving children demonstrate self-discipline. They have learned that in order to achieve pleasant results in the long term, they have to make sacrifices in the short term. One of the ways you teach children this key foundation for achievement is through the externally imposed limits that we call discipline. The other way you can teach self-discipline is through teaching the Habits of the Mind that make tolerance of frustration and delay of gratification possible. Here are four key aspects of effective discipline:

When children are young, you set the rules. As they get older, be more democratic. It is important that children are aware of a few important rules that outline their important responsibilities and specify what is appropriate and inappropriate behavior. For example, here are some rules that help guide children through homework, an activity that many would normally choose not to do:

1. Homework should be neat and completed as well as you can.
2. Homework should be started and completed on time.
3. Homework is your responsibility to do and should not be done by anyone else.
4. Communicate with teachers and parents when help is needed.

GUIDELINES FOR SETTING RULES THAT WORK

1. Decide upon a few but important rules.
2. Discuss the reasons for these rules with your child.
3. Involve your child in discussing the limits of the rules as well as fair and reasonable consequences for breaking the rules.
4. Praise your child when your child follows the rules.
5. Consistently, assertively, and calmly follow through with the consequences when the rules are broken.
6. Change the rules and expectations as your child grows up.

—P. C. Bernard & M. E. Bernard,
The You Can Do It! Little Book for Parents

The rules are set in place by you as the authority as to what is best for your child. As your child gets older, by all means discuss the reasons for rules and be prepared to be somewhat flexible in terms of how they should be interpreted by your child. As long as your children respect the rules, do not be too controlling about the where, when, and how. That's up to them.

Rules need to be consistently and persistently enforced. Your children need to know that when they follow rules, not only will they achieve better results in their schoolwork, and experience the satisfaction of doing so, but also that you appreciate their efforts and acknowledge them accordingly. Similarly, they need to know if they break house rules—for example, not handing in homework—that they will have to pay a big price, including some penalties. Do not make rules that you are not prepared to enforce. Enforcement means making sure that your children follow rules. They wear their bicycle helmets; they do their homework.

Do not blame or condemn your children when they have broken rules. The point here is to discipline without anger, which is easier said than done. If you give your child the right to be wrong and separate the doer from the deed, this will be a lot easier.

Encourage independence. More will be said about the importance of your child's becoming independent. You accomplish this by trusting your child to act responsibly. One of the greatest battles parents fight with themselves and their adolescents is over loosening up on the reins. Sometimes you can give them too much responsibility and sometimes not enough. The right amount has to do with the characteristics of each individual child. What works for one often doesn't work for another. It is important that you be flexible and attuned to the needs and maturity of each child.

> **HOME FACTORS THAT CONTRIBUTE TO ACADEMIC ACHIEVEMENT IN YOUNG CHILDREN**
> - Children have a variety of intellectually challenging activities.
> - Children participate in family decision making.
> - Parents reward children's efforts in learning.
> - Parents encourage independence.
> - Parents encourage children to socialize with a peer group that values achievement.
> - Parents communicate realistic standards for judging schoolwork.
> - Parents help their children manage their time so that schoolwork is completed.

Best Practice 4: Involvement in Education

It is so very clear that your involvement and interest in your child's education and schooling have a major influence on the shaping of expectations for achievement, including the value your child places on education. In addition, parents who show their interest at school find that teachers relate to their children on a more personal level.

Your involvement will obviously change as your child gets older. Your tenth grader will not generally appreciate your sitting in on her Spanish class helping her and others with grammar, whereas your third grader will love to see you in class. However, in spite of changes in your adolescent's reaction to parent involvement in most any aspect of his life, your interest and enthusiasm should never wander or waver. Your child needs to know that are you involved and that you care.

This idea that you can make a difference in your child's achievement in school may seem somewhat dubious. After all, your child may spend all of five seconds in a whole semester discussing school with you and may appear totally uninterested in your opinion about anything associated with school. Take heart, and beware! Our children are very sensitive to our reactions to what happens to them at school. Your constructive interest and support go a long way toward instilling in your child's mind the importance of performing well at school. Don't despair; hang in there.

Some youngsters who are not doing as well in school as they could already have one or both parents who have always shown lots of support and interest in their education. You might be the sort of parent who read to your child when she was little, attended most parent association meetings at school, baked cookies for the school bake sale, offered to have your child's science class visit with you at the laboratory where you work, promised your child the reward of the latest computer gadgetry, and did countless other things. Despite your involvement, the reports from school remain: "Jenny continues not to hand in her work and shows little interest in class. She is in real danger of failing the year."

You might be too far down the road of parent involvement in your child's education. The material below offers you the opportunity to examine the extent of your involvement and to determine whether or not it needs to be extended. If it doesn't, you'll find plenty of new roads to explore in subsequent chapters.

You might be reading this and thinking "Great. I'm an only parent— or feel like an only parent. Unless I cut out sleeping completely, I have no more time to get involved." You have a point. My advice is twofold: One, plan in advance, carving out little chunks of time during the week or weekend to spend with your child discussing schoolwork or to visit school. Two, try to find someone in your family or a family friend who agrees to take an active, regular interest in what your son or daughter is doing at school. This mentor should arrange with your child to meet on a regular basis as well as to talk on the telephone to communicate interest in your child's progress at school and to detect any significant problems or prevent them from arising.

There are a number of things you can do at home to communicate interest and demonstrate support. Showing your interest and enthusiasm for your child's projects, assignments, and what he is learning is important. You do not have to be a year-round cheerleader for your child as he goes about his work. Just have an open mind about what your child is doing, and when something takes your fancy, make sure your child can experience your enthusiasm. Do not take your child's work for granted.

Your child needs a place at home where she can study. The suitability of a place depends somewhat on your child's characteristics and age. Younger children sometimes like to work in sight of a parent who might be doing household chores or preparing dinner. Older children need a quiet, private area where they will not be distracted by noise, including that of older or younger siblings.

Whether your child should study with the radio on (or TV) depends on your child. Most cannot study as efficiently with loud music or the television on. Many students report that some music helps relieve the stress of doing difficult homework. Check with your child's teacher to determine the quality of homework handed in. If it is consistently good, then your child should probably be allowed to listen to music, but not at decibel levels that distract.

Much will be said about homework in chapter 11. For now, it is important for you to know that many underachieving children—especially those who put off doing their work until the very last minute—do not decide ahead of time when they will start their homework each evening and for how long they will work. They do their work when they feel like doing it and give up when they get bored or find it hard. With young children, you have to play a very large role in deciding with your child when homework is to be done, and for how long your child should work, and to check that it has been done properly. You will probably have to schedule a regular homework time. As your children get older, they will assume more responsibility for independently managing their own work.

There are two main attitudes you need to be weaving into your communications with your child about school as they contribute to your child's developing the Habits of the Mind that are the foundations for motivation. First, your child needs to have repeated that you expect her to do the best she can. I do not mean that she has to get a grade of A. Your expectations need to be realistically consistent with your child's talents and abilities—just beyond reach, but not out of sight!

The second attitude that you need to communicate frequently to your child has to do with the relationship between effort and success. Many children take a long time to appreciate this cause-and-effect

BEST PARENTING PRACTICES

> **RESEARCH STUDY FINDS READING ALOUD TO CHILDREN HAS NUMEROUS BENEFITS**
>
> Researchers have found a positive relationship between being read to at an early age and reading achievement, reading readiness, the development of listening skills, and early reading capability. Reading aloud allows for the introduction of new words, complex sentence structures, standard forms of English, various styles of written language, the development of sense of story, motivation to refine reading skills, and a pleasurable experience.

relationship. They may believe their success has nothing to do with them and results from the fact that what they were doing was easy or that they were lucky. If your child discounts his own efforts in his successes, attributing them to factors outside him and his control, then when he is faced with difficult, challenging work, the benefits of his previous successes will be negligible.

Another way to show your child that you are interested in her schooling is by your involvement at school. The more your child sees you at school, the more she will internalize the value of education. When your child acknowledges and accepts the goal of education, she is on the right road to success. Here are four suggestions for involving yourself at school:

Participate in school activities. Make an appearance at school. Your presence at school reinforces in your child's mind that you view school as a number one priority. During the early and middle grades, there will be opportunities to participate in class activities. Teachers will vary in their openness to your involvement, with some offering restricted opportunities and others many. Whether you volunteer to correct homework, read aloud to the whole class, tell the class about your profession, or do in-class tutoring, the key is doing something, anything. It's important! This also includes attending school events such as recitals, plays, art exhibitions, fund-raising events, and orientation

BEST PARENTING PRACTICES

> **BENEFITS OF PARENT INVOLVEMENT**
>
> 1. Children get better grades.
> 2. Children have fewer behavior problems.
> 3. Children are more goal-directed.
> 4. Parents gain confidence in how to interact with and encourage children.
> 5. Teachers are more positive toward parents who are actively involved.
> 6. Parents support and extend at home activities begun in the classroom.
> 7. Teachers learn firsthand about parents' concerns and are better able to respond to needs.

evenings. If you are unsure about how to participate, ask your child's teachers or call the parents of other children in your child's class.

When your child gets into the upper grades, you will have the opportunity to attend Open Houses, Back-to-School Nights, and fund-raising events. Many parents who attended functions while their child was at elementary school do not attend upper-grade events, feeling that they are too impersonal. However, at these events, in a fairly brief period of time, you will be able to pick up lots of useful information about different teachers, specific rules and expectations, and the curriculum that can be of great benefit to you and your child throughout the year.

Volunteer for a school committee. Today, more so than ever before, many schools offer you the means to influence decisions that directly affect your child. Numerous committees exist at school to offer schools advice about many of the programs and services that exist or are being considered. It is important that you find out about your school's committees and their responsibilities. The more knowledgeable you are about your child's school life, the more you can speak with authority to your child.

Develop good communication. It is always best if you can keep one or two steps ahead of your child. There is nothing worse for a child's morale than when his parents seem in the dark about issues concerning homework, school functions, and half or full days when school is not in session due to teacher in-service activities. Keeping yourself up to date and well informed about what goes on at school is a good stance to adopt. This involves developing a good and regular communication system with your child's school and, when necessary, with your child's teacher.

A great source of information is a school newsletter that comes home with your child. If your school doesn't have a newsletter for parents, consider volunteering to assist in developing one. Many schools today have homework hotlines that provide prerecorded messages made by teachers at the beginning of each week concerning the week's upcoming homework and extracurricular activities.

Problem solve with the teacher. The old adage "Two heads are better than one" definitely applies to helping prevent and solve problems of motivation and achievement that your child may have. If you are concerned about your child's performance at school and haven't been in contact with your child's teacher or teachers, it is time to walk down that road.

The parent-teacher conference is the traditional forum for parents to raise concerns about their child and for teachers to bring up any problems or issues. The track record of these conferences is not good. Far too many parents and teachers come away with feelings of hurt, anger, and frustration. Fortunately, it doesn't have to be this way for you. Whether you are about to attend the regularly scheduled parent-teacher conference that is typical of elementary schools, or have asked to see one of your child's teachers at any grade level, there are a few dos and don'ts that will help your conferences with teachers be upbeat and productive.

Remember, you have a perfect right to have a meeting with your child's teacher. Teachers have the responsibility for seeking parent involvement, especially for a child who is having any difficulty in school.

To begin with, you need to follow established protocol for scheduling a conference. This means that you do not just roll up to a teacher and ask to speak with her on the spot. Teachers do not like being put on the spot, and if they have over a hundred students each day, they may need a bit of time to prepare. Instead, send in a brief note with your child requesting a conference. In the note, you should briefly describe the purpose of the meeting so that your child's teacher can be prepared. It is also possible to leave a telephone message at the school for the teacher requesting a conference.

You will also want to do some preconference planning. No matter what the purpose of the meeting, it is best to go in as informed as you can be. Informing yourself involves reviewing your child's current completed assignments, noting what he has been doing, and recording any questions you might have. Spending a few minutes studying your child's textbooks will help you ask informed questions of the teacher. You might ask your child if there is anything he would like you to say to his teacher. Spending some time reading any literature your school has sent concerning school policy, programs, and parent involvement will help put you further in the picture. Be sure to familiarize yourself with your child's past report cards, noticing strengths and weaknesses and the general comments of teachers concerning behavior and attitude. Finally, make a list of specific questions you would like to ask your child's teacher. It is very easy to lose focus and get distracted during the brief time you will have for the conference.

When you meet with your child's teacher, remain calm. Be sure to arrive on time. Be friendly. If you have specific concerns about your child's achievement, discuss, in an atmosphere of mutual support and respect, how the two of you can work together to help your child, including suggestions for how you can help at home. During the meeting, if you do not understand any information the teacher presents, be sure to ask for clarification. Listen carefully, with an open mind. Try not to be defensive. After all, you both are after the same thing.

If you have any negative comments to make about the teacher, such as not following through on what she said she would do in a previous meeting, be sure to stick to your guns and speak your mind. It is generally a good idea to give a compliment before bringing up anything the teacher could perceive as criticism. Remember, teachers are human, like the rest of us. They do not like to be criticized. Do so with tact.

As the meeting time ends, schedule another time if you have not had the opportunity to have all your questions answered or if you want to follow up on any mutually agreed-upon solutions. Be sure to thank the teacher for her time and for taking a special interest in your child. Praise is a great note to end on.

Best Practice 5: Motivational Methods

Even by instituting the four best practices previously listed, you cannot guarantee that your child will be motivated in the area of schoolwork and, in particular, develop the internal desire and sense of responsibility we call academic internal motivation. "Academic internal motivation" refers to children's enjoying school learning and, in particular, being oriented to master challenging work. Research clearly shows that internal motivation is positively related to your child's achievement.

> **MOTIVATION AND HOMEWORK**
>
> What you say to your child and what you do before, during, and after he has completed or not completed his homework dramatically affect your child's motivation and achievement.

In addition, to ensure optimum levels of motivation and achievement and especially to help boost motivation in an underachieving child, you need to be able to influence your child to do work he doesn't feel like doing—work that may be boring or hard!

To be a good motivator for your child, you have to be equipped with two different types of parent motivational practices. You will use one set, internal motivational practices, when your child is happily working on certain subjects, and you will use another set, external motivational practices, when your child is working unhappily or is unwilling to work at all.

To develop both types of motivational parenting practices, it will be important for you to clearly recognize the difference between internal motivation and external motivation.

Internal motivation is in evidence in your child when your child's desire to do schoolwork comes from the pleasure associated with doing the assignment, project, or other learning activity. This type of motivation is different from external motivation. **External motivation** is seen to exist in your child when she does her schoolwork because of the payoff she receives after doing it or because of the penalty she avoids for not having done it.

> **A STUDENT SPEAKS**
>
> "What stops me from being motivated to do my work is when my parents constantly tell me what to do and when. This makes it seem like a chore. I want their support, not their dictatorship."
>
> —Elly, age fifteen

As a rule, your child will not demonstrate internal motivation in all subjects. It is more than likely that she will be internally motivated in certain subjects but will rely on or require external motivation in others. Internal motivational practices are called for when your child is interested in her work to begin with and brings with her some inner desire to do her work, and when quality or creativity rather than quantity is called for from your child. External motivational practices may be necessary when your child has little or no desire to do work in a subject, when he perceives he has little chance of being successful, when the schoolwork itself is perceived by your child to be boring or repetitive, and when quantity rather than quality is the desired learning outcome.

> **INTERNAL MOTIVATION FOR ALL CHILDREN**
>
> The goal of school and home is to insure that all children experience internal motivation in as many areas of their work as possible.
>
> —C. L. Spaulding, *Motivation in the Classroom*

This goal—helping children to develop internal motivation—is achieved through the use of teaching methods and parenting practices that are different from those designed to motivate children to do work they do not feel like doing.

Children with internal motivation hold two different sets of attitudes. First, your child perceives herself as likely to experience success in her work. Second, your child perceives that she has some influence over the way she learns. Rather than feeling that she has to do her work in a specific way, as told to her by her teacher or by you, she feels that she can decide how the work will be done, and with whom she will work.

Some parenting motivational practices that will help encourage internal motivation in your child have been highlighted by Allen and

Adele Gottfried and their colleague James Fleming in a research article dealing with the role of parental motivational practices in children's intrinsic motivation and achievement. These include:

1. encouraging your child to be persistent in schoolwork
2. encouraging your child to enjoy schoolwork
3. encouraging your child to do schoolwork independently, without too much support from others
4. providing learning activities at home that supplement schoolwork
5. communicating to your child that you expect him to put in more effort when he finds work difficult
6. providing new learning activities when your child is bored
7. spending time with her, trying to work things out, when your child experiences difficulty in understanding schoolwork
8. allowing your child to answer questions on his own without supplying answers

Key among these specific methods is the encouragement of independence. Overprotective parents and parents who take too much responsibility for their child are likely to prolong their child's dependence on them and on others. Internally motivated children excel at and enjoy activities that they accomplish on their own.

Another key to instilling internal motivation is avoiding the excessive use of external motivational methods when your child is initially interested in or is fully enjoying a learning activity or has completed specific homework assignments. External motivational methods rely heavily on the use of positive reinforcement, including high doses of praise and rewards for achievement, and the dispensing of penalties for poor achievement. In addition, external motivational methods are designed to provide support for the child. A well-designed motivational plan to encourage a child is successful partly because the child perceives the presence of promised rewards and penalties while doing the work. Independent work is not the goal of external motivational practices. Doing the work is the goal.

The problem with extensively praising your child for the work he has accomplished and for being extremely vigilant in managing homework is that after a while your child's initial enthusiasm, curiosity, and desire to do the work may start to wane. Here is an example of how praise and reward can demotivate a child:

Dorothy rewarded her third grader, Sara, for reading books. Initially, Sara enjoyed the constant pats on the back and the weekend trips to Pizza Hut as a reward for her accomplishments in reading. However, after a while, Sara became somewhat confused about her purpose in reading. Was it to enjoy herself and learn neat stuff, or was it so that she could receive a reward?

Sara's mother noticed that her daughter was less enthusiastic about reading as she entered fourth grade. She decided to beef up her incentive plan. Sara was rewarded for finishing five books in the first semester with a trip to her favorite amusement park. Soon thereafter, Sara's intrinsic desire to read a book, previously one of her most enjoyed activities, turned into boredom with reading. At about that time, her mother decided that Sara was probably interested enough to read without having to be reinforced for reading, so she stopped providing Sara with any incentives for reading. Losing the rewards she had become attached to and expected after she had done her reading assignment, Sara lost all interest in reading.

The story of Sara illustrates an important insight into effective motivational parenting practices. External motivation does not add to internal motivation to produce a higher level of motivation. The former can actually subtract from the latter.

Praise and acknowledgment do have a role to play in internal motivation. However, rewards should be directed at behavior that reflects internal motivation. When you praise your child, do so quietly when your child demonstrates curiosity, pleasure, and persistence in her reading. "I really am pleased you are enjoying that book." "You really are seeing this project through." "I like the way you are thinking about all the different ways the story could end up."

Powerful rewards and praise do, however, play a prominent role in external motivation. If your child is not making an effort in an area of schoolwork and is doing so because he finds the work hard, or boring, or a poor substitute for free time, the external motivational methods are likely to produce greater changes in your child's behavior than will internal motivational methods.

To motivate a child who feels discouraged and frustrated with his work, you will have to catch your child in the act of reading—currently a low-frequency behavior. You will want to reward him each time he reads. The selection of rewards is important. They need to be perceived by your child as extremely pleasant and enjoyable.

Essentially, there are five different types of positive reinforcement you can employ to motivate your child. Consider the following list to decide which specific aspects of your child's environment he finds rewarding and to determine which reinforcers are most likely to be effective with your child:

1. primary reinforcers: food, sleep, novelty, challenge
2. social reinforcers: praise, attention, being cuddled
3. object reinforcers: toys, comics, clothes
4. activity reinforcers: watching TV, using the telephone, bike riding, going to a restaurant, shopping, using the computer
5. token reinforcers (things that can be traded for something else the child wants): stars, points, marbles

The use of tokens bears some discussion. The idea behind token reinforcement is that whenever your child engages in the behavior you wish to encourage, he receives a certain number of tokens, depending on the quality and quantity of work. Ahead of time, the two of you will have put together a menu of reinforcers that your child can order after he has earned a specified number of tokens. The idea behind the procedure is that your child will be motivated to do work to earn a token that he can use later on to "buy" something he really wants. An example of how token reinforcement can be used in a tutoring session can be found in chapter 13.

For some children whose lack of motivation is due to a lack of self-discipline and rebelliousness, you might find that the use of penalties can increase your motivational effectiveness. If your child associates not doing work with the withdrawal of valued activities such as watching favorite shows on television or using the computer or telephone, or the presentation of unpleasant consequences such as early bedtime or curfew, he will be more likely to do the work to avoid the penalty.

You might question whether rewarding children for hard work and achievement constitutes a form of bribery. You might have heard about some programs set by local communities to reward children with money after they have improved their grades. My thinking on this is twofold. First, the ends sometimes justify the means, and in the case of helping start a child's motivational machinery, I think the end of better grades and the positive feelings and future that tend to go along with better achievement justify the temporary use of bribes. Some children who have a long history of school failure need to taste success before they can independently decide to work for it. Once they have taken their places on the playing field of achievers and experience the pleasures and rewards that naturally come from achievement, the need to continue external, artificial bribes is reduced.

The choice of which motivational practice to use, internal or external, is a tricky one and depends on a number of factors, including: your usual parenting style, the personality of your child, her age, her history of success and failure in school, what her natural interests and desires are, and what subject she is studying. Later in this book I will revisit these same issues when I discuss ways in which you can motivate your child to do homework.

In this chapter, I have covered in some detail five parenting practices that can help you parent for achievement. Again, your aim is not to be a Super-Parent or to raise the Superachieving Child. My experience with my own children and in my work with many parents of children of all ages is that these practices are solid home foundations to guide both you and your child toward the goals of success and happiness. In chapter 6, I will discuss the Habits of the Mind that help

BEST PARENTING PRACTICES

> **RESEARCH STUDY FINDS DEMOCRATIC PARENTING PROMOTES ADOLESCENT SCHOOL ACHIEVEMENT AND ATTENDANCE**
>
> In studying firstborn children between the ages of eleven and sixteen, from fifteen working- and middle-class families, investigators have found that adolescents obtained higher grades and attended school more often when their parents used democratic rather than authoritarian decision-making practices, when their parents were warm, and when their parents were not psychologically overcontrolling.

children achieve, and I will show you how to evaluate your own child's Habits of the Mind.

Putting It All Together

To summarize, here are the main parenting practices that can help you encourage your child's achievement in school:

1. Make sure that your child understands that schoolwork and, in particular, homework is his responsibility, not yours.
2. Communicate clear expectations and, if necessary, rules that spell out your child's responsibilities for doing homework.
3. It is important that your child knows that if homework is not done at a satisfactory level, she will be penalized. Don't bail your child out.
4. Persistently and consistently follow through on rules you have set for your child in the area of schoolwork.
5. Show enthusiasm for what your child is learning at school and maintain a high degree of involvement in your child's education.
6. Encourage your child's curiosity, persistence, independence,

and enjoyment of learning rather than focusing solely on results.
7. Communicate high expectations for success.
8. Teach your child the Habit of the Mind that the harder she tries, the better her achievement.
9. From an early age, teach your child to set short-term and long-term goals. Have your child see how his present schoolwork leads to the achievement of short- and long-term goals and rewards.
10. Teach your child to be an optimistic thinker and to use positive thinking when he is faced with frustrating and difficult schoolwork.
11. Teach your child how to reward herself after she has successfully completed her schoolwork.
12. While your child is doing homework, monitor—and where necessary restrict—outside distractions (TV, friends).
13. If he wants to, and doesn't find it distracting, permit your child to listen to music—especially when doing work he finds boring or difficult.
14. Teach your child to take little breaks in doing schoolwork (for an older child, ten minutes' break in every hour).
15. Be sure to schedule fun activities during your child's peak periods of work, in order to help your child manage stress.
16. Direct your child toward a peer group that values achievement.

PARENT SELF-REFLECTION SHEET: PARENTING FOR ACHIEVEMENT

1. Do you, as a rule, parent calmly (circle one)?

    mostly   sometimes   rarely

    In what situations with your child do you need to be calmer? Describe some ways you can remain calmer in these situations.

    _____

2. Do you think that you communicate sufficient warmth and love to your child?

    mostly   sometimes   rarely

    What are some things you can say and do with your child to express warmth and love?

    _____

3. Are you sufficiently firm (rules, consistency, persistence) with your child?

    mostly   sometimes   rarely

    In what situations do you need to be firmer? How could you communicate firmness?

    _____

4. Do you show interest and involvement in your child's education?

    mostly   sometimes   rarely

    Decide on two things you can do to increase your involvement and show greater interest.

    _____

5. Are you effective in your use of internal and external motivational methods?

    mostly   sometimes   rarely

    What are some ways to improve your use of either internal or external motivation?

    _____

CHAPTER 5

HOW TODAY'S TEACHER HELPS YOUR CHILD ACHIEVE

In thinking about how best to support your children's education, one of the most important factors for you to consider is how teachers contribute to your children's achievement. Oftentimes, you will have an opportunity to discuss with school personnel the placement of your child with a teacher who you believe would be best for your child. Knowing what to look for in a teacher ahead of time can help guide you and the school in this process. Aside from the general demeanor of a teacher, there are certain styles and methods of teaching that can motivate as well as demotivate your child. This chapter provides valuable insight on what makes a good teacher.

Teaching today is more difficult than ever before. Today's teacher is faced with innumerable pressures associated with school reform and change. Moreover, the students teachers face today are far more challenging than those they may have taught twenty years or more ago. Imagine teaching a class of thirty-five students with the following characteristics:

- 4 Economically disadvantaged
- 4 Diverse cultural background/Latino background
- 4 Limited English proficiency/Cambodian
- 2 Attention deficit hyperactivity disordered
- 2 Learning disabilities
- 2 Gifted
- 2 Low academic ability
- 2 Highly creative
- 1 Perfectionist
- 3 Helpless/discouraged
- 1 Peter Pan syndrome
- 2 Rebellious
- 3 Peer-conforming underachievers
- 3 No apparent features that place them at risk for underachievement

This is a challenging class, to say the least, but it is by no means atypical of many of the classes in our public schools. Moreover, with the advent of MTV and computer games, an especially heavy burden has been placed on teachers to employ curriculum programs and instructional methods that can compete with today's whizbang, highly stimulating media.

Demotivating Styles of Teaching

Just as there are some not-so-good parenting styles, there are some not-so-good teaching styles. Sometimes "not-so-good" means that the method is not helpful for certain students, although it might be helpful for others. Some teaching methods need to be totally retired.

Teacher Not Providing for Individual Success. For many different reasons, some teachers do not devote enough time to providing individual students with assignments that increase their likelihood of success. Some teachers believe that it would not be fair to provide certain students with individual programs and to give them different opportunities than other students get. Teachers of older students find it difficult to find the time to design individual programs, given the large number of students they actually teach each week.

Success in providing individual assistance requires an in-depth understanding of the learning strengths and weaknesses of each student as well as of current motivational methods for increasing internal and external motivation. You should find out which teachers find it difficult to provide individualized instruction and which are able to in case your child needs extensive individualized education.

Lack of Teacher Expectations. Students profit when their teachers communicate high expectations for academic success. Students underperform when they do not have goals that challenge them and that they can reach with some effort and encouragement. Where does your teacher set the high-jump bar for your child? Many teachers will set it at a challenging level, whereas some may set it too low or too high relative to your child's capabilities.

Some teachers started off their teaching careers with very high expectations for their students, and their expectations were fulfilled by their students' doing their work at a high level. Today, these teachers observe that their students are different from those of previous years. As a result of their students' bringing less achievement motivation to their work and failing to comply with minimal expectations for homework and classwork, these excellent teachers have lowered their expectations.

It is important for your child's achievement that her teacher set the high-jump bar at a realistic level for your particular child's capabilities. Many teachers appreciate hearing from you early in the school year about how high they should set the high-jump bar for your child. This is especially the case if they do not have your child's complete past school records or if they do not rely on existing ones to formulate expectations.

Negative Teacher Expectations Based on Student Characteristics. It is unfortunate that some teachers today subconsciously hold negative expectations of certain students based on the students' sex, race, or other stereotyped qualities. Sometimes, if your child has an older sibling who didn't do well at school or who terrorized his teacher, a teacher might form a negative expectation of your child based on his being in the same family as his older sibling.

As a consequence of negative expectations about a child, a teacher may provide less than enough encouragement and attention. In time, a self-fulfilling prophecy may begin to operate. A child who is the recipient of less teacher support because of some stereotyped characteristic may begin to think "If my teacher gives other students more attention than me, maybe I'm not really suited for this subject. What's the point in trying?" If your child is female, brings diverse cultural values to the classroom, has limited proficiency in English, has dark skin color, is developmentally disabled, or has an older sibling who was taught by your child's current teacher, it will be important for you to have your antennae out for negative expectations from your child's teachers.

Overcontrolling Teaching Style. It used to be the case that the good teacher planned highly structured lessons in which students knew exactly what was expected of them, including how their teacher wanted assignments completed, with whom they could work, and how they would be assessed. Today, because of many changes in the values and expectations that students bring with them to the classroom, many students require more freedom of choice in how they go about learning. Student perception that they have some control of how they will learn contributes to their own internal motivation. Too much planning and structure may take away initiative and instill boredom. In classes and subjects to which your child brings an internal motivation to learn, her teacher should use a less directive and structured, more student-centered style.

Highly Competitive Teaching Style. Students who lack self-motivation can profit from teaching situations in which they are faced with having to compete against their classmates. Getting your child's motivational juices flowing through individual or team academic competitions that include public displays of grades and the awarding of prizes may be just the thing for your child. However, if your child is sensitive, easily embarrassed, or anxious and has not learned to cope with losing, he may choose to opt out rather than compete. So if you are aware of the teaching styles of teachers at your child's school, and if you are aware that some employ more competitive methods than others, you will need to make a judgment about whether such methods suit the individual motivational style of your child.

Authoritarian Discipline Style. In the good old days, most students seemed to respond favorably to a strict, rigid code of classroom conduct in which the teacher handed out severe punishments for disobedience. Today, with the breakdown of many young people's respect for the authority of teachers, teachers have to work harder at earning respect. Far more students today will rebel against too much adult-imposed discipline. Teachers who negotiate and discuss class rules with students are likely to have more student cooperation than if they impose them in an authoritarian fashion.

In your child's school, some teachers will employ more of an authoritarian discipline style, while others will be more democratic, and still others will have a loose, unstructured approach. If you do have any influence over the choice of your child's teachers, you will need to decide and communicate to school personnel which style best suits your child. An authoritarian style of teaching may produce conformity, and your child may comply with schoolwork responsibilities out of fear, or your child may passively resist. If your child is particularly sensitive to others' opinions, or is used to a more democratic process of decision making used at home, it is likely that he will not be suited to a teacher who employs an authoritarian style. A laissez-faire teaching style, in which students are left to exercise their own judgments about how to act, may not suit a child who likes to play rather than work.

Oversupportive Teaching Style. This style of motivation is wonderful for self-esteem but can work against students' achievement. If frequent positive reinforcement (praise, stickers, privileges) that is not earned by a student for really trying hard to learn challenging material is provided, students may fail to develop an appreciation of the connection between working hard and achieving a good result. Moreover, some students begin to work for the reward itself. They fail to appreciate the intrinsic satisfaction that comes from learning and achievement that is motivated by their own interest and the excitement of the learning experience.

In his early years, my son was provided with bountiful amounts of praise for doing the smallest amount of work. He became quite content with himself because of the frequent "warm fuzzies" he received. However, the quality of his schoolwork did not improve when it needed to. Under a regime of too much support, I saw my child fast becoming a happy underachiever. Support and recognition are vital for supporting the learning process. However, you need to make up your own mind, when you observe your child being stickered to death, about whether such support is contributing to achievement.

Insufficient Academic Challenge. If your child is blessed with strong verbal and quantitative scholastic ability, and if she is placed in a classroom where her teacher teaches to the middle range of ability, your child is very likely to become bored and turn off. If you notice a mismatch between what your child is capable of and what she is expected to do, you need to meet with her teacher and ask for extra enrichment. Strategies for supporting an academically gifted child are covered in chapter 10.

Too Many Academic Demands. If your child is attending a school with a track record of high levels of academic achievement, with high proportions of the student population eventually attending top universities, you can expect your child to receive extremely challenging and demanding schoolwork. In some schools, there are teachers who teach more to the top end of students than to the middle.

If your child has average scholastic ability and finds that he is constantly bombarded with work that is over his head, he may begin to drown. Under these circumstances, his chances for getting good grades are lowered, and, depending on how he reacts to low grades, his motivation might be affected. If your child struggles a bit with schoolwork, he probably needs a teacher who has high expectations for all students but does not expect each one to graduate with a doctorate by the end of the year. It may well be your call in deciding whether the academic demands your child encounters in the class are matched to your child's needs and capabilities.

Mismatch of Curriculum with Student Interests. As children enter adolescence, their interests become more defined. Whether their interests are social and involve helping people, or technical and center around machines and tools and not people, adolescents' emerging interests play a big role in their motivation. Where there is a large mismatch between the natural interests of a student (e.g., artistic) and the content of his school's curriculum (e.g., traditional academic), student motivation will be lower than it would be if there were a closer match.

In chapter 8, I will present a way for you to determine your child's emerging interests and to figure out how they should dictate subject and study choices as well as leisure time pursuits. It will be important, especially if your child is struggling in school, for teachers to accommodate your child's interest as much as possible in her schoolwork.

Dull Curriculum, Dull Teaching. Current educational research into the characteristics of good and not-so-good teachers highlights the importance of teacher enthusiasm and energy to student motivation and achievement. This is a no-brainer. Regardless of your child's characteristics and needs, your child should be taught by teachers who communicate enthusiasm and excitement.

This is not to say that all teachers have to be on the shortlist for Hollywood's Most Dynamic Teachers. Some teachers who have a profound commitment to teaching and are expert in their subject areas are simply not going to make it to the shortlist. Does this mean that they are bad teachers? No. Does it mean that your child cannot learn from them? No. Students with some internal motivation may well excel under their care. However, if your child seems to require razzle-dazzle to become excited about what life and learning have to offer, lackluster teaching will not do.

Poorly Assigned Homework. Many schools do not have their homework policy right. In many schools, there is still no clear statement of the purposes of homework and the responsibilities of teachers, parents, and students that has been discussed and agreed to by staff and parents. As a consequence, many teachers, especially at the elementary level, are very uncertain as to whether to assign homework at all and how much to assign.

I am extremely unhappy about the lack of a coherent homework policy promoted by county, state, and federal government agencies. Too much is left up to the school and the individual teacher. This is not acceptable, because we know that poorly assigned homework undermines student achievement. If homework requires your child to do too much in the available time, if it is unrelated to your child's current classwork, if it has not been sufficiently explained so that your child fully understands what he should be doing, your child will likely underachieve at homework. Moreover, if your child's homework is not returned with comments within forty-eight hours, research indicates that it doesn't have much impact on student learning.

You need to make a judgment about the importance of homework for meeting the needs of your child and its role in promoting high levels of achievement. (I will discuss this in chapter 11.) Teachers vary in how effective they are at integrating homework into their daily instruction for the purposes of promoting educational achievement.

Best Teaching Practices for Building Internal Motivation

In every school I've visited, and in my own children's classrooms, I have witnessed and met incredibly talented teachers. Even though they diverge in their strengths, in the subjects they teach, and in some of their instructional and disciplinary methods, not surprisingly, they share certain characteristics in common. Research has revealed a great deal about good teaching and teacher effectiveness.

In any profession, be it driving a taxi, providing health care, or playing a sport, there are members of that profession who do not perform as well as they could, and teaching is no exception. There are teachers who are unenthusiastic, who do not particularly care about children, who are there just for the paycheck and the fringe benefits, who do not have the teaching skills or enthusiasm required to teach classrooms of diverse students and who do not care to learn how to do so, who sabotage efforts at school improvement, and who do not have the personal stability and internal personal resources that enable them to inspire children to achieve to the best of their ability. Our children would be better off without these teachers.

I believe all teachers (and parents) have a responsibility to provide for the needs of all students so that each child experiences success and a sense of belonging to the school and classroom community. I know that my students in the College of Education at California State University, Long Beach, who vary from first-year teachers to teachers with many years of experience, are passionate in their resolve to teach effectively and to make sure that their efforts make a tangible difference to children's achievement and psychological well-being.

Let's look into the classrooms of good teachers to observe those teaching methods that research and common sense reveal as leading to students' motivation and achievement. In chapter 4, I discussed the important difference between internal and external motivation and how parents need to be competent in methods to bring about both types of motivation in their children. This is equally true for teachers. Students bring with them different degrees of intrinsic motivation for different subjects such as mathematics, English, or science. Teachers need to be attuned to these differences in intrinsic motivation among students and to employ methods over the school year to enhance the natural desires, curiosity, persistence, and enjoyment of students. These methods generally involve giving students greater choices and control over how they go about learning ensuring high levels of individual success.

In this section I will describe teaching methods to look for in teachers who are likely to be successful in engendering a high level of internal motivation in your child. The first few methods represent the basics of effective teaching practice that apply to the motivation of all students. In the following section, I will discuss methods that a teacher should use with a child who has little or no interest in the subject being taught.

Develop supportive relationship with students. An effective teacher is patient and encouraging. Your child needs to be aware that her teacher is on her side. You can measure how supportive your child's teacher is by hearing from your child how her teacher reacts to her efforts in class when she is not being successful and is making mistakes. Does she feel her teacher's support at those times? Does your child perceive that her teacher expects and anticipates that she will be successful each time, or that her teacher doesn't really have such faith?

Present an appropriate level of academic challenge. An effective teacher adjusts the difficulty level of assignments and project work so that students find that, with effort and some guidance and instruction when they need it, they will be successful. An effective teacher is able to provide schoolwork that is neither too difficult nor too easy. The more your child spends time stretching and reaching to master academic material, knowing that his teacher is available when needed, the higher his achievement will be.

Make schoolwork relevant and meaningful. "Relevance," once the catchword of educational reform of the 1960s, has become accepted as a necessary condition for today's students to be internally motivated in their schoolwork. The more your child's teacher can relate the ideas that are being taught in the curriculum to the outside world, the greater the likelihood that your child will be interested.

You can get some idea of how well your child's teacher is doing in this area of teaching from the homework that your child is bringing home. If projects involve connecting your child with his culture and community as well as with his future, your child's teacher is hitting the mark. The more time your child spends studying topics in biology, history, mathematics, and English for their own sake without relating them to today's world, the greater the risk that your child will lose internal motivation.

Use cooperative learning. Many students learn better and have better internal motivation when they work in smaller groups and take on the responsibility for their own learning. Teachers who step back and act as coaches presenting students with the tools for learning are more likely to increase students' desire to learn.

Traditionally, teachers stood up in front of their class and directed all instruction. Students answered questions individually and mostly had to rely on their own resources. It is now recognized that not only does cooperative learning stimulate students' internal motivation, but because they have the opportunity to learn not only from the teacher but from their peers, they achieve better results. Your child's teacher should have an appropriate balance between presenting material in a lecture format and cooperative learning activities.

Let students participate in classroom decision making. Students who are allowed a role in deciding on basic classroom rules, whom they work with, how assignments are to be completed, when assigned homework is due, and what to do with free time are likely to feel more empowered. Research clearly shows that the more students perceive they have control over events in their lives, the greater their internal motivation. Informal discussions with your child, as well as with her friends and other teachers, will provide you with a sense of a teacher's democratic practices.

Encourage students to set goals. When students think about the goals for a particular class or unit of study, when they write down the grade they hope to achieve and other outcomes they hope to achieve, when they identify possible obstacles to achieving goals and strategies to overcome them, once again, they will feel more ownership of what they are learning.

Surprisingly, few teachers incorporate goal setting into the beginning phase of instruction on a regular basis. Sometimes, as I'll indicate in chapter 7, you can take over the responsibility of helping your child think through her immediate, short-term, and long-term study goals. Once goals are in sight, it is also easier for students to take on a fuller commitment to taking those actions that are necessary to achieve the goals.

Allow students to struggle with difficult work. When students are given the room to struggle with challenging work and to be successful, their perception that they have what it takes to be successful is increased. Increased perceptions of self-confidence in a subject bring increased internal motivation. Some well-meaning teachers, fearing damage to student self-esteem, may prematurely rescue students who are experiencing frustration about their schoolwork.

Effective teachers do not let their students drown in hard work but recognize the importance of the struggle. Frustration followed by success is the recipe for the development of self-discipline. Especially at the elementary-grade level, teachers vary in this. Regardless of a teacher's preferred teaching style, you will need to make a judgment about how much struggle is optimal for your child, and you should communicate this information to your child's teacher.

Encourage students to persist and recognize their effort. When a teacher lights up when she notices that a student is really trying hard to master material, everyone notices. The student senses that his effort is valued as much, if not more, than whether he gets the answer right. Other students in the class notice too. What screams out from research into internal motivation is that students who recognize the importance of their effort in their achievement and who apply their insight to the task of learning are likely to be achievers. Unfortunately, the grading system that your child's teacher has inherited is far more weighted toward results than to the process of getting there. If a child is working flat-out, the results will come. Some forward-thinking schools and teachers provide grades for effort.

Match curriculum with students' interests. As I will discuss in chapter 8, students who are working on materials and on tasks that are compatible with their emerging interests will experience greater motivation than will students who do work that does not interest them. While the selection of classes for a student frequently rests with the school's guidance counselor, teachers who are sensitive to differences in their students' interests, and who design instruction that takes into account different interests, have more motivated students. For example, if your child has interests in sports, he will work harder in classes that incorporate these interests.

Use teaching methods that cater to different learning styles. In chapter 10, I will describe how differences in children's learning styles influence their degree of success in learning. For example, students vary across the three main learning modalities of seeing, hearing, and doing. Effective teachers vary the way in which they present information and design instruction to cater to these differences in student learning styles. Your child will tend to experience higher motivation if his teacher employs teaching methods that are matched to his learning strengths.

Use assessment methods that cater to differences in how students demonstrate what they have learned. Just as students vary in the ways they go about learning, they also differ in the ways they best communicate what they have learned. Some students are better at displaying what they have learned in writing, others by giving a talk, and still others by demonstrating what they have learned by constructing a model or actually showing how to apply their knowledge in the real world. Good teachers tap into all three modalities. Children whose strengths are in communicating through the written word are at the greatest advantage, while those that communicate by doing have fewer opportunities in school and are at a disadvantage at testing time.

These methods are particularly designed to help unleash student motivation and potential. They help develop a culture in the classroom in which students are stimulated to excel. Teachers also need methods for teaching students who have fallen off the track or who bring little natural desire to learn part or all of the curriculum. Being aware of these methods will help you select a teacher who is equipped to help an underachieving student.

Teaching Methods for Motivating Hard-to-Motivate Students

If your child is turned off by a subject she is studying at school, she needs to be taught by a teacher who has skills not only in reawakening internal motivation, but in the use of external motivational practices. Methods intended to increase external motivation are used when a child is doing schoolwork she finds boring or repetitive, when quantity and quality are the desired result, or when she doesn't believe she has any real chance of being successful. External motivation exists in your daughter when the reason she is doing a particular unit or studying a subject is that she wishes to get a good grade or to avoid some penalty she associates with not doing well, and has little desire for or interest in doing the work.

If you think about the subjects your son is studying, you will, no doubt, be able to identify one or more that he is fantastically absorbed in and one or two that he finds difficult to study. In the latter classes, you will want your son to be taught by a teacher who has at his fingertips methods to motivate your child. Not every teacher will know these methods.

> **ONE TEACHER'S SIMPLE, DIRECT RULES FOR GETTING MANY STUDENTS TO DO HOMEWORK**
>
> 1. Students who don't hand in their homework when it is due are required to stay after school to finish it.
> 2. Students who receive a failing grade on a homework assignment are required to stay after school to correct missed items and receive additional tutoring.
> 3. Students who fail a quiz or test are required to stay after school to retake it until they pass.
>
> —L. Sonna, *The Homework Solution*

The rationale for the effectiveness of these methods is quite straightforward. Effective teachers know that, based on principles of learning and behavior (as discussed in chapter 2), behavior that is immediately and consistently reinforced tends to be repeated, whereas behavior that is ignored or penalized tends to decrease. Effective teachers also know that to increase the chances of your child's doing work and responding correctly, they may initially have to simplify the difficulty of the work to the point that with minimum effort, your child will be successful. Your child's teacher should be both calm and assertive in relating to and teaching your child. Here are a variety of methods that can motivate your child when he is not in the mood to do work:

Act calmly when students are not working. Just as calmness is the first key to being a successful parent, so, too, effective teachers do not readily lose their cool. I am not at all advocating that teachers be robots and never express their feelings. Teaching children who are resisting doing their work is extremely frustrating. Effective teachers use emotional self-management strategies so that they do not allow themselves to get too angry or guilty about their students' lack of performance.

If your child is pretty thick-skinned when it comes to criticism, then the effects of an overemotional teacher may not be too dramatic. If your child takes things personally, teachers who calmly insist that he do his work will bring about the best results.

Treat undermotivated students with respect. Respect comes in a variety of forms. In dealing with your child, who may be underperforming and possibly acting up in class, a soft reprimand will maintain your child's sense of dignity. Teachers who treat students with disrespect in their tone, manner, and actions can destroy children's sense of dignity and hope—two essential conditions for helping them get back on track.

Develop programs for individual success. Your child may need an individualized program of study in order to break through his perception of boredom or expectation of failure.

Effective teachers somehow find the time to modify their program of study to meet the needs of individual students.

Assess current level of students' learning. Before prescribing a solution, an effective teacher will use a variety of informal and formal tests to determine what your child knows and what he hasn't as yet learned. This information will be used as a basis for the design of your child's program of study.

Establish reasonable and achievable expectations. An effective teacher will not expect that on the very next lesson, your child will make up all lost ground. Rather, depending on how many steps behind your child may be, she will encourage and praise your child for taking one step at a time so that he can work up to a higher standard.

Assign work where students are successful. Success breeds more success. Effective teachers employ this rule in working with students. However, it is not easy for a teacher to have all the information required, and time available, to fine-tune a course of study in which your child will be successful. If you volunteer to help in the classroom, this sometimes helps your child's teacher find more time to be helpful to each child.

Break down tasks into simpler steps. One of the reasons your child gets bogged down and then uninterested in some projects is that she feels overwhelmed. An effective teacher helps your child break down an assignment into the following steps: a) determining what the assignment means and what is expected by the teacher, b) gathering research, including visiting the library, reviewing notes, interviewing people, making observations, c) thinking about how the information collected connects with and answers the question, d) writing an outline, e) writing the first draft, and f) writing a final draft. In chapter 7, I will show you how to help your child get in the habit of performing this type of analysis on his projects and assignments.

Good teachers recognize the importance of spoon-feeding certain students so that they have to do some work and hand it in each night rather than having the teacher wait for the student to hand in the completed project at the end of the week.

Communicate clear expectations. Your child may need to be reminded on a regular basis of the standard (quality and quantity) of work expected of her. Good teachers are adept at letting their students know clearly and concisely what constitutes acceptable and unacceptable work.

Do not accept poor work. Students lacking in motivation often seek the minimum level of work they can get away with doing to satisfy requirements. Effective teachers do not accept inferior work. Students of these teachers learn that if the work is not done properly, it has to be repeated until it reaches an acceptable level. The communication style of teachers who successfully motivate under-motivated students is assertive and persistent. They say what they require with respect, and they follow through.

Praise effort frequently. An effective teacher recognizes the central importance of poor effort in a student's underachievement. A great deal of this teacher's effort is directed at catching and praising undermotivated students in the act of expending effort rather than waiting for the final product to be handed in.

Assess progress and improvement. There is plentiful evidence that effective teachers recognize the importance of providing certain students with regular, frequent feedback on their learning progress. They recognize that when these students, after putting in effort, receive positive feedback on their learning progress, they will begin to acquire the achievement-oriented Habit of the Mind: "The more you try, the better you get." Your child's teacher should provide frequent verbal and written comments. If he is not getting them often enough, you will need to talk to your child's teacher.

Use incentives to motivate students. One way a teacher can light a fire under an undermotivated child is through the appropriate use of rewards and penalties. Teachers who offer praise and other more tangible rewards immediately after your child has completed some work he didn't feel like doing make it more likely that your child will do the work the next time.

If your child's teacher is lacking in enthusiasm for providing tangible positive reinforcement of any kind, because he believes a child should want to do the work for its intrinsic pleasure and value, you may have a problem on your hands. You may need to provide the incentives yourself, if they are not available from your child's teacher. Once again, you should discuss with teachers the importance of external incentives to your child's motivation.

Use negative consequences to motivate students. Negative consequences are not the same as punishment. Punishment is something harmful done to someone who has done a wrong thing, such as not doing schoolwork. The physical and psychological damage done to the person being punished acts as a painful reminder the next time the person thinks of doing the same thing again.

I am not an advocate of punishment if students do not do their schoolwork. However, effective teachers select penalties that are logical negative consequences for children who do not do their work. For example, not allowing your child access to some preferred activity, such as free time, until after he has done his homework may motivate your child without negative side effects.

Recognize student achievement. Effective teachers rarely take the achievements of underachieving students for granted. While they do not have to go to the extreme of being a cheerleader every time a student achieves a goal, they nonetheless understand that the more recognition students receive for achievement, the more students will choose not to resist working. Effective teachers also know how to select a form of recognition that will not embarrass the student in front of peers. Some students enjoy being proclaimed student of the month and having their name read in assembly. Others prefer that a discreet note be sent home.

These effective teaching methods will lead teachers to success in promoting student motivation and achievement in the latter part of the 1990s and beyond. Obviously, no one teacher will use all these methods. Effective teachers use many of them. You will need to judge which methods are used by your child's teachers or prospective teacher.

A word of caution: Do not go charging into the principal's office demanding that those teachers who do not demonstrate these effective teaching practices be fired. They won't be. In addition, change generally comes from sustained pressure at appropriate leverage points. The principal's office is not one of those points.

Do not photocopy this chapter and give it to your child's teacher—especially after a semester during which you think your child has not made sufficient progress. Most teachers will not take well to your well-meaning efforts at encouraging their professional development.

It is useful, however, to try to identify teachers who can accommodate your child's educational needs and interests. In parent-teacher conferences, you can offer suggestions about those teachings methods that you believe are best suited for your child. Be aware, however, that you have crossed into a territory that is traditionally the reserve of teachers. Just as some medical doctors will not be overenthusiastic about your prescribing medicine for your child's maladies, so, too, most teachers will be sensitive about your foray into their territory. When you need to make suggestions, be considerate, respectful, and mindful of a teacher's professionalism. Offer suggestions as suggestions rather than as demands. More often than not, your child's teachers will very much appreciate your interest and involvement and will come to see you as a partner in the collaborative enterprise of educating children.

PARENT REFLECTION SHEET: TEACHING STYLES AND YOUR CHILD

1. In the blank spaces below English/Reading and Math, write in all the classes/subjects your child is taking at school. Then estimate the amount of internal motivation he has for each. Also, estimate how much your child relies and needs external motivation to get the work done. Circle your answers.

How Much Internal Motivation?	Class	Requires External Motivation?
little medium a lot	English/Reading	rarely sometimes often
little medium a lot	Math	rarely sometimes often
little medium a lot	_____	rarely sometimes often
little medium a lot	_____	rarely sometimes often
little medium a lot	_____	rarely sometimes often
little medium a lot	_____	rarely sometimes often

2. Look over the list of classroom teaching methods in this book and think back to teachers who have helped bring out and develop your child's internal motivation in a class. What are some teaching methods to which your child responds favorably?

_____

_____

3. (a) In classes in which your child has relied on external motivation, what are some things (incentives, rewards) that teachers have used successfully to motivate your child?

_____

_____

(b) What are some incentives or penalties that occur to you, or that are mentioned in this chapter, that your child's teachers could use to help motivate your child?

_____

CHAPTER 6

HABITS OF THE MIND FOR ACHIEVEMENT: GETTING TO KNOW YOUR CHILD'S HABITS

For the past decade, I have been at the pulpit at every opportunity, preaching the need to teach all young people some key attitudes that I strongly believe are necessary to children's achievement and happiness. I have written countless articles in which I've stated that the typical school curriculum does not teach these key attitudes. In the past few years, I've begun calling these attitudes Habits of the Mind in order to emphasize the importance of children's using their minds in particular ways on a regular basis.

I anticipate that in years to come parents will spend more and more time helping their children form good habits of thought. Rather than concentrating on getting their children to follow rules, do homework, and play cooperatively with each other, parents will focus more on the importance of the mind in all areas of a child's life.

The next two chapters will acquaint you with those patterns of thought that help children to become achievers. These same patterns of thought also help promote children's healthy emotional life and will help them get along well with others. In chapter 7, I will describe methods for teaching your child these very basic foundations for achievement. As a result, your child will have an enormous advantage in life.

The chart below lists the eleven key Habits of the Mind. The unhelpful, bad Habits of the Mind are listed on the left, while the positive, helpful Habits of the Mind are listed on the right.

HABITS OF THE MIND

unhelpful, negative		helpful, positive
self-depreciation	_____	self-acceptance
perfectionism	_____	risk taking
approval seeking	_____	independence
pessimism	_____	optimism
external locus of control for learning	_____	internal locus of control for learning
low frustration tolerance	_____	high frustration tolerance
nongoal directed	_____	goal setting
poor time management	_____	time management
intolerance of others	_____	tolerance of others
impulsive problem solving	_____	reflective problem solving
intolerance of limits	_____	tolerance of limits

These chapters will give you a pretty clear idea of how to recognize and teach each of the eleven habits to your child.

Recently, I completed a research study that answered this question: Are the eleven Habits of the Mind I've identified more in evidence in achieving students than in students who are significantly underachieving? Teachers in three different schools that spanned grades one through twelve selected three students in each class who they judged to be achievers and three students they judged to be underachievers. Each teacher completed a questionnaire in which each rated the extent to which a student tended to think in a particular way that was characteristic of each of the eleven Habits of the Mind.

The results confirmed my suspicions. Teachers rated achievers as having far more positive, healthy, and helpful Habits of the Mind than did underachievers. This was true for each of the eleven Habits of the Mind. These results were the same when I compared gifted achievers with gifted underachievers, and again when I compared achieving Latino, African-American, and Anglo-American students with underachieving students in each of these three cultural groups. I also found the same results when I compared achieving boys with underachieving boys and achieving girls with underachieving girls.

The results speak quite clearly. If we want our children to be successful and happy, we parents should take the many opportunities we have with our children to teach them Habits of the Mind.

What Exactly Is a Habit of the Mind?

A Habit of the Mind is the tendency of a person—in this case, a child—to think in a certain way. By thinking in that way, the child experiences certain emotions and behaviors that will lead either to good motivation and school achievement or to poor motivation and underachievement.

Habits of the Mind

The drawing of the boy wearing a You Can Do It! T-shirt illustrates some of the eleven Habits of the Mind: Frustration Tolerance, Tolerance of Limits, Optimism, Tolerance of Others, and Time Management. In this illustration, there are "stick shifts" that cover different degrees to which a child has a Habit of the Mind. For example, a child may tend toward being optimistic or toward being pessimistic. He might be optimistic about math and pessimistic about playing soccer. In addition, the illustration shows that children can learn to control their own Habits of the Mind. In time, you can teach your child that she has control over the way she thinks. In *Hamlet*, Shakespeare communicates this idea very clearly: "Things are neither good nor bad but thinking makes them so."

The diagram on page 131 illustrates your child's options in how he thinks about schoolwork. His thinking is determined by his Habit of the Mind, and this thinking directly influences how your child feels about schoolwork and his actions.

Let's analyze the different parts of the diagram. To begin with, there is the box labeled "Habits of the Mind." This is the storehouse of the different habits—both the positive ones and the negative ones. The arrow from Habits of the Mind to "THINKING" indicates that the way in which your child thinks about a "SITUATION" depends upon her Habit of the Mind. A good habit such as "High Frustration Tolerance" leads to a pattern of thinking that helps children cope with the frustration of work, whereas a bad habit such as "Low Frustration Tolerance" leads to a pattern of thinking that results in poor motivation.

The dotted lines surrounding the box labeled "Habits of the Mind," as well as the line from the habits extending to "THINKING" indicate that Habits of the Mind are not always in a child's immediate consciousness. Because they are frequently well-rehearsed automatic habits, your child can be unaware of their actual existence until they are pointed out.

Different Buses, Different Destinations

I like to draw an analogy between children and their current behavior and achievements in and outside of school, and buses and their different destinations. Today's children have arrived at different destinations. Some are achieving, happy, and growing every day in many ways. Some have dropped out of school, either literally or figuratively. Different buses arrive at different destinations, and children's destinations are determined by which bus they get on in the morning. Children's Habits of the Mind are the buses that determine

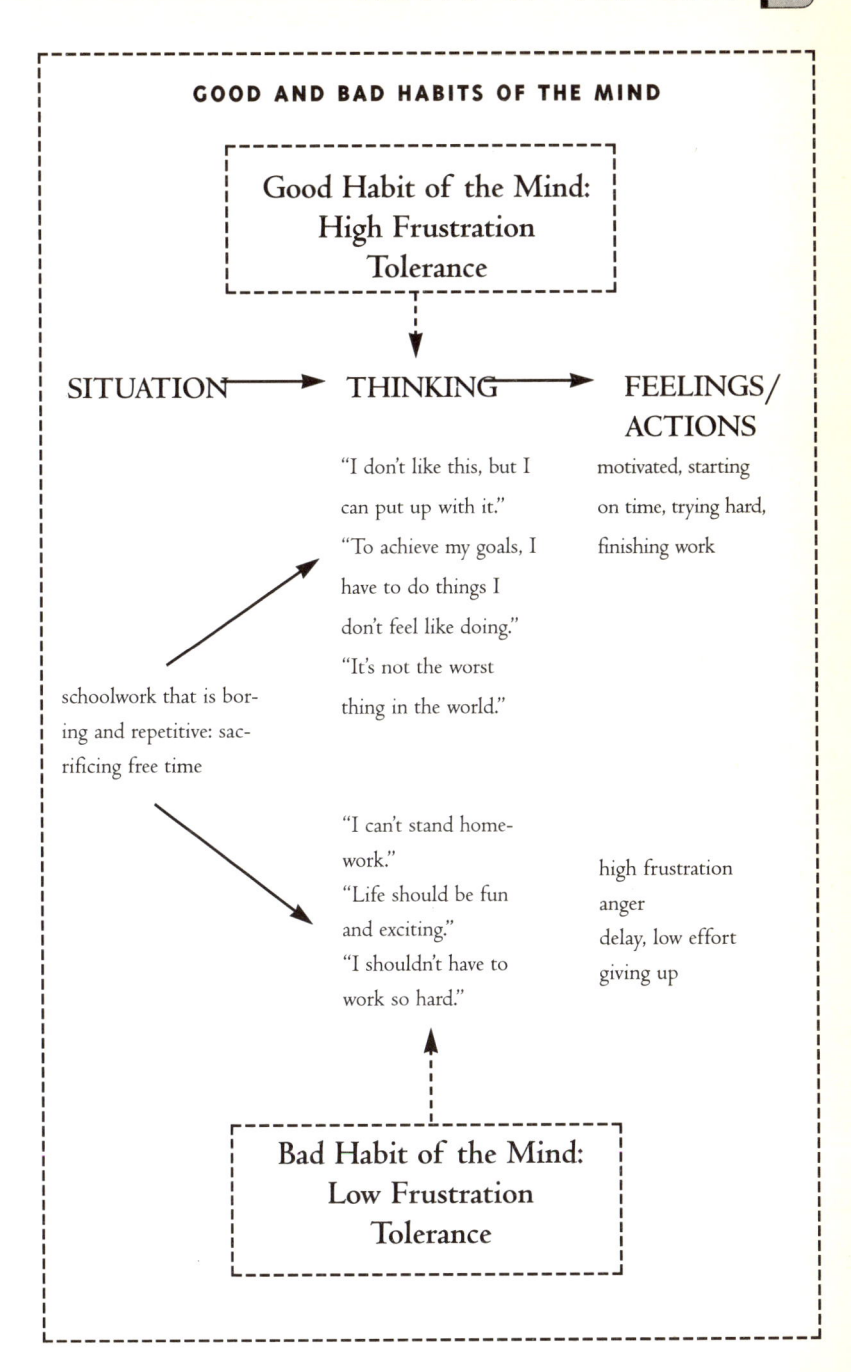

HABITS OF THE MIND

GOOD AND BAD HABITS OF THE MIND

Good Habit of the Mind: High Frustration Tolerance

SITUATION → THINKING → FEELINGS/ACTIONS

"I don't like this, but I can put up with it."
"To achieve my goals, I have to do things I don't feel like doing."
"It's not the worst thing in the world."

motivated, starting on time, trying hard, finishing work

schoolwork that is boring and repetitive: sacrificing free time

"I can't stand homework."
"Life should be fun and exciting."
"I shouldn't have to work so hard."

high frustration
anger
delay, low effort
giving up

Bad Habit of the Mind: Low Frustration Tolerance

their destinations. Bad Habits of the Mind lead to less desirable destinations, and good Habits of the Mind help children achieve to the best of their ability. Sound Habits of the Mind help children overcome obstacles that block them from realizing their potential at school and all areas of life.

In the pages that follow, you will be presented with the eleven Habits of the Mind that form the foundation for your child's success. They will help you to understand the current destination of your child. In the following chapter, you will learn how to change your child's destination by changing one or more Habits of the Mind.

Also, as you learn about each of the eleven Habits, you will be given the opportunity to examine the extent to which your son or daughter possesses each one. First, you will see a drawing that depicts a good and bad Habit of the Mind along with the names of the Habit. Next, you will be given a brief description of the good Habit of the Mind. Then you will be presented with four questions to answer concerning the extent to which your child possesses the Habit.

Don't worry if you find it difficult to know whether your child thinks in a certain way or not. It's very common for parents not to know. After all, Habits of the Mind are very private. But see if you can make an educated judgment about how each Habit applies to your child. If you are evaluating more than one of your children, you can use a different-colored pencil for each child.

You may wish to consider your own Habits of the Mind too. They are extremely important foundations for parents as well as children, and contribute not only to good parenting, but also to success in employment. Now go ahead and complete the following worksheets and indicate your child's Habits of the Mind by placing a mark at the bottom of the page.

HABITS OF THE MIND

SELF-ACCEPTANCE VS. SELF-DEPRECIATION

Self-Acceptance as a Habit of the Mind refers to the extent that your child can separate her own actions and behaviors from her own judgments of self-worth and can accept herself even in the face of lack of achievement (poor grades) and disapproval or rejection (teasing) from others.

Does your child...

___ accept herself even when she doesn't do well on an assignment or test? (Self-Acceptance)

___ avoid putting herself down after doing badly at something? (Self-Acceptance)

or

___ think of herself as a failure when things go badly (having fights, being teased, getting a bad grade)? (Self-Depreciation)

___ believe that she is a failure when she doesn't succeed at something? (Self-Depreciation)

Place a mark somewhere on the following scale to indicate your child's Habit of the Mind.

Self-Acceptance   Self-Depreciation

RISK TAKING VS. PERFECTIONISM

Risk Taking as a Habit of the Mind refers to the extent that your child believes that trying new and challenging tasks and making mistakes is a desirable and necessary part of learning rather than needing to be perfect all the time at important activities.

Does your child...

__ think that it is better to start his work even when he doesn't know exactly what to do? (Risk Taking)

__ accept that there are many things in life that he cannot do perfectly? (Risk Taking)

or

__ believe that it's better to avoid doing something until after he knows how to do it just right? (Perfectionism)

__ believe that it is not worth trying too hard on his schoolwork if he or she cannot do it perfectly? (Perfectionism)

Place a mark somewhere on the following scale to indicate your child's Habit of the Mind.

Risk Taking   Perfectionism

INDEPENDENCE VS. APPROVAL SEEKING

Independence as a Habit of the Mind is related to Self-Acceptance. It refers to the extent that your child: a) can separate her own self-worth from the negative judgments of other people, and b) appreciates that while approval from peers, teachers, and parents is often desirable, he does not need the constant approval from others to be worthwhile, to survive, and to be successful.

Does your child...

___ accept criticism by others (parents, teachers) for making mistakes or for doing poorly on an assignment or test? (Independence)

___ accept that trying hard and making mistakes on schoolwork is necessary even if it shows his teachers or you how much he doesn't know? (Independence)

or

___ believe that one of the worst things for him is when others find out that he has made mistakes on his homework? (Approval Seeking)

___ thinks that if he makes mistakes, other people will think he is stupid? (Approval Seeking)

Place a mark somewhere on the following scale to indicate your child's Habit of the Mind.

Independence   Approval Seeking

OPTIMISM VS. PESSIMISM

Optimism as a Habit of the Mind refers to the extent that your child predicts success, sees opportunity and challenge, avoids taking responsibility for failure, and does not generalize from present difficulties and setbacks to other areas of her competence, self-worth, and view of the world.

Does your child...

__ expect to be successful when trying something new or hard? (Optimism)

__ refuse to allow failure or mistakes in an activity or assignment to influence her positive evaluations of her abilities in other areas? (Optimism)

or

__ make negative forecasts about her chances of doing well in school? (Pessimism)

__ seem to spend more time thinking about what she cannot do well and has not accomplished than thinking of what she can do and has accomplished? (Pessimism)

Place a mark somewhere on the following scale to indicate your child's Habit of the Mind.

Optimism   Pessimism

INTERNAL LOCUS OF CONTROL FOR LEARNING VS. EXTERNAL LOCUS OF CONTROL FOR LEARNING

Internal Locus of Control for Learning is a mouthful. As a Habit of the Mind, it refers to the extent that your child believes that: a) learning and success is due to his own effort rather than to outside factors such as luck or ease of task, and b) effort leads to higher skill level and achievement rather than achievement being due only to inherited brain power.

Does your child...

___ when trying something hard, seem to know that the harder he tries, the better he gets? (Internal Locus of Control)

___ recognize the importance of hard work in doing well in schoolwork and downplay the importance of luck? (Internal Locus of Control)

or

___ seem to think that either you are good at something or not, and if you're not, what's the point of trying? (External Locus of Control)

___ when he doesn't do well in schoolwork, blame it on having a bad teacher, that his teacher doesn't like him, or that the work is boring? (External Locus of Control)

Place a mark somewhere on the following scale to indicate your child's Habit of the Mind.

Internal Locus of Control   External Locus of Control

HIGH FRUSTRATION TOLERANCE VS. LOW FRUSTRATION TOLERANCE

High Frustration Tolerance as a Habit of the Mind refers to the extent that your child accepts that in order to achieve goals and be successful, she sometimes has to do things that are frustrating, hard, and boring and that require putting off fun and social activities until after the work is done.

Does your child...

__ believe that in order to do well in school, she will sometimes have to do schoolwork that is hard or boring and that she doesn't feel like doing? (High Frustration Tolerance)

__ accept the idea that sometimes schoolwork will not be fun, interesting, or exciting? (High Frustration Tolerance)

or

__ believe that things will turn out okay whether she works or not? (Low Frustration Tolerance)

__ believe that when she gets frustrated with homework, that it's unfair and that she shouldn't have to do any more? (Low Frustration Tolerance)

Place a mark somewhere on the following scale to indicate your child's Habit of the Mind.

High Frustration Tolerance   Low Frustration Tolerance

GOAL SETTING VS. NON-GOAL DIRECTED

Goal Setting as a Habit of Mind refers to the extent to which your child values education as a goal, sets big long-term goals, realistic short-term goals, daily specific goals, and is fully committed to doing the things necessary to accomplish his goals.

Does your child...

___ believe that setting goals can help him do better on his schoolwork? (Goal Setting)

___ believe in the importance of committing himself to whatever has to be done to achieve the goals that he sets? (Goal Setting)

or

___ when setting goals, set them so that they are too hard or too easy for him to achieve reasonably? (Non–Goal Directed)

___ believe that nothing he does at school will help him in the future? (Non–Goal Directed)

Place a mark somewhere on the following scale to indicate your child's Habit of the Mind.

Goal Setting   Non-Goal Directed

TIME MANAGEMENT VS. POOR TIME MANAGEMENT

Time Management as a Habit of the Mind refers to the extent that your child can: a) on a daily, weekly, and monthly or semester basis successfully schedule schoolwork, homework, and other extracurricular, family, and work obligations in terms of their relative priority, and b) break down long-term, complex assignments, projects, and tests into smaller, simpler steps.

Does your child…

___ appreciate the value of breaking down a large assignment or project into smaller steps? (Time Management)

___ value the importance of planning how long homework will take and when she is going to do it? (Time Management)

or

___ when given an assignment, think: "When is the very latest I can start?" (Poor Time Management)

___ disregard the importance of planning her use of time (does it only when in the mood, doesn't use a study timetable)? (Poor Time Management)

Place a mark somewhere on the following scale to indicate your child's Habit of the Mind.

Time Management   Poor Time Management

HABITS OF THE MIND

TOLERANCE OF OTHERS VS. INTOLERANCE OF OTHERS

Tolerance of Others as a Habit of the Mind refers to the extent that your child realizes and accepts that all humans are fallible and make mistakes and that it doesn't make sense to judge another person's overall worth and value on the basis of his mistakes and/or unfair actions.

Does your child...

__ accept and tolerate people even when they act unfairly or behave badly toward him? (Tolerance of Others)

__ tolerate a teacher or you even when he believes he has been treated unfairly? (Tolerance of Others)m

or

__ seem to judge other people who act unfairly as bad people and believe he should retaliate against them? (Intolerance of Others)

__ think that everyone should treat him fairly all the time? (Intolerance of Others)

Place a mark somewhere on the following scale to indicate your child's Habit of the Mind.

Tolerance of Others   Intolerance of Others

REFLECTIVE PROBLEM SOLVING VS. IMPULSIVE PROBLEM SOLVING

Reflective Problem Solving as a Habit of the Mind refers to the extent that your child, when faced with an interpersonal problem, generates a variety of solutions to a problem, considers both the positive and negative consequences of each possible solution before acting, and considers the consequences of her actions on the feelings of others.

Does your child...

___ when faced with a problem, think ahead for a solution that can solve the problem and not get her into trouble? (Reflective Problem Solving)

___ when faced with a problem, think about the different ways she can resolve it before she acts? (Reflective Problem Solving)

or

___ when faced with a problem, find it difficult to think about different courses of action that she might take to resolve it? (Impulsive Problem Solving)

___ when she has a disagreement with someone, seem to have difficulty thinking about how the other person will feel if she says something bad or nasty? (Impulsive Problem Solving)

Place a mark somewhere on the following scale to indicate your child's Habit of the Mind.

Reflective Problem Solving   Impulsive Problem Solving

HABITS OF THE MIND

TOLERANCE OF LIMITS VS. INTOLERANCE OF LIMITS

Tolerance of Limits as a Habit of the Mind refers to the extent to which your child can live with and tolerate limits as a means not only of making school, home, community, and world a better place to live, but also of achieving his own long-term goals.

Does your child...

__ seem to think that even though he doesn't like doing schoolwork and following rules, he can stand having to do so? (Tolerance of Limits)

__ believe that he can tolerate doing schoolwork even though his friends won't like it and may think he is a nerd? (Tolerance of Limits)

or

__ seem to think that he cannot stand having to behave well, do schoolwork, and follow rules? (Intolerance of Limits)

__ believe that he shouldn't have to obey rules, do schoolwork, and behave well? (Intolerance of Limits)

Place a mark somewhere on the following scale to indicate your child's Habit of the Mind.

Tolerance of Limits   Intolerance of Limits

By reviewing your evaluation of your child, you may have a pretty good sense of your child's strengths and weaknesses regarding her Habits of the Mind. This will be useful information to have as you move on to learn ways you can teach Habits of the Mind.

Consider the following destinations and the Habits of the Mind that help your child get there:

Destination Confidence: Self-Acceptance, Risk Taking, Independence, Optimism

Destination Persistence: Internal Locus of Control for Learning, High Frustration Tolerance, Optimism

Destination Organization: Goal Setting, Time Management

Destination Impulse Control: Other Acceptance, Reflective Problem Solving, Tolerance of Limits, High Frustration Tolerance

Confidence, persistence, organization, and impulse control are all important outcomes of different Habits of the Mind that lead to achievement. If your child lacks confidence, is poorly motivated, is disorganized, or breaks rules and loses his temper often, you can often trace these negative states to unhelpful Habits of the

Mind. By teaching your child about the underlying Habits of the Mind, you can do much to help your child arrive at her destination, dealing successfully with schoolwork and relating well to other people.

CHAPTER 7

DESTINATION ACHIEVEMENT: HELPING YOUR CHILD TAKE THE RIGHT BUS

Positive Habits of the Mind are the buses that will help your child arrive at the destination of both academic accomplishment and emotional well-being. The negative ones are the buses that get children to the wrong destinations. As your child reaches higher levels of mental maturity, you can begin the process of teaching personal empowerment. By explaining to your child that her feelings about schoolwork and herself, as well as the behavioral choices she makes, depend upon her own patterns of thinking, you are developing her capacity to exert greater free will over her destination. And by teaching your child the specific Habits of the Mind that are the basis of achievement, you will be providing her with the bus that will help her to develop her potential at school and achieve to the best of her ability.

One of the greatest concerns parents have about their children is how their young ones will cope with challenge and adversity when they are away from parents and home. Habits of the Mind inoculate children against life's adversity and empower them to conquer obstacles that stand in the way of their success at school and beyond. In this chapter I present ideas that can help you instill those Habits of the Mind your child might be lacking.

Remember the Checkerboard

Several years ago my son was voted by his third-grade class as Most Popular Student. I don't know why his teacher would want her class to have such a competition. Nonetheless, I was especially pleased, since my family had just moved from Australia to the United States, and this was my children's first year in a totally new school and culture.

If you knew my son, you could see why he could win such a vote. He was, and still is, a thoughtful, warm boy who does little to alienate anyone and is quick to smile and laugh. I mention this because in spite of his endearing qualities I was surprised he had won. As he often remarked to me, he had no real friends (except Travis). No one to play with after school. No one for sleepovers. He was lonely.

I understood why on the one hand his fellow classmates were taken by him but, on the other hand, he was not much taken by them. He was very judgmental and intolerant of kids his own age. When he was eight, he found it very easy to write people off. If a boy was too loud or too quiet, if a girl did something dumb, if a classmate got into trouble, my son would think they were totally hopeless and would choose not to form friendships with them.

As a psychologist as well as his well-meaning and loving father, I was bound and determined to excise from his brain the tendency to make global judgments of people as bad on the basis of their behavior. I knew full well that this bad mental habit leads people into interpersonal difficulties and conflict. Moreover, my son was unhappy with it.

It took me several weeks to find the right occasion to challenge and change the mental habit my son was using to evaluate and judge people. I wanted to teach him that evaluating people as good or bad on the basis of their behavior is rarely if ever helpful and never really makes sense. I wanted to instill in my child the idea that people are not their behavior and should not be judged by it.

The opportunity came one evening while we were changing the sheets on his bed. These sheets were of a checkerboard pattern in various shades of green and red. One or two of the squares were in fact deep green, almost black, while a few were almost white.

The conversation between my son and me went something like this.

"Son, do you see this portion of this sheet? It looks like a checkerboard only the colors are different from the usual checkerboard. The greens and reds are in various shades, light and dark."

My son waited for the revelation.

"If you look at this portion of the checkerboard," I said, pointing to an area the size of a normal checkerboard, "you can see that it is made up of many smaller squares, each having a different shade of green or red. See, this one is a light shade of green while this one is almost black."

Sensing I was on a roll and not wishing to block my progress, my son patiently nodded.

"Here's a question." I pointed at a dark square. "Does this black square make the rest of the checkerboard black?"

"No, Dad, many of the others are still light."

"Quite right. Now, when one of your classmates behaves darkly, he does the wrong thing by you, does that mean that everything about him is dark?"

He shook his head.

"When you get upset with the classmate and won't consider him as a possible friend, aren't you really forgetting about any of his good qualities? Aren't you saying that the whole checkerboard is dark because it's got a dark square?"

While we finished making the bed, I explained that if he wanted to have more friends, he would have to learn not to be so judgmental about people who do the wrong thing and to work on accepting people even though he might not like aspects of their behavior. I was not saying he should like it when others acted stupidly or that he had to put up with it when they did. That choice was his to make. However, it only makes it harder to get along with others when you are unable to mentally separate their behavior from them as people. People are made up of countless behaviors—some good, some not so good. It makes little sense to rate them as people on the basis of one behavior that occurs in one small interval of their total existence. Evaluating their behavior as bad is fine, because it will inspire you to seek change. Evaluating them as bad people is not fine, because it is rare, if not impossible, to find people with no good behavior.

There is now a standing joke in our family when my son gets too upset with someone. In fact, if I'm not around he'll often tell his mother about an incident where he got upset but will make her promise not to tell me so that he doesn't have to face me saying "Remember the Checkerboard."

Today, my son has several good friends at his new school. We recently moved again from the East to the West Coast of the United States, and with the move our children have had to adjust to new peers once again. He is still his pleasant old self but, fortunately, has not had to run for election as Mr. Popularity. Thanks to the Checkerboard, he has demonstrated greater tolerance and acceptance of others. "Remember the Checkerboard" reveals the power we parents have in instilling in our children Habits of the Mind.

> **IT'S A NO-BRAINER**
>
> The mind-set of children is the main factor in their achievement. To help them achieve to the best of their ability, we should teach them as often as possible the Habits of the Mind that are the foundations for excellence.

Ten Guidelines for Teaching Habits of the Mind

Even if you are a natural teacher, you will find it challenging to instill in your child different Habits of the Mind. You will have to make a conscious attempt to work at it. Because parenting does not come with an instructional manual for their installation, you will need to develop some techniques for helping your child develop good habits of thought.

Guideline I. Explain to your child the Habit of the Mind before, during, and after events or situations your child perceives as difficult, boring, full of rejection, or frustrating. For example, in teaching Internal Locus of Control for Learning, you could say after your child has received a good grade on an assignment he worked hard on, "Your good grade on your book report comes from your hard work and not because it was easy."

In explaining the meaning of a Habit of the Mind to your child, you will want to take note of his level of understanding and cognitive maturity. Children who are less than eight years old will not readily be able to understand an explanation concerning the relationship between their thinking and behavior, and describing a Habit of the Mind in general terms will not have much influence on the mental makeup of a child less than twelve. At twelve or so, children develop the capacity for abstract reasoning. Children younger than eight can be told what to think about a situation but will not absorb an explanation of a Habit of the Mind and spontaneously begin to apply it to new situation. So when working with a young child, you will need to model, by thinking out loud, much of the thinking your child should use in specific situations.

Guideline 2. Expect that your child will apply the habit, so that he will come to expect it of himself and use it. You will want to go over with your child ahead of time a specific way to think about an upcoming activity or even as a prelude to his using the Habit in the real world. For example, in teaching Independence as a Habit of the Mind, you might go over with your child before she starts to work the idea that mistakes are okay to make and that she can handle it when people find out she makes mistakes and is not perfect. Then, when she does start her work and encounters some difficulty, do not step in too quickly to rescue her.

Guideline 3. Model the Habit of the Mind yourself. In teaching High Frustration Tolerance, you could throw out the garbage rather than read the newspaper. You can also use examples from your own life when a Habit of the Mind helped you to achieve a goal. For example, in my writing this book, my children have seen me set some goals in terms of how many hours I wanted to write each day. At night, they have asked me how many words I managed to write. They are learning that Goal Setting helps me achieve.

Guideline 4. Use examples from other people's lives whose Habits of the Mind enabled them to conquer adversity and succeed. For example, if you are teaching your child and he is making mistakes, you could discuss the life of Thomas Edison and how he stumbled and bumbled before achieving success. There are a variety of situations and experiences, from movies to sporting events to politics, in which you and your child witness the exploits of people who have achieved, as well as seeing those who did not succeed. Their exploits offer an endless supply of examples of good and bad Habits of the Mind that the two of you or the whole family can discuss. For example, which Habit of the Mind enables politicians to campaign eighteen hours a day during election time? (Optimism, High Frustration Tolerance)

Guideline 5. Think out loud to show how a particular Habit can help you manage in a particular situation or deal with a person. For example, when your child sees you arguing with someone else and hears the other person say something that is not nice or is disrespectful, you can teach Tolerance of Others by saying, "He's not a totally bad person, even though his behavior wasn't very nice. There are other positive things about him." You can actually be instructive and directive with your child in using the think-aloud method. You can say, "When I have a big project to do at work, to make sure I get it done in time, I think to myself, 'What are the different steps I have to take to get this project done, how long will each step take, and when do I have to start the first step?' Thinking this way helps me get the big jobs done."

Guideline 6. Praise someone else in your family for applying the Habit of the Mind you wish to teach your child. Do this within earshot of your child. For example, if you want to teach your daughter Time Management, you could say to her brother, "I really like the way you are planning ahead of time what you have to do after school rather than waiting until the last minute." I am not suggesting that you add fuel to sibling rivalry or resentment. It will be important for you to balance the praise among all your children so that all children have an opportunity to learn from one another.

Guideline 7. Praise your child when you notice him applying a Habit of the Mind. The key here is to catch your child in the act of using his head. You have to observe your child engaging in some activity that he wouldn't be able to do unless he were using a Habit of the Mind. For example, you might observe that your child has not gotten too upset with herself after losing a race for her school's track team. In teaching Self-Acceptance, you could say, "I really liked the way you didn't get too upset with yourself with your slow start. You really are learning that making mistakes is a part of learning and that making mistakes doesn't mean anything about you as a person."

Praise is one of the main tools you have to reinforce your child while he is using the Habit in different situations. For example, just because your child has learned how not to take it personally when he is teased by Larry, it does not mean that he will not be upset when someone else teases him. Habits of the Mind are normally developed over a long period of time as a result of children's seeing that they benefit from them. They need lots of encouragement in the form of praise and acknowledgment during the process of learning and applying new patterns of thinking.

Guideline 8. Challenge your child's negative, nonhelpful thinking. The goal of challenging is to get your child to change the way he thinks about schoolwork, himself, or other people. It involves discovering how his perceptions and evaluations of reality really are false and helping him change his perceptions and evaluations to those that make sense, are true, and are helpful.

Challenging is a technique pioneered by Albert Ellis for uncovering and eliminating the irrational beliefs of people that lead to extreme emotional upset. You can use the challenging method to help correct and redirect aspects of your child's thinking that are not helpful, sensible, and true and which as a result give rise to poor self-confidence, lack of motivation, and other barriers to achievement. When children are older, you can actually teach them how to challenge their own nonproductive ways of thinking.

Challenging is not the same as lecturing or arguing. It's not a question of proving your child wrong and yourself right. Rather, challenging is based on the notion that just because your child thinks something is true doesn't make it true. All people, both adults and children, have a vast number of assumptions about the world, some of which are based on fact, others on fiction. For example, years ago people assumed that the world was flat and as a consequence had great fear about sailing too far away from home. Their assumption that the world was flat was not based on fact but rather on mythology. Once the risk takers sailed around the world, they provided new evidence that challenged and changed people's existing assumptions.

In a similar way, you can challenge any erroneous idea that your child has, especially those that contribute to poor endeavor in school. If your child is a teenager, you can explain the difference between a fact and an assumption. For example, you could say that the fact that he assumes he will never finish his geography assignment doesn't make it true that he won't. Once your child gets accustomed to the idea that his assumptions may not be true, it is an easy step to challenge any of his erroneous thoughts. "Let's check this thought out; is it a fact or just an assumption that you cannot do math?"

With children of any age, you can directly challenge their thinking without their understanding the difference between fact and assumption or the idea that just because they hold an idea, it doesn't necessarily follow that the idea is true. To challenge a child's thought, you can ask any or all of the following three questions:

Does it help you to think this way?	YES NO
Does it make sense to think this way?	YES NO
Is there evidence to substantiate your belief?	YES NO

If one or more of these answers is no, the thought should probably be discarded and a new, more helpful one found to replace it. For example, suppose you see your child putting off doing some math homework and hear her mumbling about the horror of having to do it. You know that homework is boring or hard and can be a hassle, but that it is not the worst thing that could happen to your child. In the moment, though, the math homework seems to your child to be the most terrible thing that could befall her.

Looking back at the Catastrophe Scale that was discussed in chapter 4, you will see the basis for challenging your child's exaggeration of the unpleasantness of homework. You could ask her what would be worse, doing difficult math homework or getting hit by a car, breaking a leg, or having the house burn down. Once you get your child to see that she is blowing the unpleasantness of the math homework out of proportion, you can then agree with her that the homework is unpleasant to do, but also remind her that in order to achieve pleasant results in the long term, she will sometimes have to do unpleasant things like math homework in the short term. In this way, challenging can be used to teach High Frustration Tolerance.

Consider this dialogue I had with my daughter, who was having trouble getting along with one of her friends:

"You seem to be thinking that friends *always* act nicely to each other and that if someone isn't nice to you, she can't be your friend."

"Uh-huh. Friends are that way."

"But is it sensible to think that way? Is that the way friends really are? Isn't there a lot of evidence around you that sometimes even the best of friends have fights?"

"Rebecca and Julie are best friends, and they fight."

"You see, your idea that friends are always nice to each other and that when someone isn't nice to you she isn't your friend doesn't make good sense. And thinking that way only makes it harder for you to have friends. Wouldn't it be more sensible for you to think 'Sometimes even good friends have disagreements and arguments'?"

I have identified five patterns of thinking that contribute to poor grades. If you catch your child revealing these attitudes, you need to help challenge and change them to more constructive ways of thinking.

Unhelpful Attitude:	Constructive Alternative:
"Everything will turn out okay whether I work or not."	"Unless I work hard, things will not turn out okay."
"School should always be fun, comfortable, exciting, and enjoyable."	"Schoolwork is sometimes going to be difficult and boring. It's not the end of the world when it's not to my liking. I can stand it."
"My friends won't like me if I work hard."	"If by working hard I do lose a friend or two, then they were probably not true friends anyway. I can do without these types of friends."
"I must be one hundred percent successful at everything I do, or I'm a complete failure."	"Not performing well does not make me a complete failure. If I make a mistake, it only means I'm learning and that I can improve the next time."
"Nothing I do at school will ever benefit me."	"What I do at school and the grades I receive have a direct influence on my future opportunities. Working hard now opens doors in the future."

Guideline 9. Provide accurate feedback to your child when she believes she is thinking in a helpful way about a situation, person, or her

work but in reality is not. I've learned that children who are not achieving their potential and are not doing as well as others in their schoolwork tend to evaluate themselves in an unrealistically positive light. For example, they can believe they have High Frustration Tolerance and can put up with lots of hassles when, in fact, there are chores or homework to do, they weave and dodge their way out of doing them.

It takes a bit of tact to confront a child's misperception. When I catch my son having strewn his clothes and schoolbooks everywhere, I sometimes say in a nonstern, slightly sarcastic, humorous, non-put-down way, "Boy, are you a wimp. I thought you said you were tough. You can't even put your clothes away. What a lightweight." The message is registered that others' perceptions of him are not those he holds of himself.

Guideline 10. Use educational material to teach specific Habits of the Mind. There are personal development books and programs for children that illustrate different Habits of the Mind, including my *Program Achieve: A Curriculum of Lessons for Teaching Children How to Be Successful and Happy in School and Life* and the *You Can Do It! A Motivational and Personal Development Curriculum for Increasing Student Achievement and Happiness in School and Life* video. The Reference section at the end of this book will give you some more ideas on where to find additional information.

One key to teaching any or all of the Habits of the Mind is for you to have a good knowledge base for recognizing and explaining both the positive and negative habits. The more you can apply any of these habits to yourself and witness their impact on you, the more enthusiastic you will be in encouraging them in your child. After all, enthusiasm marks a good teacher. It is probably not a great idea simply to read the descriptions of the different habits to your child as a first introduction. Introduce an idea around an existing situation or activity your child is engaged in.

The "uptake" time for children in learning new ways of thinking deserves mention. While it is quite possible for you to teach the meaning of each habit in a relatively short period of time, the time it takes for a child to practice and internalize the habit is relative and sometimes can take many months—in some cases, if your child is strong-willed or adolescent, longer. If for different reasons many negative habits occupy your child's mind, much work will need to be done over an extended period of time to make your child aware of them, to understand why they are not helpful and do not make sense, and for your child to incorporate newer, more helpful habits.

In the following discussion on teaching the Habits of the Mind, focus on providing enough information on each habit so that you can explain it to your child. Once you have a hold on what each habit means, you can use the guidelines above to teach it in a variety of ways and situations. The Parent Reflection Sheets offer you a series of questions that are designed to help you to begin to teach the Habits of the Mind to your child.

Teaching Self-Acceptance

In chapter 4, I described how Self-Acceptance can help you remain calm even when your child isn't doing well at school or is goofing around and not doing homework properly. It is probably the most important Habit of the Mind you can teach your child. Just as the polio vaccine inoculates your child against the virus, so Self-Acceptance inoculates your child against the psychological insult and injury associated with mistakes, bad grades, and peer-group teasing and rejection. This is important not only for helping your child maintain good mental health, but also, by preventing your child from falling into deep despair, it will make him more able to maintain the confidence and effort that goes along with sound achievement.

You can use the diagram below to teach Self-Acceptance. It illustrates how Self-Acceptance influences children's feelings and actions in a far more beneficial way than does Self-Depreciation.

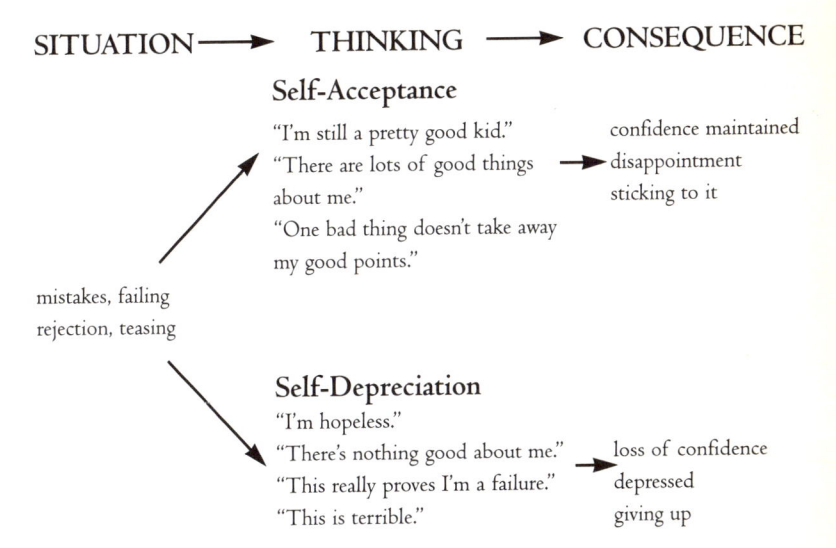

SITUATION ⟶ THINKING ⟶ CONSEQUENCE

Self-Acceptance

"I'm still a pretty good kid."
"There are lots of good things about me."
"One bad thing doesn't take away my good points."

→ confidence maintained
disappointment
sticking to it

mistakes, failing
rejection, teasing

Self-Depreciation

"I'm hopeless."
"There's nothing good about me."
"This really proves I'm a failure."
"This is terrible."

→ loss of confidence
depressed
giving up

This diagram shows how your child has options about how to think when negative things happen. Self-Acceptance leads to thinking that maintains confidence and motivation, but Self-Depreciation leads to thinking that results in feelings of hopelessness and helplessness. Self-Acceptance prevents the disappointment that occurs when your child hasn't been successful from becoming despair.

> **IDEAS THAT ENCOURAGE SELF-ACCEPTANCE**
>
> "I am worthwhile because I am."
>
> "I am made up of some good qualities and some that could be improved. It doesn't make sense to judge myself as bad because I have some not-so-good qualities."
>
> "When something bad happens, it doesn't take away my good qualities."
>
> "I accept and like who I am."

As your child gets older, you will be able to emphasize the point that his different destinations have a lot to do with his Habits of the Mind. At the same time, you will be reinforcing the idea that once we have choices as to which bus we get on, it is up to us to choose one that gets us where we want to go.

In teaching Self-Acceptance, you want to teach your child that he is made up of many positive characteristics and some that are not so good. The key for him is to learn that it never makes sense to rate himself solely on the basis of the bad things. You should challenge your child's negative thinking when you see him getting in the dumps when something bad has happened, like getting a bad grade. At these times you may say something like "You are not a D person because you got a D." Or with an older child, you may say, "Would you junk a car with a flat tire? If not, why junk yourself for not doing well in a particular class at school (or for being teased, or not being invited to a party)?"

Explain that when someone does one wrong thing, this event or behavior does not make that person a failure. Expect your child to be able to practice Self-Acceptance when suitable occasions arise. You will want to reinforce your child when you see that she isn't putting herself down when things haven't gone her way. You will also want to model Self-Acceptance. Do not be afraid of acknowledging your own mistakes in front of your child. Show that you are choosing not to be too upset by them.

Because of our human nature, Self-Acceptance does not come easily. This is especially the case for some children who are instinctively very sensitive. For some children, their tendency to put themselves down is quite strong and will have to be challenged by you and, as your children get older, by themselves. In time, however, Self-Acceptance will help all children (and ourselves) with the rough spots along the way to our personal achievements.

PARENT REFLECTION SHEET: TEACHING SELF-ACCEPTANCE

1. In your own words, what is Self-Acceptance?

_____

_____

2. List some situations in which your child has put herself down for not doing well or for having problems with her friends.

_____

_____

3. Together with your child, write down four of her positive characteristics and four of her not-so-good characteristics (at school, at home, personality, interests, skills). Then discuss with your child how people are made up of many good and not-so-good things and that you cannot really judge them as totally good or all bad. People have value because of their unique special qualities.

positive   1. _____ 2. _____ 3. _____ 4. _____
not-so-good 1. _____ 2. _____ 3. _____ 4. _____

4. Your child has just made an error in completing her work and has said, "Oh well, at least I got the other seven sections correct!" What could you comfortably say to reinforce your child for not taking the error personally and for accepting herself?

_____

_____

5. Think of yourself at home in the past several weeks. List two situations in which you could have modeled (or did) that making a mistake is okay and that you are not going to whip yourself for it or think less of yourself.

_____

Teaching Risk Taking

In chapter 8, I will suggest ways to support and encourage a perfectionistic child. For now, I want to zero in on the chief Habit of the Mind, Risk Taking, that can help combat a child's fear of trying new things or extending herself. If your child gets too upset when she doesn't achieve as well as she thinks she should, Risk Taking is a very suitable antidote.

To become an achiever or to extend her current achievement, your child will be helped enormously if she can handle the prospect of not being successful. Tackling new tasks and difficult assignments is risky for anyone because of the possibility that she might make mistakes, not know what to do, not compare well with others, or fail. Indeed, you will want your child, without prodding from you or a teacher, to attempt to do things at which she is likely to fail. If she doesn't, and stays within the comfort zone of doing things she already can do pretty well, she will never learn what she can do and cannot do. She will not grow in areas in which she has talent but is afraid to take the risk.

By Risk Taking, I do not mean taking irresponsible risks, that your child participate in highly dangerous activities at which he could get hurt. Nor does Risk Taking lead a child to risk all his marbles by trying things that appear beyond his capabilities. For example, if your child needs a certain grade point average to gain entry to a certain program or college, I would not at all encourage his taking a course for which he lacks the academic grounding or talent, in which he is likely to earn a low grade. That would be an irresponsible risk.

> **IDEAS THAT ENCOURAGE RISK TAKING**
>
> "While it's nice to do things very well, when I don't, it's not the end of the world."
>
> "I don't have to be successful or perfect in everything I do."
>
> "What's important is trying my best."
>
> "Making mistakes is a natural part of learning."
>
> "If I don't make mistakes, I'm not going to do as well at things as if I do."
>
> "It's much more important to concentrate on improving my work than on comparing myself with how other students are doing."
>
> "It's good to try things even if at first I might not be terrific."

When you teach Risk Taking, you will explain to your child that the greatest mistake she can make is to be afraid of making a mistake. Emphasize the value of striving to do your best but not demanding of yourself that you must be great all the time. Using your own experiences, model that it's not a catastrophe if you don't succeed at everything you try. Encourage your child to try new things even if he might not be successful. Do this in noncompetitive areas first; then, have him take on more competitive activities. Create a climate at home in which mistakes and less than perfect performance are encouraged, especially in the beginning phase of learning. Closely monitor what you and other members of your family say when your child does not achieve a perfect result or receives less than an A on her report card.

PARENT REFLECTION SHEET: TEACHING RISK TAKING

1. Identify areas of your child's schoolwork in which your child most shows his perfectionistic Habit of the Mind (having to do things perfectly). List any areas he may be avoiding because of his fear of not being perfect.

_____

_____

_____

2. In words that suit the maturity of your child, summarize what you could say to develop Risk Taking as a new Habit of the Mind to replace Perfectionism.

_____

_____

3. Imagine that your child has completed a task and has not done it perfectly. Write down a comment that you could make that would give your child the message that although he has not done it perfectly, that is okay and he is okay.

_____

_____

4. Is there anything that you or someone else at home does to discourage your child from making mistakes and encourage his doing things perfectly?

_____

_____

5. What can you or your significant other do to model the message that making mistakes is okay and that everyone makes them?

_____

_____

Teaching Independence

Independence is a Habit of the Mind that you may wish to teach your child if he is too concerned about what others think of him. If your child worries too much about how he is viewed by peers or adults, it is likely that he has an Approval-Seeking Habit of the Mind. Approval Seeking involves a child believing not only that he would like approval from others, but also that he needs it from people he comes in contact with, and that it is awful not to have it. The fear of rejection that is mainly caused by Approval Seeking may cause your child to conform to peers who are not working. Alternatively, he may work very much within his capabilities, restricting his creativity and nonconformity, to avoid appearing to his teacher to be a mistakemaker or troublemaker.

The important point to stress in teaching Independence is the difference between *wanting* or *preferring* another's approval and needing the approval. Explain to your child that while it's definitely nice to be liked, he doesn't need to be liked by everyone all the time. Have a discussion about the difference between wants and needs. Explain that there are a few basic human needs, things we cannot do without: water, food, air, clothing, and shelter. Those things we can survive without, such as the latest Levi's jeans or not being invited to a party, are wants. Wants are important; when your child receives what he wants he is happier. However, it is useful for your child to learn that he can tolerate and survive not having all his wants met. When others disapprove of him for making mistakes or doing his work, this will not kill him. He will survive.

Obviously, you will not hold this abstract conversation when your child is still in diapers! Until your child is around the age of eight, and his thinking is mature enough so that he can understand the difference between a want and a need, it will be better for you to help build up his resilience to situations in which his peers are teasing him or he hasn't done all that well in school. For example, if you see your son upsetting himself because he received a negative comment on his writing assignment, you can say, "I know how you feel. However, it's not the end of the world if your teacher thinks you can do better. You can stand it!"

If your child is especially sensitive to being called names and takes them personally, ask, "If someone called you a fish would that make you a fish? If not, why do you think you're a nerd because someone said you were?" When your child can see that others' opinions of her are only opinions, not facts, it will be easier for her to give up her Approval Seeking.

IDEAS THAT ENCOURAGE INDEPENDENCE

"What people think of me, good or bad, doesn't make it so."

"While it's nice to be liked, I don't need it all the time."

"If my friends want me to hang out and not work, I can still do my work anyway."

"If they don't like it, maybe I'll have to find new friends."

"It's important to stick up for what I believe and what I want to do."

PARENT REFLECTION SHEET: TEACHING INDEPENDENCE

1. Provide an example of a family member or friend who reveals Independence in his behavior. Describe to your child a time when this person did something even though he risked losing approval or being rejected by others.

_____

_____

2. Challenge the belief that your child couldn't stand it if a classmate hassled her for working hard at her schoolwork. Write down what you would say.

_____

_____

3. What can you say to your child if she appears to worry too much about what others think about her hair or clothes?

_____

_____

4. Would you describe yourself as having an Independent Habit of the Mind and not being overreliant on other people's approval? Explain.

_____

_____

5. What are some things you can encourage your child to do for which she might invite the temporary disapproval of others by doing something silly (for instance walking a banana down the street)? Once she has survived, discuss with her the fact that she now has evidence that she can stand being thought foolish by others.

_____

_____

Teaching Optimism

Optimism is a Habit of the Mind that will help your child remain confident when he is faced with difficult and challenging situations, and it will help him persist in doing difficult schoolwork. It has also been linked to good mental health. On the other hand, pessimism has been associated not only with depression but with the tendency to withhold the effort required to succeed at frustrating, difficult tasks. If you have found your child to be more pessimistic than optimistic, you will be happy to learn that there are methods you can employ to help him change.

Optimistic children predict success at their schoolwork, take the credit when they get good results, attribute lack of success to outside events beyond their control (difficulty of work) or to not having worked hard enough, do not blow mistakes or rejections out of proportion, and have Self-Acceptance. Setbacks are seen as temporary.

On the other hand, pessimistic children predict difficulty or failure in their schoolwork, think they are hopeless and incompetent when they fail, explain their failures in terms of global, unchanging, internal attributes such as lack of ability, take one setback and generalize it to everything they are doing, credit their successes to outside events (luck, ease of work), and are self-depreciators. Setbacks signal permanent failure.

One of the most common beliefs of many underachieving children is associated with pessimism. Because of a history of failure at school, children can develop the belief that "It doesn't matter how hard I try, I'll never be successful." This negative forecast for the future, combined with a disassociation of achievement from effort, is not the bus you want your child to be on. If your child holds this belief, it is vital that you work closely with your child's teachers to ensure that he begins to see that with additional effort, he can be successful. In time, success as a result of effort will help reduce your child's pessimism.

In helping your child become optimistic, you should help him take credit for the successes he has at his schoolwork. ("Your effort and ability made the difference.") When failure occurs, help him attribute its cause to temporary, internal, and specific factors over which he has

---

IDEAS THAT ENCOURAGE OPTIMISM

"Even though it may take some time, I know I can do it."

"One failure doesn't mean I'll always fail."

"Mistakes mean I'm one step closer to success."

"I've done hard things before, I know I can do them again."

"Predict success."

control. ("You didn't do as well on your algebra because you didn't spend enough time working on it.") When he has difficulty in some aspects of his schoolwork, you can help him maintain a positive view of the present by helping him focus on the things he is doing well. In terms of dealing with past failures, teach your child not to take full responsibility for them. ("That Spanish test was impossible. I would have failed it, and I speak Spanish!")

When your child is faced with a difficult task requiring confidence and persistence, ask him to think of the last time he was successful at doing something he did not think he could do. He can then use this success experience in approaching the new task. Once your child has in mind his past success, encourage him to think "I've succeeded at difficult work before, I can do it again." If you teach your child this strategy, he will have a method to boost his own confidence through the use of optimistic thoughts.

As your child gets older, you can introduce the following diagram and explain the options he has in terms of thinking pessimistically or optimistically.

SITUATION ⟶ THINKING ⟶ CONSEQUENCE

Optimism

"I can do this."
"I have the talent to be able to do this."
"Even when I goof up I know I still do other things well."
"If I keep trying, I'll do it."
"If I make mistakes, I'll just have to try harder and not rush it the next time."

⟶ strong confidence
sticking to it

difficult and challenging assignment, exam, or situation

Pessimism

"I can't do this."
"What's the point in trying?"
"I'll never be able to do this."
"I'm not good at anything."
"It's my fault this is so hard."
"If I'm successful, it's because I was lucky or it was easy."
"Failure will happen because I'm stupid."

loss of confidence
⟶ giving up

PARENT REFLECTION SHEET: TEACHING OPTIMISM

1. In which situations do you catch your child being most pessimistic?

_____

_____

2. Provide examples of people you and your child have known who are optimistic and describe situations in which their confidence contributed to their success.

_____

_____

3. Think of current or future situations in your own work and personal life that you consider challenging. How could you think out loud to model Optimism for your child?

_____

_____

4. When you catch your child thinking pessimistically ("I'm no good at math"), what could you say to challenge and change her thinking?

_____

_____

5. Think of a situation, task, or schoolwork that your child finds hard. Write down some optimistic thoughts that could increase her confidence. Discuss them with your child.

_____

_____

Teaching Internal Locus of Control for Learning

The word "locus" simply means "place." You want your child to know that the place where learning originates and is controlled is internal, inside him. And you want to instill in your child the belief that effort is the main control that he can exert over his learning and success. The more his effort, the greater the success. Lack of success comes from not enough effort. Who controls effort? Not you, not his teachers, not TV—your child does!

Many children with an External Locus of Control for Learning mistakenly believe that "Everything will turn out okay whether I work or not." This is especially the case if their parents tend to be overinvolved in their schoolwork and have helped to bail them out when they have failed to get their work finished on time. Obviously, one of the most direct routes for challenging this idea is to make sure that the next time your child doesn't do his work, things do not turn out okay. That is, stop rescuing him and let the full natural consequences of not working hard take their toll (failing a test or a class, reproaches from teacher, personal embarrassment).

One idea that you will want to combat in helping your child develop an appreciation of the connection between her own effort to her success is what has been called the fixed entity concept of ability. Some children believe that either you were born good at something or you were not, and if you were not, there is little point in trying. Children with an Internal Locus of Control have an incremental concept of ability. They believe that the more you try something, the better you get at it. It's trying, not the ability you were born with, that leads to success.

IDEAS THAT ENCOURAGE AN INTERNAL LOCUS OF CONTROL

"The harder I try, the better my success."

"The more I practice, the better I am at it."

"When I am successful, it's because I tried hard and I'm good at it."

"When I don't do so well, maybe I rushed it or didn't try hard enough."

Consider whether any areas of your own child's poor motivation can be caused by her belief that she doesn't have the talent to achieve to begin with. If this is so, you should spend considerable time over many occasions explaining to her the incremental concept of ability and challenging her fixed entity concept of ability.

I cannot stress too strongly how important it is for your child's achievement for her to recognize the importance of persistent effort. Over the years, I have tried in many ways to instill this habit in my own children. For example, once several years ago my son said he needed some special basketball cards for that evening. This was at 4:30 in the afternoon, and I knew that the stores that sold the type of cards he wanted closed around 5:00 P.M. Off we dashed to one, two, and three stores, but with no success. He looked at me dubiously. As traffic mounted, I definitely felt like giving up. However, I sensed that this was an opportunity to teach him that effort pays off in results. I knew of one last store that might still be open. Off we raced again, and we arrived at 5:20 P.M. to find the store still open, with a fresh supply of cards having just arrived that afternoon. Before my son began opening the cards, we spent some time discussing our adventure and how sometimes, not always, when you push yourself just that little bit further, you may achieve your goals.

You should also explain to your child that when she has succeeded at a task, she has a choice about the way she views that success. Two different ways of thinking about the success are:

1. She may attribute her success to luck or to the ease of the task. This type of thinking may cause her to lose motivation.
2. She may attribute her success to the fact that she worked hard and put in a lot of effort. This type of thinking leads to strong motivation.

You can ask your child about times when she was successful but attributed her success to luck rather than effort. Ask whether some of her successes might be better attributed to her own trying than to luck. Ask her about the effects on her motivation of attributing her successes to her own efforts.

Read "Out of Luck" and then ask your child the following questions:

1. Why was Jonathon's father surprised?
2. Why did Jonathon throw away his good luck charm?
3. What is the moral of the story?

OUT OF LUCK

Jonathon had been playing soccer for five months. Although he loved to play during training, he never played as well as he could in the actual games on Saturdays.

Jonathon's father told him: "You're not trying hard enough during the game. You're allowing others to control the game. If you want to play better, you will have to play harder."

Jonathon seemed to accept his father's advice, but he still didn't play well in the next three games. In fact, he didn't score any goals. Jonathon's coach started to take Jonathon out of the game, replacing him with other players.

The time came for the big game. Jonathon's team could be the first in the league, but he seemed very discouraged and was almost ready to quit. His father reminded him once more about the importance of trying hard during the game. "It's not that you are not good enough, you are. It's just that you are not making a big enough effort during the games. You can do it this Saturday if you really try."

That Saturday, Jonathon played as hard as he had ever played. The result was that he played his best game ever, scoring two goals and helping his team to victory. Jonathon's father was happy because not only was Jonathon happy, but also he knew Jonathon had learned an important lesson about how effort produces results.

Later that same day, Jonathon's father received a real surprise. Jonathon and he were playing a game in which each player tried to throw a tennis ball on a coin sitting on the ground, trying to make the coin turn over. After hitting the coin and turning it over twice in a row, Jonathon reached into his sock and pulled out a small chain. "Dad, this is my good luck charm. I had it with me during the soccer game and I scored two goals. Now, it's helping me beat you!"

Looking slightly pained, Jonathon's father explained once again that effort was the key to his son's success in the soccer game, not luck. Jonathon decided his father was right and threw the good luck charm away.

PARENT REFLECTION SHEET: TEACHING INTERNAL LOCUS OF CONTROL FOR LEARNING

1. What messages has your child heard at home concerning the importance of effort rather than results?

_____

_____

2. If you do not already know, determine whether your child has an incremental concept of ability or a fixed entity concept of ability. Ask him what he thinks about both his strong and his weaker classes. What have you found out?

_____

_____

_____

3. In which areas of your child's schoolwork would it help to remind him of the importance of the effort he was putting in?

_____

_____

4. Whom could you praise at home for demonstrating Internal Locus of Control by the way he persists at his work?

_____

_____

5. Describe a recent time when you illustrated for your child how a person's success and achievement was due to effort and not luck or ease of task.

_____

_____

Teaching High Frustration Tolerance

If you have discovered in getting to know your child's Habits of the Mind that she has Low Frustration Tolerance, it is likely that she has an "allergic" reaction to certain schoolwork or doing chores and would rather be spending her time enjoying herself. She is likely to hold one or more of the following beliefs that you can challenge and change:

"Schoolwork should always be fun and exciting."

"I should never have to do boring or difficult work."

"I can't stand doing homework or chores."

The question is how to instill High Frustration Tolerance in your child. There are several ways this can occur. It is important that your child have a set of expectations to meet. He needs to know what is expected of him in his schoolwork and that you are firm in your resolve that he will meet the expectations. The expectations or rules do not have to be onerous:

"Make an honest effort in all areas of schoolwork."

"Do your chores before relaxing or playing."

With these expectations as a guideline, you can teach your child that certain types of thinking will help him be successful in meeting the expectations, while other types of thinking will not. The habit of thinking "Homework is terrible. I can't stand doing it" is not a habit that will help your child achieve the goal. You can challenge this type of thinking by having your child put the unpleasantness of doing certain homework assignments or chores into perspective ("It's not the worst thing in the world") and getting him to see that since he has survived homework and chores before, he will continue to do so in the future.

IDEAS THAT ENCOURAGE HIGH FRUSTRATION TOLERANCE

"In order to achieve pleasant results in the long term, I sometimes will have to do unpleasant things in the short term."

"If I put off doing work today, it will only be harder to do tomorrow."

"I can stand doing things I don't feel like doing."

Being firm with your child is as important as working on his habits of thought. When you catch him perspiring mentally over some difficult assignment, you need to praise the thinking that got him there. ("See, you can tolerate it. That's real mental toughness.") But when your child dodges work and is distracted by short-term pleasantness rather than pursuing long-term rewards, you can assertively get him back on task and, if necessary, penalize him for demonstrating Low Frustration Tolerance. ("Thinking that this work can wait until you are in the mood is the wrong bus to be on. It's the fun bus to be on, but you pay the price later on. Now, no telephone until after you get on the right bus and get back to work.")

Another powerful influence that contributes to your child's development of High Frustration Tolerance is the models he encounters at home. The father in the drawing is putting off having fun playing ball with his son until after he has worked on his taxes. The more you and other family members model and demonstrate High Frustration Tolerance in actions and words ("I don't like writing this chapter on Sunday morning, but I can stand it"), the more your child will internalize this habit.

Finally, Goal Setting is a Habit of the Mind that helps encourage High Frustration Tolerance. When your child is working toward goals that he values, he will find it easier to justify the sacrifice of short-term pleasures.

PARENT REFLECTION SHEET: TEACHING HIGH FRUSTRATION TOLERANCE

1. In your own words, explain High Frustration Tolerance.

_____

_____

2. What expectations have you communicated to your child about her responsibilities for schoolwork and homework? Are you firm in your follow-through?

_____

_____

3. Your child learns a great deal from watching her parents. In your family, what would children learn from watching you and your significant other working on difficult or boring tasks?

_____

_____

4. How could you challenge your child's thinking "I can't stand this homework"?

_____

_____

5. Write down the homework that your child finds most boring to do. What can you say when you see her putting in the effort to remind her that her mind-set toward the work is helping her get through it? ("See, by telling yourself the sooner you get it done the more time you will have for fun helps you to do it.")

_____

_____

Teaching Goal Setting

Zillions of dollars have been spent over the past thirty years or more on educational research that reveals quite clearly that children who set their own goals in school are more motivated and generally achieve better results than those who do not. Why? The reasons are pretty obvious. Having a goal that she wants to achieve gives your child a direction. It helps justify in her own mind having to do work along the way that she would otherwise choose not to do. And because it is your child's own goal, she has a greater commitment to achieving it.

Unfortunately, as is the case with almost all of the other Habits of the Mind, Goal Setting is not generally taught in school. It will frequently be up to you to show your child how to set goals and to show him how setting goals on a regular basis helps him achieve good results.

You may wish to help your child set goals in different areas of her life. You may want to concentrate on educational goals such as specific improvements in grades. If your child is a teenager, you could help her develop career or work-related goals. Personal goals, the type of person your child would like to become, can also be discussed and set.

You will want to teach your child three types of goals. Long-term goals are the things your child will achieve in time. For younger children, "in time" may mean three months to a year. For adolescents, "long-term" can mean what they want to be doing in ten to twenty years. Long-term goals help bring the future into the present and will help your child see the connection between current and short-term activities and his future success. Achieving children set big long-term goals. Rather than setting small, modest goals that would meet the modest expectations of their peer group or home environment, achieving children "go for gold." Examples of long-term goals that are big include: be an excellent airplane mechanic, become the best teacher ever, graduate from high school or college, star on the school basketball team, be a fantastic friend.

IDEAS THAT ENCOURAGE GOAL SETTING

"Setting long-term goals helps me to achieve and be happy."

"Short-term and daily goals help me to achieve my long-term goals."

"When I set a goal, I will commit myself a hundred percent to its achievement."

"I will not allow myself to be distracted by outside events and people."

"Luck is not involved in achieving goals."

Achieving children also rely on short-term goals, which they set at realistic levels—out of reach, but not out of sight. Examples of short-term goals include: specific grades in specific subjects, a specific number of words correctly spelled on the weekly spelling test, writing a specific number of letters seeking summer employment, and meeting a certain number of new people. Examples of short-term, realistic goals are: get a B in math, get an A in English, get at least a C in the weakest subject, make the basketball team, spend more time listening to and supporting friends.

Daily goals involve your child's deciding how much time she will devote to different activities, how much work she will accomplish for homework, or how well she will accomplish the work each day. Examples of specific, daily goals are: do thirty minutes of practice math problems, get an A on an English research project, get started on the first part of a science project, call up friends and ask if they'd like to come over this weekend.

A SEVEN-STEP PROCESS FOR TEACHING YOUR CHILD TO SET GOALS

Step 1. Define your goal clearly (make a B in Spanish).

Step 2. List the steps to reach this goal (amount of work, skills to learn).

Step 3. Think of problems that might come up that would interfere (distractions, other commitments).

Step 4. Think of solutions to these problems (say no to distractions, have a timetable).

Step 5. Set a time for reaching the goal (end of term).

Step 6. Evaluate your progress (keep track of results on class assignments and tests).

Step 7. Reward yourself for accomplishments (go to a movie).

—Bob McCombs & J. E. Pope, *Motivating Hard to Reach Students*

In teaching Goal Setting, you will also have to introduce the important concept of commitment. There is a difference between being committed to doing something and promising to do something. A commitment is a solemn pledge to do what you say you are going to do, whereas a promise is a much lighter form of commitment that is easier to break when conflicts or distractions arise. You should emphasize to your child that a goal without a full commitment to its achievement is like New Year's resolutions, easy to break. Sitting down with your child and helping her spell out her goals for subjects in which she would like to improve can be a tremendous catalyst for improved grades and achievement. Getting children in the habit of setting goals without adult assistance is an even greater parental achievement.

PARENT REFLECTION SHEET: TEACHING GOAL SETTING

1. What long-term goals do you have for your child?

Education goals _____

Career/work goals _____

Personal goals (kind of person you'd like him to be)_____

_____

2. Does your child have any short-term goals for the next six months? If so, write down as specifically as you can what you think they are.

Educational goals (grades in subjects, awards)_____

Personal goals _____

_____

3. In which subjects would it be good to do some goal setting with your child?

_____

_____

4. In which areas of your life do you model goal setting for your child? Are there areas of your own life in which you practice goal setting as an encouragement for your child?

_____

_____

5. What are some areas of your child's schoolwork in which you could praise him for setting goals?

_____

_____

_____

Teaching Time Management

Time Management is a skill that ought to be taught more in school. It's not. If it isn't taught in your child's school, it is difficult for your child to develop Time Management as a habit. So if you find that your child could be doing a lot better in school if only she did not rush to finish things at the last minute, then Time Management will help her become more efficient.

There are two time management skills to teach your child. The first skill, *time planning*, involves the how-to of scheduling time. The second skill, *task analysis*, involves

---

IDEAS THAT ENCOURAGE TIME MANAGEMENT

"Set priorities about what's important to do."

"Break down complicated tasks into smaller ones."

"Establish a set time to start homework."

"Establish in advance how much time to spend on homework each night."

"Keep track of when all assignments are due."

"To successfully complete assignments, ask yourself: 'When is the very latest I can start the *last* step?'"

"Reward yourself for work completed."

breaking down long-term and complicated assignments and projects into simpler, smaller steps. Your mission is not an easy one, for it involves not only teaching these two skills, but making sure your child practices them enough so that she gets into the habit of using them. Obviously, the more that she sees that planning her time and breaking down complicated projects into smaller steps leads to her being more successful than when she doesn't, the greater the likelihood that Time Management will develop from a skill to a habit.

Teaching time planning is relatively easy. It involves showing your child how to use three different types of schedules: a monthly assignment calendar, a weekly timetable, and a daily schedule. This is very straightforward. Every time your child receives notification of a forthcoming test, assignment, or project, the due date is entered on a monthly assignment calendar. This way she can see on one page when things are due and when conflicts in studying for different subjects may arise. I have found that many children do not believe they have enough hours in the day to get everything done and still have time left over for fun and recreation. This is sometimes the case when a high school student is studying for exams. However, there is generally more time than children think. A weekly timetable shows children concretely how much schoolwork and free time they really have. In completing a weekly timetable, your child would start off by shading in with a colored pencil those time periods that correspond with the amount of homework his school expects of him each day and on weekends. After that, with different-colored pencils, he writes in each after-school extracurricular activity, any after-school/weekend jobs, sleep and meal times, and housework time. Time unaccounted for is his own. In addition, your child will be able to decide on the priority of the various homework tasks that he has to do each evening.

An important point to make to your child about the use of a weekly timetable is that it needs to be used flexibly. After it has been completed at the beginning of the week, when other activities and homework unexpectedly come up, they need to be incorporated into the timetable, and other prescheduled activities and homework should be shifted around. The point to stress, however, is that it is not permissible to take away from study time and not replace the time later that day or on the weekend. If your child has two hours of homework to do each school night with the exception of Friday and four hours of homework on the weekend, then twelve hours of homework need to be scheduled for that week, no matter what.

COMMON DISTRACTIONS TO TIME MANAGEMENT AND SOLUTIONS

1. Television. Solution: Only watch your favorite shows after you've done your homework. If you have a VCR, record shows that you will want to watch later.

2. Telephone. Solution: Tell your friends you'll call them back.

3. Friends. Solution: Ask yourself: "What's more important, hanging out with my friends or getting my work done first?"

The daily schedule helps your child get organized for a night's homework. By referring to his weekly timetable as well as looking at the homework that has been assigned that day at school and is due the following day, your child will have a clear idea what homework he has to do from the time he comes home from school until he goes to bed. He should write down the specific work he will do to accomplish his homework and at what time he will do it. He can schedule his homework around his other after-school commitments.

Teaching your child how to do a task analysis is much trickier. Your child can use a task analysis to help simplify the steps she has to take when she has a long-term project or assignment to complete that is due in a week or month. The two questions that frequently bamboozle students are: a) When should I start the assignment? and b) What should I do first?

In fact, it has been discovered that many underachievers ask the wrong time management question. When they receive an assignment, their typical first question is "When is the very latest I can start this assignment?" They frequently underestimate the time it takes to do the work and are forever rushing at the last minute. As a consequence, the quality of their work suffers a great deal. Unfortunately, many underachievers never learn from their mistakes. They continue to leave insufficient time to get their next project satisfactorily completed.

Once your child learns task analysis, she has the tools to work efficiently to get her schoolwork done on time without having to rush at the very last minute.

To teach your child to do a task analysis, you will want to teach him the following steps. These are almost always the same regardless of the assignment.

Step 1. Make sure you understand the assignment question and know what the teacher expects. Some children make the mistake of only reading part of the question. Others think they know what a question is asking but have misinterpreted the question. Still others have difficulty in fully understanding what the question actually means. For example, my son had to do a time line for a third-grade social studies assignment. But while he had some sense of what a time line was, he had never seen one.

Step 2. Collect necessary information (research). Most projects and assignments cannot be started until after your child has gathered the necessary information to answer the assignment question. This step is what scientists call the data-gathering step of research. This step involves your child's thinking about all the different types of resources she will need and where they are located (in-class notes, library, interviewing people).

Step 3. Think about and analyze information in terms of the assignment question to be answered. Before your child starts writing or designing the assignment, some time should be spent thinking about the information she has collected. This should be the time for creativity. For example, with the time line assignment, my son looked at the photographs of his family, the information he gathered from separate interviews with his mother, sister, and myself concerning what they considered to be significant events in his life that deserved entry on his time line, as well as his passport. Without putting pencil to paper, he spent some time considering how all the different bits of information fitted together to represent his first eight years of life. This step enables the child to tell the difference between the significant and the insignificant information she has collected and to decide what material deserves special emphasis.

Step 4. Make an outline. Your child needs to know that the grade she receives will reflect not only the quality of the information presented, but also whether it is presented in a sequence that makes sense. In a time line, a logical order is pretty much built into the assignment. The early events in your life precede the later ones until you arrive at the present day. For other assignments, more thought is required to decide how all the information should be assembled. For example, consider the following foreign language assignment: "Prepare a play in the form of a plausible conversation between two characters of the French Revolution." Before a script is written, an outline of the topics to be covered in conversation in the beginning, middle, and end would likely lead to a more sensible conversation. Sometimes, your child's teacher is willing and prepared to have a quick look at the outline to make sure your child is on track.

Step 5. Write a first draft. Most of your child's teachers will recommend that she write a first draft. Normally, the first draft takes the lion's share of time. If your child has a computer with a word processing program and if her teacher accepts computer-printed assignments, then your child will save an enormous amount of time when she comes to revise the first draft. Once the first draft has been completed, your child should review it to make sure that she has included all the information necessary and that it is presented in the most sensible order. Attention should be paid to sentence structure and to making sure that sentences are not too long and that they make sense.

Step 6. Final Draft. The final draft is the stage at which the final cutting and polishing of the assignment to be handed in takes place. Once written, it needs to be carefully edited for spelling and punctuation. Any special design features should be added to enhance its visual presentation.

It is not necessary for all task analyses to have six steps. Your child may find it more sensible to have more or fewer steps. For example, if the assignment is part of a cooperative learning project in which students learn from each other, then additional steps will need to be included.

Once your child has outlined each step, she then needs to estimate how many minutes or hours each step will take. The first step, understanding the question, usually takes a relatively short period of time, while gathering information/research takes much longer. Your child should employ the following procedure:

Starting with the last step, ask yourself: "When is the very latest date I can start the last step?" Look at your monthly or semester calendar and schedule this last step on that date. Then ask yourself:

"When is the very latest that I can start the second to the last step?" Schedule this step on that date in your calendar. Do this for each step, including the first one. Once this is completed, your child will know when she will have to start her assignment in order to do it well and hand it in on time.

I've included a sample activity page that you and your child can use to learn the process of task analysis and time planning. Have your child select a homework assignment that is due in several weeks' time and work through the steps.

YOU CAN DO IT!

TASK ANALYSIS AND TIME PLANNING

Directions: Write down an assignment or project that is due in several or more weeks. Then do the following:

1. Break down the assignment into smaller steps for completion. 2. For each smaller step, estimate the time required for completion. 3. Starting with the last step, write in the last date on which you can begin each step (use a calendar).

Assignment: _____

_____

_____

_____

Date Assigned: _____ Date Due: _____

STEPS (use only as many steps as you need)

Step 1. _____
Step 2. _____
Step 3. _____
Step 4. _____
Step 5. _____
Step 6. _____
Step 7. _____
Step 8. _____

Time Planning:

Step No.	Amount of Time Required for Completion	Last Possible Starting Date
Step 8.	_____	_____
Step 7.	_____	_____
Step 6.	_____	_____
Step 5.	_____	_____
Step 4.	_____	_____
Step 3.	_____	_____
Step 2.	_____	_____
Step 1.	_____	_____

Teaching Tolerance of Others

The "Remember the Checkerboard" teaching example presented at the beginning of this chapter can be used to teach your child to accept other people in spite of their behavior. This is not an easy mental habit for any of us to learn. When someone acts unfairly or unjustly, or we perceive that in some way we are being attacked, it is very difficult for us to think about the other redeeming qualities of the person who is acting in an unacceptable way.

The drawing of a mother yelling at her daughter about cleaning her room illustrates this point from the daughter's point of view. It is unfair of the mother to be yelling about something that has little if anything to do with schoolwork. At that moment, it would be easy for the daughter to paint her mother as totally in the wrong. However, by painting her mother all one color, as opposed to being made from many different colors, she is creating her own anger. And when and if she decides that getting back at her mother by not doing her work is

> **IDEAS THAT ENCOURAGE TOLERANCE OF OTHERS**
>
> "Teachers, parents, and my friends will sometimes act unfairly, inconsiderately, and not the way I want. That's the way people are."
>
> "People who make mistakes by not letting me do what I want are not totally bad."
>
> "People who do the wrong thing do not deserve to be punished."
>
> "People are complex, not simple, and cannot be judged as totally bad or good on the basis of their bad or good points."
>
> "I can accept that people have the right to do what they think is right, even though I think what they are doing is wrong."

making a problem for her, she will have to paint a different multicolored picture of her mother.

Encourage your child to strongly prefer fairness, consideration, and justice from others. Discourage him, however, from demanding it from others and rating others as totally bad people when they act in nonpreferred ways. Condemnation of others is equivalent to intolerance, and intolerance leads to anger and bigotry.

Here are two different thought patterns. The first leads to unhealthy and unhelpful levels of anger and rage. The second leads to frustration tolerance and assertive behavior.

These thinking patterns lead to intolerance of others:

1. "He is treating me unfairly and badly."
2. "He should act fairly and considerately all the time."
3. "I can't stand this behavior."
4. "He's a real jerk who deserves to be punished."

These thinking patterns lead to tolerance of others:

1. "He is treating me unfairly and badly."
2. "I would prefer him to act considerately."
3. "This is bad behavior."
4. "I don't like the behavior, but I can stand it."
5. "He is not his behavior. He is acting like a fallible human. How can I get him to change?"

If your child is rebellious or if he has problems controlling his temper, his behavior may prevent him from focusing on schoolwork. You can help him lose much of his anger by teaching him Tolerance of Others. Teach your child to view others' negative behaviors as only part of the person. Praise someone at home for being tolerant and for not losing it completely in the face of extreme provocation. In your home, nurture a climate of tolerance.

PARENT REFLECTION SHEET: TEACHING TOLERANCE OF OTHERS

1. In your own words, explain Tolerance of Others.

_____

_____

2. (a) Think of someone who seems to push your anger button. Write a list of some of this person's positive qualities.

_____

(b) The next time this person behaves badly, what are some things you could think of to reduce the intensity of your anger?

_____

3. Imagine that your child is furious about something his teacher has or hasn't done (picked on him in class). Write down some things you could say that might challenge some of the things he is thinking that are creating his anger ("I can't stand it!").

_____

_____

4. Have your child provide the name of someone who presses his anger button. Then, have him list the person's good points and not-so-good points. Explain that people are made up of many good and not-so-good qualities and that bad ones do not take away the good ones.

_____

_____

Teaching Reflective Problem Solving

More than twenty years ago, Dr. George Spivack and his colleagues Jerome Platt and Myrna Shure conducted an intensive study into why young people kept getting into trouble, having fights, stealing, skipping school, and, as a consequence, were underachieving at school. At that time, it was thought that the aggressive behavior of young people was caused by unresolved conflicts with their parents and that unconscious motives were causing their problems.

These investigators, who worked with many adolescents, failed to find deep, mysterious psychodynamics at play. Rather, they found that many young people who get into lots of trouble are doing so for far simpler reasons. It appears that many young people do not think about the consequences of their behavior before they take action. This failure to think is not caused by limitations in intelligence. Rather, it appears that some adolescents, because of their temperament, their negative experiences in school, the influence of their peer group, and, sometimes, negative influences at home, have never been thought to be reflective; that is, they act on impulse.

If you find that your child gets into more than his share of trouble, it may well be that he has an Impulsive Problem Solving Habit of the Mind. When faced with interpersonal problems or people who he perceives treat him unfairly, rather than reflecting on the best way to communicate his frustration and seek change in constructive ways, he may lash out or impulsively do the first thing that pops into his mind.

There are three related mental habits that you can teach your child to help him become more reflective and, as a result, stay out of trouble. They are:

1. Alternative Solution Thinking: This habit involves your child's thinking of a variety of possible ways to deal with unfairness, frustration, and not getting what he wants before taking action. The greater the number of alternative solutions he can generate, the more likely he will be to come up with a good solution.

2. Consequential Thinking: This habit involves your child's thinking through the likely consequences, both good and bad, of each alternative and selecting one that looks the most promising in terms of reduced risk of negative consequences for himself and a high probability of success.

3. Thinking of the Feelings of Others: Developing the habit of thinking about the impact his actions will have on the feelings of another person will help your child solve problems in a positive fashion.

Young people vary in the extent to which they have acquired these habits of thought. Because of good parenting practices (modeling) and temperament (flexibility), some children seem to develop these habits naturally. Others tend to react to problems without considering alternatives, their consequences, or the feelings of others.

It would be nice if you could just redirect your child's mind by inserting a new computer program. Unfortunately, because of some children's strong instinctive tendencies toward impulsiveness, it can

> **IDEAS THAT ENCOURAGE REFLECTIVE PROBLEM SOLVING**
>
> "It helps me to think before I act."
>
> "The best way to solve a problem is not always the first one I think of."
>
> "It helps me to think of different ways to solve a problem."
>
> "I need to think of the positive and negative consequences of my actions before I act."
>
> "Thinking about how the other person will feel if I act in a certain way helps me choose the best way to act."

take a long period of persistent parental efforts to influence an impulsive child to become more reflective in habit.

There are several strategies you can use to teach your child Reflective Problem Solving. You can catch him in the beginning stages of a conflict and have him think of different courses of action. You can also have him think at the time about the negative things that will happen if he gets too mad or breaks a rule. Asking your child "How do you think your friend will feel if you do that?" also increases his interpersonal sensitivity. It will be important for you to model all three Reflective Problem Solving Habits in difficult situations that your child sees you encounter. Praising your child when his actions show greater increases in reflectivity is crucial. He needs to know what aspect of his behavior you are appreciating and how he got there (for example, by reflecting on the best way to act).

My daughter, Alexandra, having a sweet nature, comes across the following problem at every new school that she starts (she has been in six schools in her eight years of life). Because she has a different background and comes from another country, her fellow classmates often

> **QUESTIONS TO ASK YOUR CHILD IN A CONFLICT WITH ANOTHER CHILD TO ENCOURAGE REFLECTIVE PROBLEM SOLVING**
>
> "What happened?" or "What's the matter, because that will help me understand the problem better."
>
> "How does _____ (other child) feel?"
>
> "How do you feel?"
>
> "Can you think of another way to solve this problem so neither of you will be angry (so he won't hit you, etc.)?"
>
> "Is that a good idea or not?"
>
> (If it's a good idea) "Go ahead and try that."
>
> (If it's not good) "Oh, you'll have to think of something different."
>
> —M. B. Shure, *Raising a Thinking Child*

find her interesting and very friendly and all seem to want to play with her. What then happens is that as she forms closer bonds with some of her classmates, which narrow down to close friendships, she finds that they want to keep her friendship all to themselves, and when she chooses to play with one of her friends, another gets jealous, and the exchange of words between the two can get nasty. This creates friction that lasts for several days. My daughter becomes upset, as she would like to be friends with more than one or two of her classmates. I discussed with my daughter alternative things that she could say when a friend starts to say "You like so and so better than me" or "If you play with Tara I'm not going to be your friend anymore." We came up with alternative scripts such as "You can join us if you like" or "I'll play with you after I'm finished with this game with Chrissy"—keeping a pleasant smile on her face and not getting into a hostile battle. Initially, she found her friends got nastier, but in time they soon found out that it wasn't in her nature to have favorites, and that she wasn't trying to play one friend off against another, so they could then share each other's friendships. Often, diplomatically ignoring her classmates' comments helped too.

With an older child, a more structured teaching approach can be used. After a conflict that ends badly for your daughter, have her work out alternative courses of action she could have taken, the positive and negative consequences of each, and how her behavior might have affected the other person's feelings.

Teaching Tolerance of Limits

Learning the importance of following rules and accepting limits is vital in order for your child to develop the self-discipline necessary for him to be achieving. Children need to see that following rules and behaving appropriately helps them achieve their own goals, including getting good results in school. Rule breaking and poor behavior lead to unpleasant consequences, including poor school performance. In addition, we should teach children that by following rules, they protect their own rights and those of others.

> **IDEAS TO ENCOURAGE TOLERANCE OF LIMITS**
>
> "Following rules helps to protect my rights and makes home and school better places to be."
>
> "When I follow rules, it helps me to achieve my goals."
>
> "It's not the end of the world to have to follow rules and behave well."
>
> "I can live with rules I don't like."
>
> "Following rules related to schoolwork gets me what I want in the long run."

In order to help develop your child's Tolerance of Limits, you need to establish or reinstitute a limited set of important house rules that are suitable for your child's age. These should deal with schoolwork, relating to siblings and other family members, household chores, and other aspects of your basic home economy. Once these rules have been discussed and agreed to by all members of the house, you can start getting your child in the habit of thinking about the negative consequences of breaking rules or behaving badly and the positive consequences of following rules and behaving well. Maximize the rewards for following rules and, if necessary, maximize penalties for breaking rules and behaving badly.

Explain clearly the wisdom of learning what behavior is and is not acceptable in different classrooms with different teachers and with other adults with whom your child comes in contact. Indicate that her success in that environment often depends on how well she learns to tolerate rules and limits she doesn't like.

> **ADVICE FOR THE REBELLIOUS CHILD**
>
> Schoolwork does not require you to sell your soul.

When you notice your child putting up with rules she finds unfair or behaving well in provocative situations, provide plenty of praise and recognition. The time to challenge your child's belief that she cannot stand following rules that restrict her freedom or that she thinks are dumb is when she is putting up with them.

You should teach your child assertiveness skills for dealing with rules she doesn't think are fair and for handling conflict situations. If your child has a quick temper, then Tolerance of Others and High Frustration Tolerance are Habits of the Mind that will help your child

> **WHAT IS ASSERTIVE BEHAVIOR?**
>
> A good alternative to being aggressive or to being passive is being assertive. When you're assertive, you state clearly and directly your honest feelings, thoughts, and desires, as well as your hopes for the future. You stick to the facts and make your own choices.
>
> When speaking assertively, rather than raising your voice or mumbling, you use a confident, warm, and yet firm voice. Wear a relaxed expression and look at the person to whom you are speaking.
>
> Assertive behavior consists of sticking up for your own rights without taking away the right of someone else to be treated with dignity and respect.

calm herself down when she is faced with limits she has to follow but finds unfair or disagreeable.

Finally, you need to make it clear to your child that he has choices as to whether he does or doesn't put up with limits and rules. Make it clear that no one can make him do anything. Make it clear that he has the final responsibility for behaving well or not behaving well. As a result of this understanding, your child will begin to see that he has only himself to blame for the negative consequences that ensue from his making the wrong choices.

**PARENT REFLECTION SHEET:
TEACHING TOLERANCE OF LIMITS**

1. List those limits and rules that you find disagreeable and that govern your life.

    _____

    _____

2. What are the strategies you use to put up with them even though you dislike them?

    _____

    _____

3. With your child, list the rules and limits that are not negotiable and that he hates the most.

    _____

    _____

4. Discuss with your child ways he might put up with the rules and limits. What does he think would help him tolerate rules he does not like?

    _____

    _____

5. What would be the negative consequences if your child followed all nonnegotiable rules? Discuss what his friends would think of him. Discuss what strategies he might use to cope with the negative consequences of following rules.

    _____

    _____

CHAPTER 8

HOW YOUR CHILD'S INTERESTS DRIVE MOTIVATION AND AMBITION

Recently, I was watching my daughter play tennis when I heard a grunt off to my immediate right. It came from a disgruntled-looking father who had just seen his daughter totally miss the tennis ball and fall flat on her behind.

"She's hopeless," he moaned. "I wonder how many more lessons it will take for her to connect."

"As many as it takes," I thought, sympathizing with the daughter.

His monologue continued: "I really want her to learn tennis. Tennis builds character. And these days, top universities are looking for well-rounded students, students who show more than just straight As."

I nodded, thinking that here was a father who might be bringing about the wrong results with the right intentions. He was trying to mold his daughter into what he thought was right for her, rather than being guided by her interests and talents.

"Why, when I was growing up," he went on, "I never had the opportunity to play tennis. My parents had the money but never encouraged me. I'm not going to make that mistake. Boy, it's amazing we turned out as well as we did!"

Nodding, I wondered how long it would be before his daughter told him what to do with tennis.

I believe that parents can be of great help to their children by exposing them to a range of activities in different areas. Parents need to answer this question: "What sorts of activities accommodate my child's interests and talents, and which do not?" This is a different approach from deciding ahead of time on the basis of your own interests and talents what your child should be doing and not doing, which subjects and majors he should be taking, which leisure activities he should select, and what sort of job he should be working toward.

You need to be guided by your child's emerging interests, which are critical features of your child's motivation and ambition. Interests express your child's preferences for certain activities, work situations, and people, and they express an aversion to other types of activities, work situations, and people. Your child's interests also partly determine the extent to which your child develops certain work and interpersonal skills.

Interests differ from child to child, including between those children from the same family. The types of interests that characterize your child are influenced by many factors, including his natural talent, the interests being modeled by you and other family members, and the extent of the opportunities that he has had to experience different activities and learn the different skills that go along with different interests.

By the time your child reaches the age of eight, you will be able to discern the formation of various interests. Does she like to be with people or work alone? Does she like to work with her hands or her mind? Does she enjoy being outdoors or onstage? Does she take pride in the orderliness of her room or her creativity in designing her room?

In this chapter, I will describe six different categories of interests, called types, that you can use to describe your child's pattern of interests: Realistic, Investigative, Artistic, Social, Enterprising, and Conventional.

Learning to recognize your child's pattern or type of interests will help you guide and encourage your child in a number of areas: selection of high school subjects, selection of a program of study at a junior college or four-year college or university, participation in leisure time activities, and choice of career.

In raising our children, my wife and I try to leave behind any stereotypes about what boys and girls like to do. We encourage our children to participate in areas they initially may not choose because of a lack of previous experience or familiarity. As our children get older and as we learn more about their patterns of interests, we get better at helping them select activities that they enjoy and at which they succeed. We also try to be sensible about how long we encourage our children to persevere in an area before agreeing to throw in the towel.

For our son, the flute lasted six months, while our daughter continues at her piano. We are pursuing drawing lessons at the nearby art center for our son while our daughter embarks on her second year of soccer. Our son chooses to continue working on his school's newspaper while our daughter works at her tennis. I also would like to give them experience with manual activities such as woodworking, mechanics, and gardening to see where their interests lie.

If you help your child get the match right between her interests and her selection of activities and experiences that accommodate her interests, you will see your child's star rise. To do this, you will need to know something about children's interests. Fortunately, there is a theory developed by a psychologist, Dr. John Holland, of Johns Hopkins University, that provides a clear understanding of how to recognize your child's pattern of interests and that will help guide you and your child in the selection of school subjects, courses of study, job settings, and even leisure time activities so that her motivation and ambition are maximized. It all has to do with matching your child's interests with the appropriate environments.

> **MATCH YOUR CHILDREN WITH SUITABLE ENVIRONMENTS**
>
> Matching your child with school subjects, programs of study, leisure time activities, and career tracks that call upon their interests and talents leads to a strong desire in your child to achieve. On the other hand, when your child finds herself having to pursue activities in which she has no natural interest or skills, motivation and ambition wane.

Holland's Hexagon

John Holland's theory about people and the choices they make in study, leisure time, and careers is worth knowing. In order to appreciate the detail of his theory, you need to acquaint yourself with four basic assumptions:

Assumption 1. In our culture, people, including older children and adolescents, can be categorized as one of six types: Realistic, Investigative, Artistic, Social, Enterprising, and Conventional. Holland indicates that these types are abstractions, in the sense that no person exemplifies any one type. Instead, a person resembles a few of the types and does not resemble others. My description of each type, later in this chapter, will help you determine which type your child resembles the most.

Assumption 2. Most occupations in our culture can be categorized by one or more of the same six types: Realistic, Investigative,

Artistic, Social, Enterprising, and Conventional. As with people, these types are abstractions in that no one occupation exemplifies one type. It is also possible to categorize subjects offered at high school, programs of study at colleges and universities, and leisure time activities using the same six categories.

Assumption 3. Generally speaking, most children will select school subjects, leisure time activities, programs of study in higher education, and occupations that will accommodate and be consistent with their interests. These environments will allow them to exercise their skills, express their attitudes, and take on enjoyable problems and roles. For example, an Investigative type who is interested in exploring and understanding biological, physical, or cultural phenomena will seek Investigative occupations and programs of study that provide the opportunity to do this.

Assumption 4. People's motivation, achievement, and satisfaction in school, at work, and in their leisure time pursuits are determined by the degree to which their interests are accommodated by their subjects in high school, course of study in higher education, occupation, and leisure time pursuits.

If you want to help your child achieve success and satisfaction at school and beyond, then you need to be guided by his interests (not your own interests) and help match your child with environments (study, work, play) that are consistent with his interests.

An examination of Holland's Hexagon will enable you to make judgments regarding matching your child up with different environments and, in particular, maximizing good matches and avoiding bad matches. One basic principle that should guide this matching process is what Holland calls **congruence.** The more your child's interests match the types of activities involved in a subject or program of study, the greater the congruence. The distance between the different

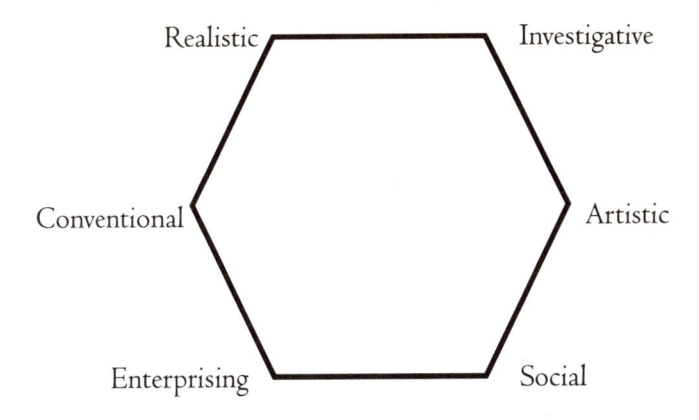

```
        Realistic ─────────── Investigative

  Conventional                     Artistic

        Enterprising ─────────── Social
```

types in the Hexagon reflects the degree of congruence. The shorter the distance between any two of the six types, the greater their similarity is assumed to be. This principle holds both for a person's interests and for types of environments. The closer the types are, the more they have in common. For example, Investigative types have most in common with Artistic and Realistic types and least in common with Enterprising types. High congruence occurs when your child is in a study, leisure, or work environment that accommodates his interests (for example, Investigative child in an Investigative program of study).

A child whose interests are Investigative will tend to be more satisfied when taking Investigative subjects in school (biology, physiology, chemistry, geography), Investigative programs of study at a university or college (agricultural plant pathology), working at Investigative occupations (surgeon, museum curator), and enjoying himself at Investigative leisure activities (flying, working with animals, nature, board games). He will be poorly suited to environments and activities that do not accommodate his interests.

In looking at Holland's Hexagon, you can see that the code farthest away from Investigative is Enterprising. A child with Investigative interests would be least well matched and have the poorest congruence with Enterprising school subjects (journalism, home economics), Enterprising programs of study (special education administration, advertising), Enterprising occupations (lawyer, politician, furniture assembly supervisor), and Enterprising leisure activities (entertainment, games of chance, gourmet cooking).

Once you know your child's dominant pattern of interests, you can use Holland's Hexagon and principle of congruence to help steer her in the right direction. You should search for environments and activities that are closest to your child's interests as represented in the Hexagon. If your child has Realistic interests, you will be guided toward practical, hands-on activities rather than buying/selling Enterprising activities or curing/teaching Social ones.

Holland describes in detail children's interests and the characteristics of different programs of study and occupations. In fact, he encourages people to describe their interests in terms of the three they most closely resemble. By classifying school subjects, programs of study, leisure activities, and occupations by not one but three of the different categories, you will be able to zero in on very specific environments that have a high degree of congruence with your child's specific interests. If you are interested in a finer breakdown of your child's interests, see Holland's works, listed in the Reference section of this book.

Just because your child's interests and a program of study or occupation have congruence, your child's success in that program of study or occupation is not automatically ensured. Other factors that will determine your child's degree of success are whether she has the necessary intelligence or special abilities to learn the material or do the job, whether she can acquire the necessary knowledge and skills, whether she will enjoy the way people who are in a program of study or occupation live their lives, and whether funds are available for study or future job training. You should ask your child whether she can actually picture herself being happy in a particular course of study or occupation and ask other members of your family and friends whether they think she can be successful.

> **CHILDREN'S INTERESTS AND EDUCATIONAL ACHIEVEMENT**
>
> High educational aspirations and educational achievement go along with all six types of interests. Children with Realistic interests have the least motivation in formal learning (studying at the library, for instance) whereas children with Investigative interests have the greatest.

Let's have a look at Holland's six types of interest. I will describe the interests that correspond with each type. I will also provide some examples of school subjects, higher education programs of study, and leisure activities that accommodate each specific interest. I will present higher education programs of study in three categories. Programs in Category 1 are generally offered at the post-bachelor's level and result in a graduate professional degree. Programs in Category 2 reflect study typically offered in a four-year college or university and may require postgraduate study. Programs in Category 3 are generally offered in junior or community colleges.

This discussion is based on materials written by Holland and his colleagues and published by Psychological Assessment Resources in Odessa, Florida: *The Educational Opportunities Finder* and *The Leisure Activities Finder*. If you want your child's interests to be formally assessed, you should contact your school's career education department or school counselor. If you are interested in learning about careers, I recommend Holland's *Occupations Finder*.

As you read through descriptions of each of the six interest patterns, see if you can locate the two or three that most closely resemble your child. Be aware that some children's interests are more clearly defined than others. If your child is right in the middle of the "No" period of adolescence, it may, at present, be difficult to discern his specific interests.

Realistic Type

Children with Realistic interests can be found tinkering with tools and machines or working on a farm. You might have noticed them pulling apart and then rewiring the family stereo or spending hours working on their bicycle. Realistic types often enjoy being outside, going camping or canoeing, raising flowers or vegetables, or just walk-

YOUR CHILD'S INTERESTS

ing through a forest. They like it down and dirty. A person with Realistic interests tends to be honest, practical, persistent, have good common sense, be fairly self-reliant, value monetary rewards, and appreciate seeing tangible results for his efforts. Realistic types tend to develop mechanical and technical abilities but may not acquire strong social skills.

Work activities that Realistic types prefer are:

- building
- handling
- operating
- repairing

It is likely, if your child has Realistic interests, that depending on his skills and abilities, he may find satisfaction in the following subjects at school: agriculture, family studies/home economics, woodworking, technical studies, clerical studies, math, and science.

After high school, Realistic types should consider the following programs of study:

Category 1: engineering, conservation, aquaculture management, agricultural production, cartography, biotechnology

Category 2: agricultural work and management, forestry, biological technician, electrical and computer technology, baking, appliance repair

Category 3: cabinetmaking, aircraft mechanics, automotive technology, electrical work, machining, construction technology, butchering, truck/bus driving, sheet metal work, logging

In terms of your child's leisure time, consider exposing him to the following types of activities and experiences: mechanical activities, crafts, cooking, nature, woodworking, adventure, making models, gardening, animals, automobiles, fishing, water sports, and needlework.

Investigative Type

Investigative children enjoy asking questions, carrying out investigations in a logical fashion, reading books on science, working with numbers, drawing charts and graphs, and keeping budgets. Some young people's Investigative interests are directed at biological or physical phenomena, while other young people are more attracted to the study of culture and history. The scientist locked up in her laboratory or the brainy mathematician calculating obscure equations are prototypical examples of Investigative types of interest. Investigative types tend to be cautious, curious, independent, introverted, and rational, and are viewed by others as intelligent and somewhat socially aloof. Rather than being attracted to power and financial accumulation, they value the acquisition of knowledge and learning. Children with Investigative interests are very comfortable studying in academic environments (such as libraries). While often lacking in leadership ability or selling skills, Investigative types often have well-developed mathematical and scientific abilities.

Investigative types enjoy:

- discovering
- experimenting
- inventing
- thinking

School subjects that accommodate Investigative interests include: agriculture, art, woodworking, math, science, and technical studies.

Examples of Investigative higher education programs of study are:

Category 1: medical microbiology, medicine, acoustics, educational testing and research, epidemiology, international economics, optometry, psychiatry

Category 2: aviation science, archaeology, physical sciences, geography, horticulture, marine biology, computer science, surveying

Category 3: hydraulics technology, ornamental horticulture operations, respiratory therapy, acupuncture, private aircraft piloting, data processing

You will want to give your child opportunities to participate in the following areas of leisure time pursuits: animals, animal preservation, gardening, science, flying, nature, and board games.

Artistic Type

Artistic types of children may enjoy writing poetry or articles for magazines. If they do not have good writing skills, artistic children may prefer painting, drawing, sculpting, pottery, or visiting museums and art galleries. Those

Artistic children who actually produce art rather than just appreciating it tend to be nonconformists who hate cleaning up their rooms and, as adults, working 9 to 5. Artistic types tend to be disorganized, emotional, impulsive, impractical, intuitive, and nonconforming, and resemble people who have right-brain dominance (see chapter 10). The Artistic type prefers creative ideas and self-expression to being organized or making lots of money and often has well-developed artistic, musical, or writing skills.

Artistic Types are attracted to:

- creating
- composing
- expressing
- imagining

Subjects in school that correspond with Artistic interests include: English, foreign languages, social studies, home economics, art, music, and business management.

Higher education programs of study that are congruent with Artistic interests are:

Category 1 and 2: architecture, cinema, comparative literature, teaching art, teaching foreign languages, music conducting, social psychology, graphic design

Category 3: general art, drawing, metal and jewelry making, play/screenwriting, auctioneering, business communications, radio broadcast technology

The Artistic type of child will naturally respond positively to the following types of leisure activities: art, music, craft, food, entertainment, performing, dancing, and collecting.

Social Type

Children with Social interests like to be involved with people, like to meet new people, and generally make friends easily. They often can be seen helping others, working on group projects, and doing volunteer work for social or community agencies. As their interests mature, Social types become more attracted to teaching, counseling, or helping others. Social children often volunteer to be camp counselors or take a leadership role in Scouting. Fairness and serving others are predominant values in Social types. They are characterized by patience, understanding, warmth, generosity, helpfulness, and cooperation. Social types develop good interpersonal skills rather than manual or technical ones.

Social types are attracted to:

- healing
- helping
- supporting
- teaching

Subjects at school that a child with Social interests should consider include a wide variety and will depend on what her other interests are: English, family studies, social studies, math, industrial shop, and business finance.

Higher education programs of study that accommodate Social interests are:

Category 1: child development, occupational therapy, podiatry, clinical psychology, rabbinical or other clerical studies, continuing education administration, public policy analysis

Category 2: home furnishing consulting, naturopathic medicine, criminal justice, nutritional services, instructional media design, speech pathology, teaching

Category 3: medical radiology technology, dietitian assistance, elder care, practical nursing, cosmetology, bartending, air traffic control, paralegal work, teacher aide work

Types of leisure activities that may be attractive to a Social child include: a variety of sports, physical fitness, martial arts, table games, nature, bowling, social games, performing, crafts, biking, skiing, racquet ball, water sports, nature, card games, ball games, and travel.

Enterprising Type

Enterprising children could sell refrigerators to the Eskimos. Generally blessed with verbally persuasive abilities, Enterprising types enjoy being with people and like having good times. They can be described as adventurous, ambitious, argumentative, attention getting, energetic, impulsive, optimistic, self-confident, and talkative.

Enterprising types value financial and social success and are happiest when driving red sports cars or large gray Mercedes. They get turned on by risk-taking activities and being given or assuming responsibility for their own actions. Typically, Enterprising types, except for business majors, dislike the tedium of study. Scientific, intellectual, or complicated study is avoided. Rather, the true Enterprising types like to go out and sell, using their persuasive abilities to help further their own goals as well as those of an organization.

Enterprising types prefer:

- persuading
- promoting
- risking
- selling

School subjects viewed as matched to Enterprising interests include: accounting, business finance, and business management.

Higher education programs of study that accommodate Enterprising interests are:

Category 1: forest management, industrial management, information sciences, business teaching, financial planning, special education administration

Category 2: merchant marine, broadcast journalism, executive assistance, office supervision, travel and tourism, clinical social work, food administration

Category 3: building management, clothing worker, fashion modeling, entrepreneurship, hairstyling, umpiring, emergency medical technology, franchise operation

Types of leisure activities that potentially appeal to Enterprising children include: performing, entertainment, business, games of chance, cooking, and investing.

Conventional type

Conventional types are 9-to-5ers. They prefer following an orderly routine in which what is expected of them is clearly spelled out. Conventional children are good at doing detailed behind-the-scene work such as organizing a fund-raising benefit or being the secretary of a club or organization. They may enjoy preparing food, planning a dinner, or working in a kitchen. Some Conventional types are attracted to office practices and enjoy typing letters, using copying machines, and working at a desk. Conventional types tend to be conforming, conscientious, inflexible, obedient, persistent, and practical. They value making money and being thrifty as well as acquiring power in social or business affairs. Lacking in artistic abilities or sensibilities, Conventional types tend to develop advanced clerical or numerical skills.

Conventional types prefer:

- administering
- organizing
- planning
- processing

Conventional higher education programs of study are:

Category 1 and 2:   computer programming, accounting
Category 2:   legal and medical administrative assistance
Category 3:   printing, dry cleaning, card dealing, court reporting, data processing, library assistance, food service, reception work

Types of leisure time activities that appeal to children with Conventional interests include: collecting (toys, tools, cards, stamps), needlework, craft, card games, and computer games.

A number of years ago, I was contacted by a distressed father who was concerned because his son, Carl, had apparently lost his motivation to study. The father was wondering if the recent divorce had created such turmoil in Carl that he couldn't bring himself to study. "If it's my fault, I want to know what I can do to help."

Of course, some children develop strong emotional reactions to a divorce and, for a time, stop working. But this was not the case with Carl. At fifteen, he was able to accept that his parents were not getting along. Though his father instigated the divorce, Carl held no grudge.

I administered a test to determine Carl's pattern of interests. It turned out that Carl was very strongly dominated by Artistic interests. Apparently, his current academic curriculum, which had no art class, was boring him to tears.

Carl's father was relieved and reassured to learn that Carl was not suffering unduly because of the divorce. He wanted to know what he could do to help Carl pass his last two years of school and to encourage him to go on to college. I explained to Carl and his father that Carl would probably do much better in an environment that accommodated Artistic interests. Carl's father mentioned that Carl's skill at drum playing and drawing had prompted him to consider a transfer from Carl's present school to another school he knew of that specialized in art and music but still maintained an academic emphasis. I encouraged Carl and his father not only to visit the school and speak with students, but also to visit colleges that had Artistic programs of study. I believed that if Carl could see that by doing the best he could on his current academic work he could qualify for an Artistic program of study with similarly minded students in the long term, his motivation might improve dramatically.

Six months later, I received a call from Carl's father thanking me for my practical advice. Carl had transferred to a new school and was doing much better at his work. Visits to several colleges gave Carl a long-term goal to shoot for that helped him tolerate and succeed at his academic subjects.

A successful resolution of a problem, thanks to Dr. Holland's hexagon.

PARENT REFLECTION SHEET: YOUR CHILD'S INTERESTS

1. Describe your own interests, using Holland's six categories of interest. List the two or three types that you most closely resemble. Then, describe your child's interest pattern.

	Your Interests	Your Child's Interests
Interest One	_____	_____
Interest Two	_____	_____
Interest Three	_____	_____

2. List the school subjects that you believe best accommodate your child's interests.

_____

_____

3. List the higher education programs of study that would accommodate your child's interests.

_____

_____

4. List the occupations that are congruent with your child's interests.

_____

_____

5. List the leisure activities that are congruent with your child's interests.

_____

_____

6. What are some new activities that you should propose to your child, to expose him to experiences that are congruent with his interests?

_____

CHAPTER 9

How Your Child's Traits of Personality May Contribute to Underachievement

If all the children in your child's school who are not achieving their potential in their schoolwork were on the same academic playing field, you would notice that they would be wearing many different uniforms. While they all share the characteristic of having a discrepancy between their scholastic capabilities and levels of achievement, the reasons for the discrepancy vary. In this chapter, I describe eight traits of personality we can discern in children that put children at risk for underachievement at school. See if you can spot which of these types of children your child most closely resembles. You may notice that your child resembles more than one type. After each description, I will list some tips for helping that particular type of child. On the various lists, place a check next to those that seem to hold some promise for working with your child.

I have excluded from this description children who are underachieving due to severe personal problems that can accompany difficulties at home, such as depression or severe conduct disorders. For these children, underachievement is a secondary problem. They need help with their personal problems from a mental health practitioner.

If you have a child who is underachieving, it will be useful for you to understand what makes him tick. Why is it important for you to know? Because by recognizing the specific needs and idiosyncrasies of your child that make him different from other children, you will be able to locate solutions that have been shown by research and experience to help your type of child. Fortunately, by employing the strategies suggested below, as well as by teaching your child different Habits of the Mind, you can help promote the development of helpful traits of personality.

Personality Traits and Underachievement

Your child's traits of personality, her enduring patterns of perceiving, relating to, and thinking about the environment, including school, homework, and herself, contribute greatly to her success—or lack thereof—in school.

As you read and think about your son's or daughter's personality, you might be wondering why your child is turning out this way. If you are like me, you will have to work hard at challenging your own idea that anything less than optimal development of your child is caused by some defect in your parenting.

Explanations of the reasons that children develop personality traits that lead to underachievement vary from expert to expert. I am less concerned with the "why" than with the "what" of helping parents help their children reach destinations other than underachievement. Suffice it to say that personality stems from a variety of influences, including your child's biological temperament, your parenting practices, cultural effects, peer-group influences, and experiences at school.

Dependency Trait. Does your child worry a lot about making mistakes and about what others will think if she is not successful? Does she have a high need for approval? Does she have a history of being reluctant to try new things on her own? Does your child want you around her when she is attempting something new or hard? Does your child ask a lot of questions before or while doing a project? Does your child seem to be very comfortable in doing things when she knows she will be successful while avoiding stretching out beyond her immediate or proven capabilities? Dependent children are forever asking their teachers lots of questions and frequently show their teachers their work before handing it in. The most telltale sign of this personality trait is that this child is much too preoccupied with how others will judge her if she makes mistakes at her work.

When dependent children are young, their need for approval and their anxiety about mistakes lead to the avoidance of doing work independently. Because of their fear of disapproval from others, they impose on themselves low expectations for achievement. By only attempting activities within their range of competence, they protect themselves from the ridicule and rejection they perceive they will receive from others.

Dependent children often try to manipulate their parents and teachers to get out of doing work they fear they won't be able to do very well. The more they can get others to give them help, answer the hard questions, and do the work for them, the less they risk. If your child seems to rely a great deal on others, ask yourself whether her dependent behavior is really her subconscious attempt to avoid doing work and risk not having it done right.

Dependent children can experience even greater problems of underachievement as they enter adolescence. Girls, in particular, can choose not to extend themselves in certain subjects because they fear that boys will ridicule them for being hardworking and achieving.

Some academically gifted and creative children underachieve because of their preoccupation with what others think of them. These children strive for conformity, viewing it as a safe way to avoid the critical gaze of their peers and adults. Unfortunately, by seeking the safer course, they avoid extending themselves in areas of their natural strength.

The lack of motivation for doing homework can be traced in some children to excessive preoccupation with others' opinions. Several years ago I was asked to work with a seventeen-year-old boy, Gary, whose parents had just discovered that he had not handed in any laboratory assignments in physics and was in danger of failing. His parents held the opinion that Gary was lazy. For several weeks, I discussed with Gary the negative consequences of not handing in his assignments and the positive consequences of catching up on his missing assignments. I also helped Gary to keep in perspective the unpleasantness of doing the laboratory reports. He seemed to recognize the issues involved and expressed a strong desire to pass physics, because he wanted to study science in college. Much to my own frustration as well as that of his parents, Gary still resisted handing in his assignments.

Changing tack, I asked Gary: "What would happen if you handed in the first of the four incomplete reports?"

"It wouldn't be very good," he mumbled.

"What do you mean?" I prompted.

"I mean that I'm not very good at physics."

"And suppose that the assignment wasn't very good, what would be so bad about that?"

Gary appeared to be sinking down in his seat. "The teacher would find out that I am not very smart. He'd think I wasn't a very good student."

"And how bad would that be?" I asked, expecting that Gary wouldn't exactly love the idea of his teacher's poor opinion.

"Horrible."

With this new insight, I helped Gary see the connection between his approval seeking and the degree of anxiety he was experiencing about handing in work that contained many mistakes. Gary admitted that he would rather not hand in his assignments, and have the teacher and parents think he was lazy, than hand in work that was poor and have people think he wasn't very smart in that subject. For Gary, it was easier to live with someone thinking he was lazy than thinking he was stupid. Reducing his effort was a great smoke screen for Gary in protecting his sense of self-worth, which he attached to people's view of his overall intelligence.

I helped Gary challenge his belief that his teacher would think he was stupid as opposed to the fact that he needed more time to learn the material. I also challenged Gary's idea that his self-worth could be determined by what others thought of him.

"While it is nice when Mr. Stevens thinks highly of your physics ability, does that mean you absolutely must have his good opinion, and that if you don't, you'll die, shrivel up, and disappear?"

Over the next weeks, I chipped away at Gary's tendency to take personally others' opinions of him. Gradually, he came to accept that being afraid of his teacher's negative evaluations was only hurting him. By working on his self-acceptance, he was able to change his thinking enough to actually hand in his last assignment on the last day of class.

Not all children with a dependent personality trait underachieve. Sometimes, a child will be driven by the need to please others by achieving well. Some children, however, get tripped up in subjects in which they anticipate not doing well and when they anticipate not being able to please the teacher or parent. If you have a dependent type of child who is underachieving, here are some tips for helping her:

1. Remind yourself that the dependent behavior of children often is subconscious manipulation of parents and teachers in order to get out of doing work in which they might make mistakes. Do not allow this to happen. Do not do the work for them.
2. Communicate to your child that the responsibility for doing work is squarely in his court.
3. Use the Praise, Prompt, and Leave procedure when your child approaches you for help with his work. Praise your child for anything in connection with the work he has already done or for being prepared to start work. ("I'm glad you have a pencil.") Prompt the first or next step that your child should be taking on the assignment. Then, before your child has time to ask another question, leave.
4. Do not project on to your child that he cannot stand the frustration of hard work. Remind yourself that he can stand the stress of not knowing what to do. Moreover, if you are concerned about damage

to his self-esteem, know that it is more damaging if a child is protected from the struggle and, as a consequence, never experiences the success that comes from overcoming obstacles. Independent achievement is one of the greatest sources of a positive self-concept and self-confidence.

5. Do not give your child too much attention when he is expressing negative feelings about schoolwork.
6. Allow your child to struggle with difficult activities without rescuing her. Remind yourself that with the struggle comes confidence.
7. Teach your child not to judge or evaluate his work until after a certain period of time.
8. Work on developing a home environment that encourages mistake making as a healthy, natural, and desirable part of learning and attempting new activities. React positively to her when your child reveals her mistakes.
9. Communicate the expectation that schoolwork is to be done independently of adult help.
10. Provide recognition of your child for when he works independently of the help of others.
11. Do not nag your child about schoolwork. Nagging prolongs dependence.
12. Give your child a vote of confidence: "You can do it!"

To modify this trait of personality, the strongest medicine you can provide is to teach two Habits of the Mind: Self-Acceptance and Independence. (See Chapter 7.)

Perfectionism Trait. Does your child secretly or quite publicly reveal that he has gotten it into his head that he always must do things perfectly? If you do, you are faced with a big challenge. It can be extremely difficult, depending on your child's strength of conviction, to change a perfectionistic trait of personality.

You might be wondering why perfectionism puts children at risk for underachievement. Don't they strive to do all things perfectly? Unfortunately, perfectionists are extremely good at making predictions about where and when they will or will not be perfect. When they anticipate not being perfect at some work, a loud alarm bell rings in their head. At these times, perfectionists sense danger and a threat to their feelings of self-worth. The louder the bell, the more likely it is that they will take evasive action. The typical evasive actions of perfectionistically inclined students are: a) choose not to compete, b) reduce effort. If they choose not to compete, then, of course, they will be not underachievers, but nonachievers. Gradually, children with perfectionistic traits can reduce their range of activities to those they do well and avoid all those in which they predict lack of success.

In school subjects, if your child anticipates that his grade might not be so good, he drops back on his effort. With less effort, your child has an automatic excuse for imperfection; namely, "I didn't do well because I didn't try very hard." Many perfectionistic children have this excuse of not trying always ready, just in case the result doesn't turn out very favorably.

As you know from your observations of your child, or if, in fact, you yourself have perfectionistic traits, life can be hell for a perfectionist. Before starting an assignment, many perfectionists agonize endlessly about where to start and leave the completion of the assignment until the very last minute. Anxiety and stress can be almost endless companions of a perfectionist.

I once worked with Richard, who at fourteen was a dyed-in-the-wool perfectionist. Rather than causing him to drop off his effort as a defense against his not being perfect, his perfectionistic tendencies drove Richard to overwork to the point of exhaustion. Sometimes he studied five hours a night! Richard became so tired from his work that he would suffer such an extreme case of swollen glands and fever that he missed weeks of school at a time. Ironically, the result of the missed schooldays was suboptimal educational achievement.

I struggled with Richard to get him to work less, not more! Knowing that he had strong scholastic ability, I felt confident that cutting back on the hours he spent studying would cause his health to improve, as he wouldn't be so tired and would not compromise his grades.

Richard was a hard egg to crack. While many perfectionists do not grow up in homes in which heavy expectations for academic achievement are placed on them, or where one or both parents are themselves perfectionistic, in Richard's case there was lots of pressure. His mother was a perfectionist, all his brothers were in college, and both his parents were professionals.

The perfectionist's main Habit of the Mind is called Perfectionism. I described in chapter 6 how it involves your believing that you should always do things perfectly, that it is terrible to make mistakes, and that to prove your self-worth, you need to do things perfectly.

The main difference between Dependence and Perfectionism Traits of personality is that the former leads children to fear making mistakes due to the perception that others will think badly of them, while the latter leads to fears of making mistakes because of these children's own tendency to evaluate themselves poorly for not living up to their own standards.

The goal in working with Richard, as it is for working with most perfectionists, was twofold. One goal was to help Richard modify his expectation that he should be perfect. When perfectionists stop "shoulding" on themselves and start concentrating on trying to do the best they can, they no longer need to have an excuse for not being perfect, and they attack their work with appropriate vigor. They also tackle new activities in which there is a realistic possibility that they might fail or be just average. In this case, I had Richard work on preferring but not needing to be perfect. He started to accept the idea that "It's preferable to be the best I can, but not being perfect does not prove that I am a failure or hopeless."

My second goal in helping Richard was to help him set realistic goals and expectations for himself. I indicated to Richard that perfection is a rarely attained state, and that while striving to be the best he can and setting very high long-term goals can help him realize his potential and achieve well, striving for a state that is hardly ever reached is a bad formula for success.

Five years after I worked with Richard, he ran up to me one day at the university he was attending, where I was a professor. He announced proudly that he had gotten into the program of his choice and that he was still working hard at balancing his schoolwork with fun. He also mentioned that his recurrent illnesses had pretty well stopped the year I worked with him.

With all underachieving children, if we want them to excel, we have to rise to their occasion. Here are some tips, some of which come from my own experience and some from a wonderful book by Miriam Adderholdt-Elliot called *Perfectionism: What's Bad About Being Too Good?*

1. Help your child become more aware of the negative costs of demanding perfection, including the avoidance of activities she anticipates not doing perfectly and the reduction in effort at subjects that cannot be avoided.
2. Teach your child about famous people (for example, Thomas Edison) who stumbled on the road to success. Explain that these people needed to take risks and make mistakes in order to succeed.
3. Have your child list the things he has always wanted to do but has been afraid of not doing perfectly. Have your child agree to try one of these activities.
4. With your child, identify areas of weakness. Have her try activities in these areas. When she has attempted such an activity and stumbled, point out that she now has evidence that she can stand doing things imperfectly.
5. Encourage your child to stop obsessing about his poor grades.
6. Encourage your child to participate in activities unrelated to school.
7. Teach your child that there is a continuum of achievement; achievement isn't an all (perfection) or nothing (complete failure) event. Help your child set goals at a place on the achievement continuum where she doesn't have to be the best in order to learn something and have fun.
8. You can help your child tackle long-term projects and assignments by suggesting that he hand in the beginning portion (beginning

paragraph, outline) well in advance. Explain that what's important is that he does some work, not that the work be done perfectly.

9. Help your child see homework tasks as a series of parts that have to be completed one after another, rather than as a whole chunk that must be completed perfectly.
10. Remind your child of the importance of having all materials necessary for completing that portion of the assignment on hand.
11. Encourage your child to get organized by laying out or outlining the different parts of work that have to be done.
12. Provide small rewards as she completes each portion of an assignment.
13. Help your daughter enjoy the pleasure of doing new activities. Encourage her to reward herself for trying new things.
14. Help select teachers with a noncompetitive style of teaching (public announcements of grades, contests).
15. Make sure your own expectations for your child's work are not too high or rigid.

Keep in mind that the need to be perfect may lead to high levels of achievement in areas in which your child anticipates success. For that reason alone, it is difficult for your child to give it up. There is a payoff. You should explain and demonstrate to your child that needing to be perfect really works against her interest in doing things well or perfectly. In different ways, show your child that being afraid of making mistakes and avoiding doing things she anticipates not doing well prevents her from learning what she can do and what she cannot do. She needs to see the downside.

Helplessness Trait. Was your child a bit young when he started school? Is he a little bit immature, always taking a bit longer to catch on in reading, spelling, or math? Does he have a learning disability that contributes to his delay in learning? Does your child seem a step behind classmates in catching on to material presented in class? Does your child just seem to be getting the material when his teacher moves on to the next unit? Has your child experienced some difficulty in early learning? Did your child have difficulty breaking the code of reading? Does your child feel frustrated when initially presented with new material?

If you are answering yes to some of these questions, your child may develop a trait of personality called Helplessness that leads to feelings of discouragement about school and his likelihood of ever being successful. This type of child is frequently bright and has the capacity to do much better in school than he is doing, but because of his negative experiences in school and having to play catch-up in various classes, he may have acquired several extremely unhelpful patterns of thought. He might believe that no matter how hard he works, he is never going to be successful. (Many children who are achieving well in school have a clear sense that the key to their success is effort and perseverance.) Your child may also have a pessimistic outlook on his future success, seeing only negative outcomes. Further, if he is sensitive by nature, your child may tend to take his difficulties in school personally and may develop low self-esteem.

Angie was a tenth-grade student who had stopped trying in math. "What's the point in trying? I just wasn't born with a math gene," she replied to my concern about her not even having bought the math book for the new school year.

I laughed to myself when she made the comment. Just the other day I had been at a school barbecue and had met a father who was telling me how happy his daughter was at school. "She's doing great in English and drama. Her math isn't very good, but that doesn't matter to her mother and me. She never really had much math genetic material to work with. As long as she's happy, we're happy."

I looked at Angie and noticed that she had some resemblance to the father I had shared a hamburger with—without the beard.

"Whoa, Angie. Somewhere you got the wrong idea that either you're born to be a natural mathematician or you're not, and if you're not, what's the point in trying?"

Angie looked at me with surprise, as if I really didn't understand. "It's my older brother who's the math whiz. In math, he's like a duck in water. I can't swim, and I'll never be able to swim. Why buy a new bathing suit so I can drown?"

Angie's mind-set concerning math was the lead factor in her underperformance. Unless that changed, she would continue to underperform. It took about a month of working with her teacher and parents for me to see changes in Angie's application and eventual success in math. We pretty much followed the Parent-Child SOS I described in chapter 2. Her teacher temporarily provided her with less demanding work and less of it to do. Angie's math teacher and mother arranged a weekly phone call to keep tabs on Angie's efforts. I left it up to Angie's father to raise his own expectations for his daughter and to encourage Angie's Internal Locus of Control for Learning. ("The more you try at something, the better you get.") He began teaching his daughter to attribute her difficulties in math to her lack of effort rather than a lack of ability.

Here are some recommendations that can help you reinvigorate a child who feels discouraged about schoolwork and has developed a sense of helplessness:

1. Encourage your family to see your child in a positive way. Help them by noticing and commenting upon his strengths and interests.
2. Show interest and excitement about noncurricular areas of your child's skills and talents.
3. Show enthusiasm and support when your child expends effort on learning.
4. Expose your child to a variety of extracurricular activities and hobbies in which she is likely to be interested.
5. Do not prevent your child from engaging in extracurricular activities as a penalty for poor effort or results in school. Any activity in which your child is being successful can boost your child's overall confidence and act as a catalyst for renewed interest in schoolwork.
6. Communicate your belief that your child will be successful.
7. Explain that a key to success is the belief that the harder a person tries at something, the better she gets. Provide real-life examples.
8. In various areas of your life, reinforce the connection between effort and success, and discuss this with your child.
9. Meet with your child's teacher and ask her to design assignments in the short run that ensure that your child will be successful without having to expend vast amounts of effort. It will also be important that your child has time to practice newly acquired skills before having to move on to the next unit.
10. Help your child set short-term, realistic goals for short-term assignments.
11. Help your child see progress toward the achievement of goals.

Sometimes a graph helps a child see that effort actually results in forward progress.
12. Help your child to evaluate her own progress, basing her evaluation on the amount of material she has learned and not on a comparison with other students in her class.
13. You may wish to arrange tutoring for your child in areas of weakness.
14. Having your child tutor a younger student in areas of your child's strength can boost your child's own sense of achievement.

Angie's parents' task was to help Angie develop self-efficacy in areas of schoolwork in which she is weak. High self-efficacy is Angie's belief that she has what it takes to be successful in math. Angie's increasing successes in math and her seeing that her own efforts led to this success was what was needed for Angie to pass math and achieve a grade of B at the end of her senior year. I think that Angie's father in particular learned how mind-set—what I call Habits of the Mind—is more important than genetic potential when it comes to a child's success in school and in life!

Peter Pan Syndrome. Does your child seem to go through periods of having the best of intentions to do work but slackening off effort as the semester rolls on? Does your child procrastinate, especially in the area of academic work? Does your child give up easily or lose interest quickly in school without seeming too concerned? Does your child have a knack for forgetting homework? Does your child make up many excuses for not doing well at school without appearing too upset? Does your child seem pretty content even though her schoolwork is not very good except around report card time? Does your child have pretty good relationships with adults, family, and peers? Does your child overestimate how well he is doing academically?

If these descriptions fit your child, you're seeing what Harvey Mandel and Sander Marcus, in *The Psychology of Underachievement*, described as the Non-Achievement or the Peter Pan Syndrome. They cite it as the major factor responsible for the greatest number of underachieving students in high school and college.

These frequently good-natured children can be a real puzzle to their parents. If a child is anxious, despondent, or hostile, for whatever reasons, then we can use this to explain the lack of a child's application to her schoolwork. However, children who manifest the Peter Pan Syndrome are perplexing, because on the one hand they say they want to do better at school, and yet, despite any attempts to help them change course toward better achievement, they still end up putting in insufficient effort—and there doesn't appear to be any cause for their underachievement.

Experts in the field who study the characteristics of underachieving children have slowly begun to understand these children. These experts also call this syndrome the Non-Achievement Syndrome, and they have discovered the possible explanations for this group's apparent lack of motivation to achieve. These reasons became all too apparent to me over a decade ago when I was working with twelve-year-old Ian.

Ian was the youngest child in a family with two siblings in college, a father who was a bank manager, and a mother who used to teach grade school. I met with Ian and his mother at my university office. His mother had explained to me before the meeting that Ian had scored quite high on his school's test of both verbal and mathematical aptitude. She went on to say that she often spends a great deal of time sitting with Ian to help him get his homework done, but she was returning to the classroom and feared that she would no longer be able to provide sufficient support to Ian in the future. Her concern was Ian's incessant excuses for not doing his work. In the latest parent-teacher conference, Ian's teacher had expressed great concern about Ian's not doing his homework.

After finding out about Ian's many interests and talents, including computers and comics, I turned to exploring Ian's goals. Ian did not appear to be at all concerned about his underachievement, although he said he would like to get better grades to please his parents.

"What would you like to be doing after you graduate from high school?"

Ian shrugged his shoulders. "No idea."

This surprised me, because with his capacity for school learning and the background of his family, college was a natural destination for him. "What about college?"

Ian shook his head and emphatically stated, "No way."

I invited Ian to sit in my chair and view the serene university scene below, with students lounging on the grass, laughing and seemingly carefree. "Ian, have a look out this window. This is one window to your future. In a few years, you can be here enjoying life, just like these students. And I know you have the talent to do so."

Ian's response revealed more insight than many students with Peter Pan Syndrome have at his age: "But for me to get here, that requires seventy-two more months of project work. I hate project work. I want to have fun while I still can!"

I discovered with Ian what is common to children with Peter Pan Syndrome. He had a strong motivation in his life. The motivation was to underperform. By doing his schoolwork well, he would reveal to others his true capabilities. Once he started to do his work, he would have to leave the comfort of childhood and take on the responsibilities of adulthood. Afraid of growing up and afraid of revealing his true talents to others, Ian used his considerable verbal talents only to come up with many creative excuses for why he had not done his work. Ian's fear of giving away the pleasures of childhood crystallized in his avoidance of and revulsion for project work.

Drs. Harvey and Dorothy Mandel, Director and Associate Clinical Directors at the Institute of Achievement and Motivation, York University, Toronto, Canada, along with Dr. Sander Marcus, a consultant child psychologist, have spent many years studying what they refer to as the Non-Achievement Syndrome Student. They concur with the experience of parents of these children, that motivating these children actually to do their work is problematic. They describe in their writing methods that have worked in changing the achievement patterns of many types of underachieving students but are unsuccessful with the Ians of the world: a) Bribery ("You can have the car if…"), b) Nagging ("Have you done your homework yet?"), c) Begging and Use of Guilt ("Do you know what your poor grades are doing to your father's heart?"), d) Punishment ("You're grounded"), e) Last-Minute Rescues ("I had to type his paper at the last second *again*—how could I have refused— after he finally finished it,") f) Sympathy ("It's not that bad; you'll probably do better next term"), g) Medication ("He's so tired, maybe he has a thyroid problem,"), h) The Study Skills Approach ("Here's a study schedule that works"), i) The Changing Courses Approach ("Let's try a different curriculum"), and j) The Family Therapy Approach ("What did we do wrong?").

The key for you in helping a child, who is highly motivated to avoid success, and for whom low grades do not cause a problem but solve the problem of having to achieve and grow up, lies in your refusing to take responsibility for your child's school performance, and letting go. Realizing that the more responsibility you take, the less responsibility she takes is the beginning change that you need to make to help change your child's pattern of underachievement.

Here is a series of steps that Drs. Mandel, Mandel, and Marcus recommend for working with the Peter Pan Syndrome child. As you'll see, they require a parent to be fairly direct and confrontational with her child. You must have intestinal fortitude to follow through on the process of adult disengagement from a child's area of responsibility.

1. Do not become discouraged if your child does not follow through with what he promised to do.
2. Do not provide your child with solutions to his problems. Give the responsibility to your child.
3. Make an agreement with your child concerning the goal of getting better grades.
4. Offer your child assistance in helping him achieve.
5. Obtain from your child or your child's teachers information about specific work requirements, the assignments your child has completed, and those he hasn't completed.
6. Discuss this information with your child. Record the specific problems and excuses that he uses to explain his failure to finish it. Record the exact details of the problem that hinders your child's

achievement of better grades, including how often the problem has occurred in the past.
7. Inform your child of the consequences that will ensue if the problem continues. Confirm whether your child still has the goal of getting better grades.
8. Ask your child to generate different solutions to the problem that is blocking his path to better grades. Discuss things that could interfere with each solution and have your child come up with countermeasures for dealing with the interference. Give your child the responsibility for thinking through the steps necessary for solving the problem.
9. Ask your child what he proposes to do now in light of the discussion about specific solutions. Once your child selects a solution, discuss the specifics of when, how, and how long it will take for your child to implement it.
10. Do not expect your child to have done everything in the proposed solution. Continue the process of confrontation and have your child identify solutions and make plans to implement them until progress is evident.
11. As your child begins to take on more responsibility, use less confrontation and be more supportive. Help your child answer questions about himself and his future.

Ian's mother and I helped Ian look at the positive consequences of obtaining a college education and the negative consequences of not earning a degree. He accepted that getting a degree would help him and said that he was prepared once again to try harder, even with his project work. We gave him the responsibility for working out the plan to achieve his goal of getting better grades and for overcoming the perceived obstacles along the way. While not abandoning him, his mother backed off considerably from trying to solve problems for him. In time, Ian discarded his chronic excuse making and began to take pleasure in seeing his own progress toward his goals.

Low Frustration Tolerance Trait. Do you have a child who gets easily frustrated by work she finds boring or hard to do? Have you thought of your child as lazy? Does your child appear to have an allergy to hard work? Does your child put off doing homework to the last minute? Does your child seem drawn to playing and having fun? Does your child rush through her work, doing only the minimum? Does your child seem disorganized and have trouble managing time?

Albert Ellis helped to coin the term "Low Frustration Tolerance" to describe people who procrastinate at important tasks, not necessarily because they are afraid of failing but because they believe they cannot tolerate frustration. Translating his theory to children, I have witnessed large numbers of children who are underachieving who have this unhelpful Habit of the Mind: "School should always be fun and exciting and never boring. It's unfair and awful to have to do boring work and sacrifice play time. I cannot stand homework. School is a totally bad place when it requires me to do work I find unexciting or boring."

Low Frustration Tolerance as a Habit of the Mind leads students to feel very frustrated and angry about homework they find boring or hard, and as a result they put off doing it. Low Frustration Tolerance is a driving force behind academic procrastination (see chapter 13). If you want to increase your child's academic motivation, you will frequently have to do something about his Low Frustration Tolerance, as I discussed in chapter 7.

Early in my counseling career, in the late 1970s, I worked with a young boy, Adam, and his mother and father. He was referred to me because he was not doing a lot of his homework, and he was being extremely unhelpful around the house. Adam, age eleven, was certainly bright enough to do his homework quite successfully. His parents were fairly well off financially, and Adam was well provided for materially by his family. His parents were at their wits' end to know what they could do to light a fire under Adam.

In one of the sessions, his parents were complaining about Adam's daydreaming and how he just dumped his clothes and schoolbag when he got home. The straw that appeared to break their back was an incident they recounted in which Adam would not get out of the bathtub to come down to dinner. They called him and waited and waited and waited, as his food got colder and colder and colder. Eventually, his father went upstairs and encountered Adam still sitting in a rather cool bathtub. His rather heated interrogation of Adam concerning why he was still sitting in the tub, and why he let his food get cold, produced only a vacant look and "Dunno." Adam's parents turned to me, the so-called expert, for illumination.

At the time, I was only beginning to become aware of the impact of child Low Frustration Tolerance on poor schoolwork. I was, however, interested in helping children such as Adam tune in to their thinking as a means for understanding and altering their approach to work.

I distinctly recall being extremely frustrated by my own inability to elicit from Adam the reasons for his sitting in the bathtub long after it had served its function. I could also sense his parents' frustration with me.

"Adam, what was going through your mind as you sat in the cold water and heard your mother calling you down for dinner?"

Adam remained deathly quiet, and it seemed like the dead of night in my office. I could feel my brow perspiring with the pressure of the moment.

"Adam," I persisted, "what where you thinking?" Still no response.

"Adam, imagine yourself back in the tub . . . your mother is calling from downstairs . . . you feel the cold water all around you . . . you smell chicken in the air . . . and you notice you're not moving . . . What are you thinking?" His mother, father, and I held our breaths and waited. The ticking of the clock on my desk was the only sound.

I could see a new glimmer in Adam's eye as he became aware of his own thought process. His lips parted and moved, and very quietly, as all three of us bent forward to listen, Adam whispered, "I was thinking, 'I can't be bothered.' "

Those four words telegraphed great meaning to me, and as I later explained to him and his parents, this revealed the existence of Low Frustration Tolerance as a Habit of the Mind. He wasn't angry with his mother for some past injustice or depressed because he felt that his parents loved his brother more than they did him, or anxious about an upcoming meeting with the counselor. No, not at all. No great psychodynamics were at work here. Adam merely had not learned or had not been taught the Habit of the Mind necessary to put up with frustration and to delay gratification. He was in some real sense still a baby.

The key to helping these children is teaching them High Frustration Tolerance. Many of the steps incorporated in the Parent-Child SOS (see chapter 2) apply especially well for these children. Rules with consequences, consistency, and persistence are what these children need. Basically, your child needs to know that no matter how hard or boring the work is, she is going to have to do it no matter how loudly she complains or cries.

Adam's parents began instituting a policy at home of "Get the work done first before watching TV or playing on the computer." Upon hearing the new policy, Adam sternly announced, "I won't love you anymore if you make me do this." Fortunately, his mother was used to Adam's antics, and quickly shot back, "Fine. Don't love me. Just do your homework." Adam never carried through on his promise, and because his parents were consistent, Adam started to become more self-disciplined. Once you can tolerate the thought of your child's not loving you all the time, it is much easier to institute stricter measures at home that may well invite your child's disapproval.

If you believe that your child has Low Frustration Tolerance, here are some methods for increasing his self-discipline (see chapter 7 for additional suggestions):

1. Help to organize your child's home study area by making a checklist of materials that she needs to take to school and home each day.
2. Check your child's notebooks on a regular basis to ensure that papers and work are correctly organized.
3. Help your child break down long-term assignments into easier, simpler steps.
4. Help your child schedule assignment steps on semester/monthly calendars and weekly timetables.

5. Make sure your child gets into the habit of checking that he understands the specifics of an assignment before beginning work.
6. Inspect the finished homework product and do not accept poor work. Sloppy or incomplete work has to be redone.
7. Discover the type of reinforcement your child prefers (activities, telephone time, clothes) and use them as a temporary incentive for doing schoolwork.
8. Provide strong verbal praise and use other reinforcements immediately after your child has put in effort on work he finds boring or hard, including proofreading and editing work.
9. Negotiate a behavioral contract on which the work to be done for a week is written down, the reinforcement and penalties that would ensue for completion/lack of completion are agreed to, and the signatures of you and your child appear.
10. Encourage your child to join an existing work-oriented peer study or study skills group.

All people, including your child, experience low frustration tolerance in certain areas of their lives whether in education, work, family/personal life, or self-improvement. We all have a tendency to dodge discomfort and frustration if we can. The reasons for this are not altogether clear, although the genetic makeup of humans, the unique biological temperament we were born with, the style of parenting we were exposed to, or that our child is exposed to, and the community and culture we live in all contribute. While you can help yourself and your child overcome the impact of low frustration tolerance by increasing the range of pleasurable activities in his life and reducing the boring ones, to be achieving in school requires a fair degree of high frustration tolerance on the part of your child.

Rebelliousness Trait. Do you have frequent arguments with your child about homework? Does your child frequently break rules concerning doing schoolwork? Does your child believe that he should be able to do what he wants to do? Does your child openly defy your requests that he do homework? Does he have difficulty living within limits? Does he act impulsively, rarely thinking about the impact of his actions on the feelings of others? Does your child appear to think that he should be able to do what he wants, and that no one can make him do anything he doesn't want to do? If so, your child may be developing into a rebel. Being a bit of a rebel could be seen as a good thing. Too much rebelliousness often leads to underachievement.

Some children perceive injustice in many of their parents' actions. Others may have parents who, for different reasons, are too hard on them and too strict. Current researchers investigating early childhood temperaments have noticed that even within the same family, some infants are born with feisty and demanding temperaments. For some adolescents, the onset of puberty, with its galloping hormones, can provide too much fuel for a child's desire to be independent.

If you have such a child who argues a lot and who, because of his difficult behavior, is constantly punished by parents and teachers, she may decide to fix your wagon, getting back at you and her teachers by not working. Or she might just decide that she shouldn't have to live by anyone's rules including yours, and drop out of school.

Mary was a ninth grader who was referred to me for refusing to do her homework. Her parents expressed helplessness in getting her to do her schoolwork as well as doing household chores and described the extremes of their own behavior, from giving up to yelling and punishing. Nothing seemed to work. Her well-meaning parents described few problems with their other younger children.

It took almost a semester to get Mary back on the playing field of achievement. Most of this time was spent in encouraging her parents to be clearer and firmer in following through on the expectations they held for all their children. Her father would do most of the yelling at Mary, while her mother felt her husband was being too harsh and protected her by giving in somewhat to her daughter's demands. Mary was very skilled at using her temper to get her way. Her parents would give in to just calm Mary down.

Over the weeks, her parents developed a strong united front. Any disagreements between them were never discussed in front of Mary. Her father recognized the importance of calming down first and communicating his desires to his daughter assertively. Her mother agreed to stop protecting her daughter as much and to be equally firm with her daughter about following rules. Her parents presented Mary with a set of homework rules for discussion as well as the consequences of Mary's following and breaking the rules. They steeled themselves to cope with whatever Mary might throw at them when they instituted any penalty. The first time they withdrew Mary's telephone privileges when she failed to complete her history assignment, Mary screamed and broke her study lamp and her new CD. Still, her parents hung in there, saying, "Your responsibility is getting your work done. Access to your privileges has to be earned by doing your work."

Because of somewhat inconsistent parenting between her parents over the years and the lack of follow-through, Mary had developed a sense of having great power over her life, the power to choose to do whatever she wished. It took many months of pain and family disruption before the family righted the power balance. Mary came to accept and respect her parents as the ultimate authority at home.

Gaining back and exerting power and influence with your children when they have rebelled against schoolwork is no easy task. Here are some suggestions for helping them find their way back:

1. Maintain your emotional control by focusing on your child's disobedient behavior and not on your child.
2. Do not engage in routine power struggles and arguments with your child. Take your wind out of her sails.
3. Discipline with dignity by not saying things in ways that contribute to your child's feeling bad about himself.
4. Meet with your child's teacher and enlist her cooperation to have your child's classmates be supportive so that your child does not feel alienated from the group.
5. Offer your child many opportunities to demonstrate to you and to his teacher and class what he does know and can do well.
6. Use humor to defuse potential conflict situations.
7. Establish a goal or agreement with your child that she will do better in school by discussing the positive consequences of doing well and the negative consequences of bad grades.
8. Draw up a behavioral contract in which your child agrees to work on his assignments for a specific amount of time each day and week. Be sure the contract outlines the rewards for achieving the goals and the penalties for nonattainment. Ensure that the rewards and penalties are sufficiently powerful to act as motivators.
9. Discuss with your child's teacher the use of a daily report card in

which her teacher evaluates your child's behavior and quality and quantity of homework and your child brings home the card each night for your signature (see chapter 11).
10. Explain to your child that she has the choice and responsibility for whether or not she does her schoolwork.
11. Encourage your child to work with peers who have an achievement orientation.
12. Identify an older child or adult whom your child respects, who can take an active interest in your child's educational progress, and to whom he can report on a regular basis.

If you have a rebel at home, one who acts without thinking and is quick to get angry, teaching him more reflective ways of thinking and a greater tolerance of limits and of others (see chapter 8) will be of enormous assistance.

Peer Conforming Trait. Do you have a child who, while not a founding member of the Antiachievers Club, nonetheless hangs out with the so-called friends who inaugurated the club? Is your child in a grade at school in which it is "uncool" to achieve? Does your child appear to be putting in less than optimal effort on his schoolwork because he is afraid that if he did his work and got good grades, his friends would reject him? Does your child worry a lot about what his friends think about him?

As I indicated in chapter 1, there is enormous pressure on children in some schools not to do too much schoolwork. Children start to tease each other about doing schoolwork as early as third grade. Kids who do their work and do it well are thought to be nerds. This pressure can be unrelenting and peaks around ninth grade. In some schools, gangs physically intimidate those students who are not in the gang and who are inclined toward achievement. I've heard of kids' having to smuggle their books under their shirts to avoid harassment.

I remember working with a young man, Ryan, who had developed a Peer Conforming Trait of personality. While capable of a great deal better effort and success than he was currently showing, Ryan was a member of a peer group who were not achieving well in school. If Ryan did well in class, it would make them look bad. While Ryan wanted to do well in school, he also was afraid of the consequences if he did.

"What would happen?" I asked.

"I don't know. I guess they wouldn't want me around."

"You mean," I said, feigning surprise, "that if you did better in class your friends would blow you off?"

"Yeah, none of my friends are doing well in school."

"But who pays the price for you not doing well?" I asked.

"I do. My parents are on my back, and maybe I won't be all that successful when I get out of school."

"Have you ever put it to the test? Done well and see if you still have friends?"

"No," he replied.

"Well, why not test your idea that no one will want to know you if you do well? Why not get as good a mark on your next math test as you can, and see the reaction? If there is nothing more than being hassled or teased, then, no big problem. If your friends do toss you out, then you have to ask yourself, 'Are these really friends?' Would true friends reject you for trying to achieve your goals? Perhaps it would be a sign that it's time to get new friends."

Ryan took the challenge and got a B on his next math test rather than the usual low C or D. While one member of the elite set of underachievers spat on his locker and refused him entry to his card game, by and large Ryan noticed that he could retain many of his friends and still do well at school.

One of the main ways to help a child to extract himself from a group of underachievers is to tackle his Approval-Seeking Habit of the Mind and encourage, instead, Independence. Teach your child that while it's nice to be approved of, it's not the end of the world if his friends disapprove of him for certain behavior. He can tolerate rejection.

In helping to modify your child's Peer Conforming Trait, you should consider adopting the following approach:

1. Discuss with your child her long-term occupational goals and the importance of success at school for their attainment.
2. Offer your child an opportunity to express a desire to do well in school in order to please himself, important people in the family, or other significant people in his life.
3. Point out the negative consequences that will ensue if your child continues to hang out with her current peer group and doesn't do much schoolwork.
4. Ask your child what would happen if he started to work harder and do better in school. Establish that in his mind his peers would reject him.

5. Explain to your child that her belief that her friends would reject her is probably wrong, even though she might be hassled.
6. Ask your child whether he would be willing to put his belief to the test by working harder and monitoring the effect this has on his friends.
7. Ask your child what it would mean about her friends if they did reject her simply because she chose to work toward better grades in school. Would they be real friends?
8. Point out that real friends would not reject her for working toward her chosen goals. State that if they do, it might be time for your child to look for friends who accept her right to decide how to approach schoolwork.
9. Explore with your child the possibility of alternative friendships and peer group.

I hope that these insights into your child's personality will provide you with new ways to help your child achieve, despite personality aspects that might be holding him back.

HOW TO SAY NO AND KEEP YOUR FRIENDS

1. Check out the scene to determine if the situation is likely to lead to trouble.
2. Understand the consequences, good and bad, for making a particular decision. Weigh the pros and cons. Decide whether or not to go along with your friends.
3. If you decide to avoid getting into trouble instead of going along with the negative peer pressure, take action. Suggestions include: just say no, leave, ignore them, make an excuse, change the subject, make a joke, act shocked, come up with a better idea about what you can do.

— S. Scott, *How to Say No and Keep Your Friends*

YOUR CHILD'S TRAITS

PARENT REFLECTION SHEET: YOUR CHILD'S TRAITS OF PERSONALITY

1. Place a check next to those traits of personality that describe your child.

   __Dependency   __Perfectionism   __Helplessness

   __Peter Pan Syndrome __Low Frustration Tolerance

   __Rebelliousness   __Peer Conforming

2. List your child's positive traits of personality (outgoing, honest, truthful, helpful).

   _____

   _____

3. Which Habits of the Mind could you teach your child to help modify those personality traits that are contributing to underachievement?

   _____

   _____

4. What are some other practical things you can do to modify these traits?

   _____

   _____

5. Which of the parenting practices described in chapter 4 would suit your child's personality traits?

   _____

   _____

6. Which teaching practices have helped your child learn? Communicate these to your child's present teacher(s).

   _____

CHAPTER 10

How the Way Your Child's Brain Operates May Contribute to Underachievement

Imagine you are back in grade school. Imagine a school very much like the one you attended when you were growing up. Picture the same classrooms, the same teachers, the same playground. Imagine everything being the same, with the exception of the way students are taught. In this imaginary school, all teaching is done in song and dance, as well as painting, drawing, and sculpture. Subjects such as biology, Shakespeare, and algebra are taught using performing or fine arts. No books are in evidence, and teachers do not spend any time lecturing in class. My question is this: If you attended this imaginary school, who would be among the top achievers, and who would be among the underachievers? How would you yourself perform?

My guess is that the top students would be those with artistic aptitudes and interests well above average. Those parents with strong musical, creative aptitudes, whose homes encouraged early and continued exposure of their children to musical and artistic activities and experiences, would likely have the highest achieving children.

> **NO TWO CHILDREN ARE ALIKE**
>
> A recent Texas Education Agency survey found that 95 percent of secondary teachers in academic classes taught primarily with the lecture method. But research tells us that only 25 percent of students have auditory strengths and benefit from a lecture method of instruction, and 30 percent are visual learners who need to see slides, overhead projections, or pictures to learn. As many as 15 to 20 percent need hands-on experience, and 30 percent respond to a mixture of several different teaching methods.
>
> —C. Fuller, *Unlocking Your Child's Learning Potential*

The formula for predicting success would be similar to the one used today. The more that a child's aptitudes, interests, and learning styles are matched with and catered to by the dominant teaching methods of a school, the greater her achievement. Conversely, the poorer the match between a child's aptitudes, interests, and modes of learning and his teachers' modes of teaching, the greater the likelihood of underachievement.

We know that the way your child's brain operates, her capacities for different types of thinking, as well as the way she finds it easiest to take in information, plays a central role in the extent to which your child will demonstrate her potential at school. Certain children bring with them aptitudes and learning styles that are suited to school learning.

Scholars have looked at the thinking and learning styles of people in different ways. Gregorc has observed four different ways that people, including children, approach learning, including whether they think concretely or abstractly and whether they are more logical, sequential, or random in the way they combine bits of information.

Witkin has described differences in children's learning styles in terms of whether they depend on, or require a great deal of support from, the surrounding context to make sense of what they are learning (field dependent) or do not rely on or require aid from the information surrounding what is to be learned (field independent). Kolb has described how children can approach new situations primarily through feeling or thinking. Gardner has proposed seven types of intelligence: linguistic, logical, musical, spatial, bodily/kinesthetic, interpersonal, and intrapersonal. Carbo has analyzed children's reading styles in terms of global versus analytic dimensions. Most recently, Sternberg has outlined the following three different thinking styles of children and adults that parallel the functions of our government: legislative (creative, planning), executive (implementing, doing), and judicial (judging, evaluating).

The following characteristics associated with the way your child's brain operates will normally give your child an advantage in achievement in learning from curricula traditionally taught in our schools:

1. has high linguistic, logical, and spatial abilities
2. is able to process information sequentially
3. is able to operate at an abstract level
4. learns well when seeing and hearing
5. approaches learning through thinking
6. has a good balance among all three branches of learning: planning/creating, doing, evaluating

In this chapter, I will describe six types of children who are at risk for underachievement due to different ways their brains operate. When teachers cater to their individual needs by providing the type of curriculum and instruction that capitalizes on children's cognitive strengths rather than being aimed at weaknesses, then these children will excel.

Round Pegs in Square Holes

My experience in working with children who have cognitive abilities and learning styles that are not well matched to the traditional school curriculum is that they face considerable frustration and many obstacles to their success. It is not difficult for them to feel like round pegs in square holes. Some feel large amounts of stress in trying to keep up with their peers, while others feel undermotivated due to the boredom of being underchallenged. If your child resembles one or more of the following types, it will be important for you to provide him with the Habits of the Mind previously described that will help him cope with the frustration in school that he will inevitably experience, no matter how good his teachers are. There are also particular strategies you can employ with your child to help ensure greater success in school.

Left Hemisphere, Right Hemisphere

Your child's brain is divided into a right and left portion called the right hemisphere and left hemisphere. The hemispheres are connected by a set of neural fibers called the corpus callosum, which helps carry messages to and from each hemisphere. Each hemisphere is responsible for certain types of thinking, and each has a unique way of processing information.

The left hemisphere is primarily responsible for verbal learning, relying on words to describe and analyze experience. The left side likes to listen and talk, prefers automatic routines, has good capacity for verbal short-term memory, and enjoys analytical and sequential learning experiences. It carries on logical analysis of relationships, especially keeping track of sequences of information. It solves problems by breaking them down into parts. Left-brain functions are most suited to schools today.

The right hemisphere is the more emotional of the two sides of the brain and includes artistic and musical expression. The right brain employs visual images rather than words to represent experience and leads to the development of spatial rather than logical relationships. It solves problems by looking at the whole and using hunches. The right brain is receptive to holistic, simultaneous hands-on learning experiences. The right side sees wholes, prefers doing and manipulating the environment to listening and talking, prefers novel sensory input, and has a good memory for sensory experience. Right-brain functions are most suited to the imaginary school that is organized around art and music.

We know that due to a host of factors, children vary in terms of which side of the brain dominates thinking and learning. If your child is strongly right dominant, it will be crucial that he is placed with teachers who understand and cater to his thinking and learning style. We also know that children's learning relies on both sides of the brain. We need to help all our children to use both sides of the brain to learn, solve problems, and be creative.

Caution: Do Not Label Children by Their Behavior

In reading through and thinking about the information that follows, it is important that you remember not to label your child by behavior. For example, the fact that your child demonstrates certain behaviors that are described as attention deficit hyperactivity disorder does not give us license to use the words "attention deficit hyperactivity disorder" to label your child.

Children are not their behavior. Behaviors come and go as a result of many influences. Moreover, although children share similar behaviors, it doesn't mean that they share other behaviors. Describing clusters of children's behaviors with the words "attention deficit hyperactivity disorder," "learning disabilities," "academically gifted," "below-average academic ability," and "learning styles" helps us to locate educational and parenting methods that cater to the individual child. If children are labeled, they can become stigmatized. Others may treat them as if they have some permanent disease or abnormality and may lower their expectations and change the quality of their interaction with your child.

Attention Deficit Hyperactivity Disorder (ADHD)

Between 3 and 5 percent of children in the United States have been found to exhibit difficulties in attention, impulsivity, and hyperactivity. We know that far more boys than girls exhibit ADHD behavior and that many of these boys and girls are extremely creative and intelligent. More than one third of children with ADHD behavior show significant improvement in adolescence. Be sure to consult a pediatric neurologist or educational psychologist if you believe your child has ADHD behavior.

The group of behaviors we label ADHD include: failure to think before taking action, difficulty in following complex instructions, inability to wait, difficulty in following a schedule, disorganization, and the frequent loss of items (DSM-IV, American Psychiatric Association). A child may exhibit difficulties in concentration without being overactive, or he may have difficulties in sitting still. One of the central problems of children demonstrating ADHD behavior is in staying connected with a task that is difficult and has no immediate payoff. Children manifesting these behaviors frequently have difficulties in interpersonal relations. They can be a real handful for adults.

As you probably know, medication (usually Ritalin) is often prescribed to help children to be less impulsive. There is some argument that too many children whose behavior teachers and parents have difficulty managing are being medicated. However, research does seem to indicate that a majority of children who actually demonstrate ADHD behavior do profit from medication.

There are a number of areas to concentrate on in working with your child. Many of these will be familiar to you if you have received professional advice from a pediatric specialist, school psychologist, or teacher.

You will want to provide external structure characterized by predictability as well as physical outlets. Tips for providing structure include:

1. Make sure your child has regular exercise.
2. Make sure your child has adequate sleep.
3. Give your child a nutritionally sound diet.
4. Reserve mornings for the most important learning.
5. Have a calm bedtime routine.
6. Use consistent rules.
7. Make your expectations clear using simple statements rather than questions.
8. Help prepare your child for changes to new activity.
9. Practice simple daily routines.
10. Design an incentive system for helping your child remember things.
11. Teach your child relaxation techniques to help control hyperactivity.

12. Focus your attention on positive work behaviors and try to avoid commenting too much on what hasn't been done well.

You can manage your child's distractibility through the use of priorities, directions, and the removal of distractions.

1. Organize the backpack and notebooks.
2. Have an area set aside for the next morning's materials and messages.
3. Encourage your child to stay on task.
4. Use simple, short, positive directions showing what to do instead of what not to do.
5. Provide visual clues to remind your child of what is expected.
6. Provide a regular time and an organized area for homework.
7. Limit and balance extracurricular activities.

Strategies for managing impulsivity are centered around teaching social skills and building self-confidence. Tips include:

1. Build on your child's strengths.
2. Teach game-playing skills, taking turns, and making choices.
3. Encourage sports that don't center on competition (karate, dance) and that encourage self-discipline.
4. Teach friendship skills (making requests, giving compliments, less rough play).
5. Model Goal Setting.
6. Teach Reflective Problem Solving.
7. Make sure your home climate is one of reason, hope, dignity, and tolerance.
8. Find ways to give your child positive attention (allow participation in hobbies).
9. Spend special time for you and your child to build a positive relationship.

Having regular contact with other parents of children who demonstrate ADHD behavior can be of enormous assistance in finding out firsthand how best to care for the needs of your child.

Learning Disabilities

In order to be able to read, spell, and do math, children need to be able to break a code. They need to be able to decipher symbols represented by letters and numbers. To read, they have to be able to say "aaah" when they see a printed letter "a" and be able to discriminate between similar sounds such as associated with the letters "g" and "p." They need to be able to associate meaning with the sounds they are pronouncing. To perform the basic operations of addition, subtraction, multiplication, and division, children also have to think in symbols represented by numbers. Thinking with numbers and letters involves the use of a variety of basic learning processes such as auditory perception, visual perception, and short-term memory.

Approximately 3 to 5 percent of students who have difficulties learning to read, write, spell, and do math appear to have some delay or disruption in these and other basic learning processes. This makes it harder for them to break the code. These have been called learning disabilities. Children who have been described as dyslexic cannot break the code due to disorders in one or more of the basic learning processes. Many children with learning difficulties have average or above-average intelligence.

For these children, school can be quite a psychologically grueling experience. Many children have not acquired the basic academic skills that are necessary to keep up with the advancing curriculum and their peers. They struggle with subjects that require reading and flourish in areas that involve more practical, hands-on learning aptitudes. If you have a child with learning disabilities, you have experienced the anguish of many parents who see their children suffering inevitable failure experiences at school. Both you and your child need professional and peer support.

Each of the Habits of the Mind can also help protect your child from the stress of schooling. Helping your child develop the independent ability to manage his frustration and anger, do work he finds difficult to do, be organized, and cope with mistakes and failures will provide your child with the foundation for learning at school and for being successful later.

Here are some guidelines that can help your child manage with school and the rest of his life. You will see that I've organized suggestions in three categories that require your attention: a) the emotional climate, structure, and routine of home, b) support for schoolwork, and c) the cultivation of your whole child. Focusing on these areas can help you to help your child develop his potential in all areas.

To establish a positive home routine and emotional climate:

1. Work at staying calm, patient, interested, and encouraging.
2. Try to minimize any negative effects concerning labeling your child may have experienced (for example, if he has been labeled as dyslexic) by separating his self-worth from his performance at school.
3. Encourage your child to talk about his frustrations at school.
4. Set clear and simple routines in your child's day.
5. Be consistent with rules and routines.
6. Spend extra time explaining things to your child.
7. Use lots of eye contact when explaining things.
8. Have your child repeat instructions to make sure he has understood them.
9. Before your child has to make a big change such as attending a new school or taking a special class, make sure you have a long lead time to familiarize your child with what to expect.

To support your child's schoolwork:

1. Help your child organize places to store his possessions so that he knows where things belong.
2. Make sure your child has an organized study area in his room or in another quiet part of the house.
3. Help your child break large tasks, assignments, and projects into smaller steps and to work on each gradually.
4. Help your child organize his study materials. Help him make outlines of important points and details from class lectures.
5. Make sure your child understands the details of directions for assignments. Teach him the skill of making sure he understands questions before proceeding to answer them.
6. Help your child schedule his schoolwork and leisure time.
7. Help your child to set daily, short-term, and long-term goals.
8. With your child's teacher, provide opportunities for your child to experience small successes.

9. With the help of a professional, investigate the child's learning strengths and communicate these to your child's teacher.
10. With your child's teacher, help provide your child with active learning activities incorporating teaching methods of multisensory intake (visual, auditory, tactile, kinesthetic).
11. When your child is feeling sad at having failed something, help remind him of previous schoolwork he has done well.
12. Point out that what is being learned both in and outside the classroom and stress that the process of learning is more important than grades.
13. Encourage your child to read to a younger child on a regular basis.
14. Find out if your child enjoys listening to radio programs and to books recorded on audiocassette.

To cultivate the whole child:

1. Expose your child to a wide variety of sporting, artistic, outdoor, cultural, community service, and other activities.
2. Notice which activities your child is attracted to and shows some aptitude for. Place your resources (financial, time) and his energy in those areas.
3. When your child is thirteen years or older, have a professional conduct a formal assessment of his vocational interests as well as his specialized aptitudes.
4. Show genuine enthusiasm for your child's nonschool accomplishments.
5. Take time to expose your child to theater, art, and music.

It is comforting to note that many children who underachieved at school due to learning disabilities go on to be very successful professionals, business people, and humanitarians. It appears that, once again, the Habits of the Mind enabled them to manage the frustrations of school and to find a good match between their talents and interests and an occupational setting.

Creative Thinking

It is not easy to define what is meant by the terms "children's creativity." Sometimes we use the term to refer to artistic talent, as when a child plays a musical instrument or paints a picture. We also use the word "creativity" to refer to children who march to the sound of their own drummer, nonconformists who live outside the boundaries of convention. I have already discussed the interests and dispositions of the Artistic child in chapter 8. In this section, I will describe children blessed with the ability to think creatively or divergently.

While many academically gifted children are highly creative, it has been found that more than 50 percent of highly creative children do not possess superior scholastic ability. Indeed, some artistically creative children, as well as those with specialized aptitudes such as computer literacy, are placed in classes for children labeled as learning disabled.

Dr. Paul Torrance has identified four dimensions of creative thinking:

1. Fluency: The ability to generate many ideas about one topic or subject.
2. Flexibility: The ability to shift one's thinking and perspective.
3. Elaboration: The ability to use details to expand upon an idea.
4. Originality: The ability to generate new and imaginative ideas others have not thought of.

In her outstanding book *Your Child's Growing Mind*, Dr. Jane Healy provides other signs of creative thought including absorption in activities, persistence in working or playing, an unusual ability to see patterns and relationships ("Monique and Abbey probably act that way because they are shy"), an ability to combine things or ideas in new ways ("If I turn the gate on its side and put it against the box, it could be a ladder"), the use of analogies in speech ("I feel as bouncy as a ball"), an ability to see things in new or different ways ("What if the road moved and not the cars?"), a tendency to challenge assumptions or authorities because of a reasoned-out difference of opinion, an ability to make independent decisions and to take action, an ability to shift from one idea to another, strong intuition, the willingness to go out on a limb and take risks, an interest in new ideas, and the enjoyment of thinking alone.

While all children demonstrate aspects of creative thinking, some creative children, the nonconformists, seem to think beyond the given and are continuously pushing the envelope. Because of their urges to pursue their own yearnings, sometimes they alienate themselves from their peers. Sometimes, nonconforming, creative children are unwilling or unable to live with the boundaries set for others, and, as a result, these children underachieve. If your child not only has the capacity for divergent thought but has difficulty fitting in, you will be called upon to provide constant support and encouragement.

In raising a creative thinker, it will be important to support your child when her talents are not being recognized at school and to help provide out-of-school activities and interactions with you and with others that offer your child the opportunity to exercise her creativity. Some ideas to help boost a creative child's achievement or help her excel follow. You will observe that these tips deal with helping your child adjust to being creative as well as providing creative stimulation.

To encourage Self-Appreciation and Self-Acceptance:

1. Explain that some classmates will tease and hassle him for his eccentric behavior. He should not think that at these times his classmates do not like him.
2. Encourage your child to accept himself even when others are giving him a hard time.
3. Because your child's creativity may cause her to stand out from other classmates, help her appreciate her uniqueness.
4. Remind yourself that your child will often have ideas that are different from everyone else's.
5. Encourage your child to express her views even if they seem to you to be without merit.
6. Do not try to change your child by encouraging her to behave in ways that everyone else is behaving.
7. Expect that your child will do the unusual and take more risks than the average child his age.

To provide creative outlets and stimulation:

1. Encourage interactive game playing, imaginary play, and hobbies. Provide a multitude of material with which to design, build, and create things.
2. Provide a variety of stimulating experiences for your child.
3. Rather than providing the answers yourself, provide your child with opportunities to figure out things herself.

4. Use more open-ended questions ("What do you think about that?") rather than closed-ended questions ("Do you think that is right or wrong?").
5. When asking your child about a recent experience, ask questions that require a descriptive answer ("Tell me about . . . ").
6. When your child asks seemingly bizarre questions, take the time to provide answers.
7. Help your child to excel in at least one creative area and help him share his creative achievements with others.
8. Locate a mentor to take an active interest in your child and appreciate her creative way.
9. Locate peers who not only will accept and value your child's creative ways but who will model an achievement orientation.

The key to raising a creative child successfully is for parents to acknowledge and appreciate her for what she is and not to feel uncomfortable or embarrassed that their child may not fit in with the status quo.

Academically Gifted

Traditionally, the term "academic giftedness" refers to children who score in the top 2 or 3 percent on intelligence tests. These are the students whose brains are designed to cope with highly demanding academic tasks. Frequently, but not always, these children have one or more parents or a member of the extended family who is also academically gifted. With the decline in the use of intelligence tests in schools as a result of legal rulings concerning their bias against certain cultural groups, the criteria for admittance into school classes for the gifted have broadened considerably. Children who possess exceptional leadership skills or extraordinary talent in the arts are considered by some to be gifted.

You wouldn't think that a child who has vast scholastic abilities would be at risk for underachievement. However, within any group or class of gifted children, between 10 and 15 percent underachieve. While this percentage compares favorably to the rate of underachievement in the general population of students, nonetheless, if your child falls within the underachieving group, your level of concern is very great.

Some gifted children underachieve because their scholastic capacities so far exceed the academic demands provided in their classroom that they lose interest. If their teachers do not provide them with challenging material after they have completed their assigned work,

---

GIFTED CHILDREN SUFFER

Writing in the Roeper Review, James Delisle of Kent State University reports that gifted children suffer if they know they are disappointing their parents or teachers. Risk for underachievement occurs when gifted children evaluate themselves in terms of their failures rather than in terms of their successes.

but rather just give them more of the same, children will realize it is not in their interest to get the work done too quickly.

Of course, there are other reasons that an academically gifted child might underachieve. My own research indicates that scholastic brain power is not enough to ensure a child's achievement. What appear to be more important are a child's Habits of the Mind. So, if your examination of your child's Habits of the Mind as described in chapter 6 reveals certain weaknesses, these weaknesses could lead to the loss of confidence, lack of motivation, disorganization, or inability to tolerate limits that leads to underachievement. While researchers in the early part of this century found that gifted children as a group were better adjusted than were children of average academic ability, some gifted children lack the positive habits of thought that other nongifted children possess.

James Alvino and the editors of *Gifted Children Monthly* write in their book *Parents' Guide to Raising a Gifted Child* about the negative effects parenting can have on the motivation of gifted children. These experts argue against pushing children to do more and more, including completing schoolwork perfectly. Detrimental effects can be avoided when you convey your satisfaction with what your child has done rather than focusing on what she has not accomplished. Forcing a gifted child who is a perfectionist to try activities in which there is a high likelihood that he will not be able to perform perfectly can backfire, leading to inertia. Rather, giving your child choices in the selection of new activities that he might be interested in or competent in doing reduces fear and resistance. Your use of reinforcement also may have a bearing on your child's motivation. If you reserve your praise for your child's best work, you may be unintentionally communicating the idea that less than perfect work is not acceptable. You might also be increasing the pressure on your child to do more and more. Rely on the steady encouragement of your child's efforts at learning, improvement, and mastering new material.

If your child does not appear to be fully developing his potential, there are some general strategies that can help you encourage your child to extend himself in new areas: a) Teach Self-Acceptance, Risk Taking, and Independence so that your child can cope with her imperfect side (average grades, comparison with other students) as well as coping with unfavorable judgments of others (teacher disapproval of child's nonconforming ideas), b) reinforce in your child strengths rather than weaknesses so that she is more prepared to try new tasks and perform old tasks in creative ways, and c) teach emotional independence by giving your child choices that require her to make decisions within an existing structure of family rules and responsibilities. Encourage your child to set her own goals and to plan how to achieve them.

Here are some specific hints to help an academically gifted child who is not achieving her full potential:

1. Even though your child is academically gifted, do not expect perfection.
2. Do not place your child under too much pressure to perform well.
3. Encourage your child's leadership potential. Respect and support existing leaders in your child's school and in your community.
4. Allow your child as much freedom as possible to decide how to do his work.
5. Meet with your child's teacher to try to eliminate repetitive drill and practice exercises.
6. Discuss with your child's teacher how the content of the curriculum can be based on your child's interests rather than on areas he has already mastered.
7. Make sure your academically gifted child has plenty of encouragement to explore areas in which she is not gifted.

8. Help your child value originality rather than doing things perfectly.
9. Be generous in your support and encouragement of your child's achievements in areas that do not interest you.
10. Help develop your child's ability to describe things using all five senses ("How did the meal taste?" "How does the choir sound?").
11. Educate yourself about your child's special aptitude, what it means to be academically gifted, and what opportunities are uniquely your child's.
12. Involve your child in team competition like the U.S. Academic Competition.

"Average" Academic Abilities

Whereas some children bring with them to their schoolwork advanced scholastic aptitudes, other children bring advanced talents and aptitudes in other areas. There are children who are fantastically talented in nonschool domains but have weaker academic abilities than do their peers. For example, in chapter 8, I described children who were fantastically talented in working with their hands but were not so fantastically talented in doing traditional schoolwork.

Children who struggle to keep up with academic demands are, of course, at risk for underachievement. As they enter the upper grades, the struggle for success becomes greater and greater. It takes a rare spirit among these children to maintain enthusiasm and the belief in self. Once a child becomes discouraged and begins to believe that "It doesn't matter how hard I work, I'll never be successful," the likelihood of underachievement is great.

The keys to helping a child who struggles with academic material are fourfold. First, it is vital that you teach him Self-Acceptance, as outlined in chapter 7. It is especially important that he not take difficulties in schoolwork personally. Second, you need to reinforce constantly your child's Internal Locus of Control for Learning so that no matter how slow the success, your child continues to value the importance of effort in learning. Third, you need to work closely with your child's teachers to ensure, as much as possible, that they design your child's assignments to maximize his success. Fourth, you need to monitor your child's work closely and provide, when necessary, external motivation to help him get through the difficult parts. The immediate solutions for the underachieving child, as described in chapter 2, are a basic blueprint for helping your child achieve to the best of his ability. Other tips are:

1. Ensure that expectations for your child are high but realistic.
2. Help your child to see that solid effort, not outcome, deserves the best rewards.
3. As much as possible, make sure that your child's teacher is gearing instruction to your child's actual level of skill rather than to what other students in his class have learned.

4. Discuss with your child's teacher assigning work so that your child can achieve, with effort, success a majority of the time.
5. Help your child break down complex assignments into simpler parts.
6. Communicate clearly what you expect of your child in terms of quality and quantity of homework.
7. Do not accept poor work.
8. Where necessary, employ a positive incentive scheme for motivating your child to do work she finds especially hard or boring.
9. Establish regular and frequent communication with your child's teacher.
10. Encourage the full development of your child. Acknowledge your child's nonacademic strengths.
11. Provide your child opportunities to find out what he is good at by exposing him to a variety of recreational and extracurricular activities.

Once again: Whether you are parenting a child who is academically talented or one who is below average in scholastic ability, if you take notice of and accommodate her strengths and interests and help her to accept herself with her differences, you will provide your child with the necessary encouragement to be successful.

Diverse Learning Styles

Over the past years, it has been noticed that students have differences in the way they take in information that is taught in class. Experts who have studied children's learning styles have come up with a host of ways to describe these differences among students. The most popular for describing learning styles is in terms of learning modalities. It has been concluded that some students learn better by seeing what they learn (visual learners), some learn better by hearing (auditory learners), and some learn better by doing (kinesthetic learners).

A child who is a strong **visual learner:**

- is a good observer of details
- likes TV and video games
- can put things together without using directions
- takes pride in the way he dresses
- learns more from reading than from listening
- takes many notes in class

A child who is a strong **auditory learner:**

- likes to listen to CDs or the radio
- remembers the words to songs
- thinks out loud when doing math problems
- learns better from listening to a lecture than from reading
- is very good at describing feelings in words
- is good at discriminating musical sounds

A child who is a strong **kinesthetic learner:**

- likes to build things and play outside
- likes to get hands dirty
- mind wanders while listening to a story or a lecture

- is very active
- moves with music
- expresses strong feelings in body language rather than words
- learns best from practical activities
- enjoys physical contact

Getting frustrated with your child if he does things differently from the way you do them or if he takes a longer time to "get it," having low expectations of your child that you subtly communicate, expressing keen disappointment with your child for not achieving, or misinterpreting your child's failure to complete work as straight-out defiance can only undermine your child's achievement. Here are some ideas for helping a child whose learning strengths are not well suited to traditional classroom instruction:

1. Do not equate your child's success with how well she performs in school.
2. Celebrate your child's distinctive strengths and respect his individuality.
3. Provide opportunities for your child to explore activities that call upon her distinctive learning style.
4. Meet with someone at your child's school concerned with placing students with teachers. Ask that your child be placed with a teacher who emphasizes visual teaching (organized, creative physical environment, whole language approach) and kinesthetic/tactile teaching (interactive, hands-on activities and materials, learning applied to the world around).
5. Meet early in the school year with your child's teachers and educate them about your child's preferred learning style. Help work out a plan to overcome any weaknesses.
6. Discuss suggestions for modifying your child's learning environment, including changing class seats, using visual aids, and tape recording important lectures.

7. Discuss alternative forms of assessment besides written essays (make a poster, construct a model, make an oral presentation).
8. Educate your child about her preferred learning style so that she can prepare for areas of difficulty and seek out activities that promise success.
9. Provide support in your child's area of weakness by providing automated learning equipment (calculators, word processors) and tutors.
10. Employ learning activities at home that capitalize on your child's dominant learning style and build up weaker areas (auditory, kinesthetic/tactile, visual).

SUGGESTIONS FOR HELPING BOTH HEMISPHERES WORK TOGETHER

Games that combine visual and verbal cues (Simon Says)

Visualizing pictures from listening or reading (make a "mental movie")

Describing actions with words

Verbalizing intuitive discoveries ("How did you know that?" "What clues did you use?" "What came into your mind first?")

Describing problem-solving experiences ("Can you tell me how you did that puzzle?")

Memorizing math facts to music

Spelling words backward, remembering number sequences backward

Keeping the score of the game in your head

Cooking by following recipes

Watching TV and then retelling the story in order ("First they found the treasure, and then . . . ")

— J. M. Healy, *Your Child's Growing Mind*

The point needs to be made that you need to be your child's number one advocate. Take the knowledge of how your child's brain operates and put it to good use. First, at home, show your child how aware you are of her distinctive thinking and learning style and show your appreciation. Once your child accepts who he is and does not fear making mistakes or doing the wrong thing, half the battle is won. Second, at school, collaborate with teachers in an effort to compensate for your child's weaknesses and to enhance and utilize her strengths. The third step is working on the development of your whole child. Provide your child with new experiences in which she has an opportunity to learn what she is good at and what she is not so hot at. When home and school work together to encourage the fullest development of a child, based on the individual needs and characteristics of a child, most children will overcome problems and will excel in one or more areas.

PARENT REFLECTION SHEET: HOW YOUR CHILD'S BRAIN OPERATES

1. Place a check next to the characteristics that describe how your child's brain operates.

__ADHD __learning disabilities

__creative thinking __academically gifted

__"average" academic abilities __diverse learning styles

2. Describe what you think are your child's distinctive strengths in the way he thinks.

_____

_____

3. In your own words, describe what you could say to your child to describe the unique way he goes about learning and for him to accept himself while being different from many other students in his class or school.

_____

_____

4. What practical things can you do for your child to help cater to the way his brain operates?

_____

_____

5. What are some things teachers have done in the past that have helped your child learn? Communicate these to your child's present teacher(s).

_____

_____

CHAPTER 11

GETTING HOMEWORK RIGHT

Homework is controversial. Everyone has an opinion about it. Some parents think their children have too much homework, while others plead for more homework.

Homework attracts stress. Parents get stressed if they find their children being assigned homework that appears to take hundreds of hours to complete and may interfere with family time together. Children get stressed about the amount of homework they are assigned and the time in which they have to complete it. Some parents and children have ongoing fights over homework. Pitched battles over homework can give rise to so much friction that the resulting tension can sour relationships between parents and their children.

Homework is one of my "hot buttons." I find that it doesn't take too much for me to work myself up about homework. I'll explain my concerns here.

Research indicates that well-designed homework leads to higher levels of student achievement. This relationship appears to be strongest at the high school level. That is, all other things being equal, students who get regularly assigned homework do better at school than students who do not. This relationship interests me. I am extremely concerned that all schools and, in particular, those schools that my children attend, incorporate policies and programs that research indicates promotes achievement. Since homework is an area that research indicates is an important leverage point for influencing achievement, I believe that all schools should have a coherent homework policy and related set of practices.

> **THE EFFECTS OF HOMEWORK**
>
> 1. The time spent on homework influences the achievement of students from elementary grades through high school.
> 2. Time spent doing homework affects homework in a variety of subject areas.
> 3. Homework can have a strong impact on the achievement of low-income students.
> 4. Homework is one of the few variables affecting student achievement we can exploit.
> 5. The positive effects of homework exist for both high- and low-ability students.
> 6. It has been shown that students in grades five and six who do homework outperform those who do not.
>
> — D. E. Olympia et al., "Homework"

Homework also potentially occupies a significant amount of our children's overall academic learning time. Our children spend a certain number of hours studying at school and a certain amount of time doing work at home. We know that the more hours children spend actively engaged in academic learning tasks the greater their achievement. Sometimes, homework occupies a large percentage of your child's academic learning time. For example, if your child is in tenth grade, he spends an average of seven hours a day at school. Perhaps six out of the seven hours are spent studying. At home, he should be doing approximately two hours of homework. This means that at least 25 percent of your child's engaged academic learning time is spent doing homework.

Most schools do target student achievement in their mission statement as one of the themes that define their existence and purpose. However, far too many schools have gotten homework wrong. Far too many schools do not have a homework policy that spells out the value and purposes of homework. Far too many schools do not spell out the differing homework responsibilities of parents, teachers, and students. Too many schools have not sought support of their homework policy from teachers and parents. Far too many do not have ongoing communication with parents concerning how they can best support their child in doing homework.

> **RESEARCH INDICATES THAT HIGHER ACHIEVEMENT AND HOMEWORK ARE ASSOCIATED WHEN HOMEWORK IS:**
>
> 1. graded or commented upon
> 2. contains positive comments
> 3. is followed by either reinforcements or penalties
> 4. is reviewed or checked by parents

As we move to more decentralized, site-based school management, individual schools and local school districts are left to make policy in the area of homework. I am not sure this is a good idea. Several years ago, I was discussing homework with an elementary school principal who was complaining that she had to advise her staff to cut back on the amount of homework they were assigning, as the amount far exceeded the amount being assigned at the neighboring middle school. Teachers have told me that they do not assign much homework because most of their students' parents do not support the idea of having homework. This seems to me like the tail wagging the dog. Best practices in educational research should govern school policy and programs, not whether homework is popular with parents or is out of favor in a nearby school.

I do not want to paint all schools with the same brush. Some schools have their act together and have spent many hours discussing homework policy and communicating on a regular basis with parents. What I am saying is that too many schools have left this very important area unattended, and, as a consequence, students, teachers, and parents are not getting homework right.

Before providing some ideas for managing homework. I will present my view of what a typical homework policy should state, and I will describe the respective responsibilities of students, parents, and teachers.

Homework Policy

Let's start with a clear statement about what homework is and what it is designed to accomplish. I've been helped in the formulation of these ideas by an overview of homework by D. E. Olympia, S. M. Sheridan, and W. Jenson, in *Home-School Collaboration*. Homework can be conceived as serving two separate purposes: academic development and personal development.

Homework is work assigned to be done during nonschool hours and designed to extend classroom learning, including **practice** (repetition and drill), **preparation** (groundwork for future classwork), **extension** (application of skills and ideas to a new task), and **creative work assignment** (original use of previously learned skills).

Homework provides experiences for children to learn the Habits of the Mind (attitudes and life skills) that are essential for success and happiness in school and later life (optimism, high frustration tolerance, time management, self-acceptance).

It is useful to remind ourselves that for our children, homework is the first job that they do for someone else rather than for us. It affords a wonderful opportunity for them to learn and for us to encourage not only their learning of academic skills and knowledge, but also work and mental habits that will help them be what they want to be. Successful completion of homework can encourage your child to view himself as an achiever and independent learner.

Some children, even those who are academically gifted, can use homework to consolidate the information their teacher presented in class that day. I know that when my son was younger, it would help him to review with me the basic mathematical operations he was learning in class.

Responsibilities

To my way of thinking, homework is a shared responsibility among children, teachers, and parents. Once school and home accept the value of homework, then each party has distinctive responsibilities.

These are the homework responsibilities of students:

1. Homework is to be done at a high realistic level commensurate with child's abilities.
2. Homework is to be completed independently of parents and friends.
3. Homework is to be submitted on time.
4. When problems arise, communicate with teacher and parent.

These are the homework responsibilities of parents:

1. Communicate the purpose and value of homework.

2. Show interest, enthusiasm, and support.
3. Provide a suitable study area.
4. Communicate high, realistic expectations for the quality of homework.
5. Communicate the importance of effort to homework.
6. Ensure that your child knows ahead of time when homework should be started each night and how much time should be spent on homework.
7. Make sure that homework is supervised by someone to make sure it's done and to prevent cheating.
8. Praise your child's efforts at homework.
9. Encourage your child's desire to master material, to persist at homework, to be curious about it, and to derive pleasure from homework.
10. Communicate with someone at school if problems occur.

These are the homework responsibilities of teachers:

1. Homework should be assigned so that it can be completed within a reasonable time.
2. Children should be told how much time they are to spend on homework.
3. Assigned homework should reflect and be related to the current content of instruction.
4. The purpose of homework assignments should be clear.
5. Homework should be graded immediately with relevant feedback provided.
6. Children should be allowed optional ways of doing classroom assignments.
7. Homework should maximize success.
8. Children should be able to complete the homework independently.
9. A variety of homework should be assigned, and excessive, repetitive drill work should be avoided.

10. Homework should be assigned regularly.
11. There should be regular communication with parents about the content of homework for the forthcoming period of instruction.
12. There should be regular communication with parents when problems arise with individual children.

It is my belief that if schools used this sample school homework policy as a blueprint to be modified for their student population and parent community, and if this list of responsibilities were implemented by all parties, all of us would start to get homework right.

Motivating Your Child to Do Homework

The highly conscientious, achieving child will dodge fewer assignments than the underachieving child for whom academic procrastination is a way of life! But as sure as night follows day, all children will try to get out of doing some degree of their homework. Unfortunately, when children avoid homework, the amount of learning is reduced, their future opportunities appear threatened, and we parents are required to take a stand in one form or another.

I have a fairly simple model of homework management that is based on simple principles of child development. When children are young and in early grades, we parents should be somewhat involved in establishing limits so that children know exactly what is expected of them. This involves determining pretty much where your child will study, for how long, the level of work that is and is not acceptable, rewarding or penalizing your child's efforts, and being quite firm and assertive with your child about doing his schoolwork. This approach, which I call the **Structured Approach**, includes the use of external motivational methods to help your child do what he does not feel like doing and internal motivational methods when your child is initially attracted to his work.

As children get older, homework management becomes much more child directed. I call the second approach Self-Responsibility. It places

> **PARENTAL GUIDELINES FOR HELPING A CHILD WITH HOMEWORK**
>
> - Help develop the habit of your child's doing homework in a proper study area.
> - Instill the value that homework must be completed on time.
> - Make sure that your child understands that homework is his responsibility to complete independently.
> - Using clearly stated expectations and motivational strategies (praise for effort, goal setting), encourage your child to do her homework at a high standard.
> - Provide help only on request.
> - Show interest in what your child is learning.
> - When your child fails to complete homework at a satisfactory level, communicate your expectations assertively and, if necessary, use appropriate penalties such as not being allowed favorite activities until after homework is satisfactorily completed.

the homework ball squarely in your child's court. Rather than providing the structure and motivation yourself, in Self-Responsibility the decision for doing or not doing the homework and how it is accomplished is left up to your child.

Depending on the age of your child as well as the methods you have used with your child, you may decide to elect one or more of the other approaches to homework management. If your child is a teenager and you have had a fairly tight leash on her schoolwork, and yet you find that homework is still not being done, you may need to shift to the **Self-Responsibility Approach.** If you have tended to use a Self-Responsibility Approach with your twelve-year-old, you may need to tighten up quite a bit and use the Structured Approach.

The Structured Approach to Homework

This approach applies a combination of principles of reinforcement and assertiveness to the area of managing your child's homework behavior. Using this approach, your aim is to show your child the basics of how to do it so that in time she will have the skills and confidence to take total responsibility for doing it herself. Here are some of the components of the Structured Approach:

Provide a suitable study area for your child. Sitting in front of the TV and having the radio blaring is out, as a rule. Many older children do find that listening to music while doing homework motivates them to do work that is hard or boring.

When your child is in the first couple of years in school, it is okay for him to work in your immediate vicinity. Make sure your child has a place where he can neatly store his homework materials, including work he has brought home from school. In later elementary grades, the suitable study area will usually be in his room. While it is advised that children get used to doing their homework at their desk, some children really do it much better while sitting on their bed. You need to be guided a little bit by your child's style.

Help your child to manage time. Some children—especially younger children—have difficulty keeping track of time. Life can be a great buzzing, swirling mass of confusion. Help your child get in the habit of knowing how much homework he has to do on a given night and deciding when he will start the work after he has come home from school. Helping your child separate the forest from the trees will provide a solid foundation for his being more independent later on to manage his time himself.

Do not accept poor work. Many children know that they rush their work, and they hope that you will not notice or that you will let it pass. One day not too long ago, my son showed me an interview he had conducted the night before and had written down to hand in to his teacher the following day. It was a mess. Reminding myself to stay calm, I gritted my teeth and gave him the option of rewriting the interview before school began or going to school and suffering the consequences. He took the latter course but managed to rewrite it during a free period. My children know that substandard work is not acceptable.

TIME MANAGEMENT—A SHORTCUT METHOD FOR YOUR CHILD

When you are tempted by distractions when you are doing your homework or are about to start it, think of it in the following way. Ask yourself: "How important is . . ."

- this dance
- watching television
- playing tennis
- reading this magazine
- talking on the phone
- combing your hair
- doing nothing

. . . compared to your goal of being a success tomorrow?

Remind your child that it is her responsibility to do the schoolwork, not yours. Surprisingly, children of all ages think that when push comes to shove, you will end up doing their work for them. Even my wife and I have sometimes been guilty of doing a bit too much of our children's social studies homework projects. I know that it is important to make a special point to my children and myself that it is their work, not mine.

Firmly communicate expectations. I hope you can hear yourself saying to your child, "No matter what, the work gets done." Many children have an elaborate set of excuses for postponing their work until later: "I can't concentrate"; "I don't have to work so hard early in the semester"; "My teacher stinks"; "I don't know what to do"; "I forgot my books"; "I did some of it in school."

Be prepared to be a broken record. When your child turns on the excuses, simply say over and over again in a firm, quiet, yet forceful way, "You have to do it."

Praise effort frequently. Do not make the mistake of withholding praise until your child has completed her homework. You should teach your child that the process of doing the work is as important as the product. Some parents give their children fantastic rewards for getting good grades, but it is better to extend your praise and recognition at times when your children are submerged in the pleasure and pain of their work.

Use positive incentives. If you are using a structured homework approach to light a fire under your child, you will want to reward not only your child's efforts but also his achievements, however small or large. When you see your child doing the work, give him immediate praise. It is fine to promise your child a reward or extra privilege for completing his homework before he embarks on work he usually gives up doing. Once your child begins to experience the pleasure of being successful, you will be able to drop away tangible incentives and weave in more praise for effort.

Don't be afraid to use penalties. Some children respond better to penalties than to rewards. Identify privileges and valued possessions you could withhold from you child until after he has done his work (no friends over, no telephone, no going out).

The idea you want to get across to your child is that schoolwork is his number one priority. If your child goofs up, he pays the price. Your responsibility as a parent is to make sure your child does the work. Your preference is not to be the tough guy; however, you will not allow your child to be distracted by anything pleasurable or to have free time when homework has not been accomplished.

Draw up a behavioral contract. If your child is not doing homework, consider a contract. Sometimes, going to the extreme of writing down and having both of you sign a contract that specifies the work that your child agrees to do, the reward he is to earn for completion, and the penalties that will be incurred for failure to complete the work, will motivate your child. Seeing things in black and white above both of your signatures gives the homework outlined in the contract the status and aura of a legal document, which even young children sense has greater importance than doing "stupid math."

Communicate with school. As I have indicated, working as a partner with your child's teacher can be of enormous value, and communication is an important part of this partnership. Children today are more than capable of pulling the wool over their parents' and teachers' eyes concerning homework. Between "I have no homework" and "My great-grandmother got married last night," our little angels have been known to play off school against home. Once you start a dialogue with your child's teacher, your child will have fewer places to hide.

YOU CAN DO IT! SCHOOL-HOME CARD

Student Name _____

Week Beginning _____

0 = poor 1 = fair 2 = good **PERIOD**	Monday classwork / behavior / homework / initials	Tuesday classwork / behavior / homework / initials	Wednesday classwork / behavior / homework / initials	Thursday classwork / behavior / homework / initials	Friday classwork / behavior / homework / initials
1					
2					
3					
4					
5					
6					
7					

DIRECTIONS: The You Can Do It! School-Home Card is a way that parents and teachers can cooperate and communicate together in an effort to motivate students to achieve better in school as well as behave better in class. It can be used to increase the quality and quantity of work done in class and at home as well as to help students learn how to behave more cooperatively in class.

STUDENT RESPONSIBILITIES: Collect card each week; take card to teacher at the end of every class for grading and initials; present card to parent(s) at home; work hard at making improvements in homework, classwork, and/or behavior.

TEACHER AND PARENT RESPONSIBILITIES: Teachers and parents discuss with student areas of work and/or behavior which can be improved; provide concrete examples of acceptable work and/or behavior; collaborate with student on specific short-term weekly work and/or behavior goals; specify level needed to be achieved for student to receive different grading; teachers rate students at the end of each class (0 = poor, 1 = fair, 2 = good) and initial card; parents (and teachers) may provide small daily and larger weekly rewards for small improvements in student work and/or behavior, parents and teachers may communicate questions, answers, and general comments to each other in the space below.

ADDITIONAL COMMENTS

MONDAY	Teachers	_____
	Parents	_____
TUESDAY	Teachers	_____
	Parents	_____
WEDNESDAY	Teachers	_____
	Parents	_____
THURSDAY	Teachers	_____
	Parents	_____
FRIDAY	Teachers	_____
	Parents	_____

I have developed a form to provide parents and teachers with specific daily information about a child's classwork, homework, and behavior. The form can be used with children between the ages of six and sixteen. A one-week period should give you an idea of where any problems lie. Usually, your child's teacher will initiate the use of this form in a meeting with you and your child. Your child's teacher will explain that the form provides your child with the opportunity to get back on the track and to prove to himself and others what he can do. At this meeting, your child learns that he has the responsibility to take the form to his teacher at the end of every class for grading and initials and to show it to you every day after school. On the form, the teacher grades your child's homework, classwork, and behavior on a three-point scale (0 = poor, 1 = fair, 2 = good). At the meeting, the teacher explains to your child the criteria he has to meet to earn a grade of poor, fair, or good. Your responsibility is to check the form each day, provide appropriate comments on the grades your child received, and, if necessary, provide rewards or penalties, depending on the total number of points your child has earned during a week. Parents and teachers write comments on the back of the form as the need arises.

At the end of one week, all three of you can see areas of schoolwork that are good and areas that may still require improvement. Sometimes, being held publicly accountable for his work and behavior will lead to radical improvement in your child's approach to school.

If after a week your child has earned a sufficient number of good grades, you can institute a token reinforcement program at home so that at the end of the following week, depending on how many points he has earned, your child earns certain privileges. Failure to earn sufficient points may lead to the withdrawal of preferred activities (see chapter 12 for a more detailed description of a token reinforcement incentive scheme).

A highly structured approach is required when your child appears unable or unwilling to accept personal responsibility for doing homework. As the material in the next section suggests, if we parents stop becoming overinvolved with our children's homework, many will take up the challenge to grow up.

Self-Responsibility

Today's well-meaning parents believe that it is our responsibility to make sure that everything turns out okay for our children. In the 1970s and 1980s, parents were saturated with advice from experts on how to be better parents. The better parenting advice promoted, out of concern for their children's self-esteem, centered on how people could parent with fewer mistakes. It has been argued that the consequence of this advice is that parents have assumed huge amounts of responsibility for their children's social, recreational, and academic life. And as parents assumed greater responsibility, children began to assume less and less.

This brings us to the area of homework. It does appear that some parents, with the best of intentions, have appropriated too much responsibility for seeing that their child does homework and does it well.

John Rosemond has written eloquently about how, because of parents' overinvolvement, it is no surprise that so many children appear unable to do homework on their own. Rosemond, in his book *Ending the Homework Hassle*, illustrates the pitiful state of our parenting by describing a variety of games that parents and children play at homework time.

The "Great Homework Hunt" has the mother or father going through great contortions trying to figure out just exactly what Billy is supposed to be doing for homework. In the "Parenting by Helicopter" game, parents supervise Billy doing homework in the kitchen, always hovering over him, encouraging and bribing Billy to do things he can already do. In "Billy Plays Dumb," he acts like he's lost his brain. He forgets things he knew days before, and the speed with which he does homework makes it clear it's not getting done thoroughly. "The Homework Marathon" is played out over an entire evening, when a twenty-minute homework assignment can take three hours. Finally, Billy and his family play "We're a Bunch of Bananas." After hours of trying to cajole Billy to do his work, Mom has a meltdown, Billy starts screaming, and Dad becomes furious with Billy. Billy's mother jumps to Billy's rescue, which leads to Dad's going bananas, and the night is ruined for everyone.

BACKING OFF

1. Set up a regular study time.
2. Ensure that the house is free from distractions.
3. Insist that your child does work for a certain period of time each evening.
4. Leave your child alone.

—L. A. Sonna, *The Homework Solution*

While I hope that these games are not being played in your house, Rosemond provides food for thought. Are you too involved with your child's homework? Do you hover? Are you encouraging dependence? Are you sending negative messages about your child's ability to do schoolwork on her own?

Rosemond's solution is found in what he calls the "Consulting Parent," who is available when needed, assigns responsibility for homework to the child, encourages independence, and gives positive messages. Rosemond advocates that parents back off and allow their child to do her work all by herself. He advises parents to limit their involvement to clarifying or reinterpreting homework questions, demonstrating a particular procedure, and reviewing or checking work for accuracy and adequacy.

As an overall management approach to homework, Self-Responsibility has you maintaining and communicating high expectations for achievement but handing the responsibility for actually doing the work to your child. Make sure that your child knows how to schedule time, has a place to work, and senses your interest in and enthusiasm for what he is learning. However, your child knows that you trust him to be able to do his work, and he also knows that if he does not understand what to do, or wants feedback on what he has done, you are available.

If you have a child who is underachieving, the upshot of the Self-Responsibility Approach is that you may need to back off completely. It has been said that it is difficult to cure a problem if you continuously compensate for it. Backing off means allowing the responsibility for doing homework to fall squarely on your child's shoulders. By cutting the umbilical cord, you will be allowing your child to do it on his own. Backing off means that your child decides whether or not he will do homework, when he will do it, and how well he will do it. Backing off means allowing your child to walk into class not having done the homework or having produced an inferior product. Backing off means allowing your child to bear the consequences of failure. When your child learns that it isn't much fun to fail, nor is it in her interest, she will begin to motivate herself to do the work for her own sake, not for yours. And when that happens, the homework hassle will have ended.

Rosemond indicates that five out of ten underachieving children whose parents use the Self-Responsibility Approach start to assume personal responsibility within four weeks. For the children who do not, Rosemond advocates the use of the Structured Approach I described earlier in this chapter.

If you decide to adopt the Self-Responsibility Approach with your child, you may well find that for the first two or three weeks the problem gets worse. This frequently happens when parents stop compensating for their child's problems. This will be a difficult time for you, and you should seek the support of your spouse or partner to help you maintain your hands-off attitude.

PARENT REFLECTION SHEET: GETTING HOMEWORK RIGHT

1. In your own words, what is the purpose of homework, and what is its value? Communicate these ideas to your child.

_____

_____

2. What are your observations about whether your child's teachers assign homework consistently? Does there seem to be a school-home policy that has general support?

_____

_____

3. Does your child's school communicate enough with parents about homework?   __Yes   __No

What are some things you would like to know more about? Contact school for answers.

_____

_____

4. How would you describe your homework management methods? Do you employ a Structured Approach, a Self-Responsibility Approach, or a combination thereof?

_____

_____

5. What are some ways you can improve your homework management?

_____

_____

Chapter 12

Tutoring Boosts Achievement

Many children go through one or more periods of their schooling when they feel overwhelmed by the material they have to learn. Sometimes, a child misses out on a period of schooling due to sickness and arrives back at school having to play catch-up. Sometimes, the problem is simply taking a class that is in an area of academic weakness. Some children take a long time to develop the degree of reading proficiency necessary for them to perform well in the many subjects that require reading, such as social studies and English.

There is another group of children who do not quite get what they are being taught in a given class the first time around. These children frequently do not have a linguistic, logical, and sequential learning style. Rather, they approach learning material in a more global, intuitive, or hands-on fashion. Or your child's teacher may have rushed through parts of a lesson, leaving your child somewhat bewildered. It is also possible that the explanation and directions provided by your child's teacher were not as clear as they could have been. Children who have learning difficulties will take longer to learn from written material than do their classmates.

The most common reason that your child might have fallen behind in his academic skills, however, has to do with her motivation and the time she spends actively engaged in learning. Sometimes, for all the different reasons discussed in this book, your child will put off doing his schoolwork or will give up too soon (see chapter 13).

Tutoring Is a Powerful Intervention

The facts are laid out for all to see. Children who receive tutoring do better on the material in which they have been tutored. As a secondary benefit, tutoring can lead to enhanced feelings of self-esteem in the children receiving tutoring. We also know that high achievement is associated with schools in which parents are actively involved in tutoring children both in the classroom and at home.

INDIVIDUAL ATTENTION INCREASES THE LEARNING OF ALL

When children receive individual attention, many develop the inspiration to achieve. Some children use the motivation of wanting to please another to overcome the barriers to learning.

Types of individual attention include:
- mentoring (someone outside family meets on a regular basis with child)
- peer tutoring in class (same age, cross age)
- parent tutoring at home
- academic tutoring by someone outside of home (teacher, university student)
- school-home communication
- teacher-parent individualized learning program

Who Is Qualified to Tutor?

Tutoring is an appropriate intervention for children of all ages. In the lower grades, parents frequently can provide the tutoring. When children enter adolescence, sometimes a familiar person outside of the house can provide tutorial support. When a child enters his last couple of years in school and is taking very demanding high school subjects, a college student or a teacher can provide after-school instruction. In fact, many teachers are interested in earning extra income after school by providing individualized tutoring for children of all ages.

There are some desirable characteristics of a tutor, and there are certain people whom you should not select as a tutor. To be effective, the interaction between your child and the tutor needs to be relaxed and supportive. Some parents, be they mothers or fathers, would not make appropriate choices. For example, if a father is very frustrated with his child or highly anxious because of his child's lack of progress in school or because of behavior problems, then he should not tutor his own child until he makes changes in the way he relates to his child. In instances when both parents are too busy or stressed, an older sibling can often serve as an effective tutor.

As children grow older, some become less receptive to their parents and do not view being tutored by them as a positive experience. In this case, you might seek the tutoring services of an older child in the local community whom your child looks up to. Selecting a tutor of the same sex sometimes works well.

Parents as Tutors

If you and your child are going to work together, it will be important for you to be aware of some dos and don'ts of good tutoring. While tutoring your child does not require that you have a teaching certificate, your own attitude toward your child as he is being tutored will have a large influence on how beneficial your child will find the tutoring.

Working with your child will be a bit like trying to teach your husband, wife, or significant other how to drive a car. To be a good driving teacher, you should have a positive, confident, and relaxed mental approach, have selected an appropriate time and place and suitable vehicle for your driving lesson, know quite clearly what driving instructions to give the learner, and know what to do and say when the learner makes a mistake or does not understand what to do.

So, too, in learning to drive successfully, a learner should have a positive and self-confident mental approach and should be able to cope with the frustrations of making mistakes without worrying too much, losing confidence, or giving up. In addition, it is more likely that someone will learn to drive easily and readily if he remains calm and relaxed during a driving lesson.

Here are some tips to ensure that your work with your child not only will result in a successful outcome for your child, but will be enjoyable for both of you.

1. Before you begin tutoring, do some things to make your child feel good about you and your relationship. There is little point in tutoring your child if you are having major conflicts and heated disagreements. In fact, you will want to consider whether you are the best person to be working with your child.

If your relationship with your child needs some sweetening, consider doing the following: a) stop nagging your child about not doing homework and chores, b) listen to your tone of voice with your child, and if it is a bit harsh, change it to a tone you would use with someone else's child, c) make an extra effort to find some things your child is doing to be positive about, d) spend more time listening to your child rather than offering advice, and e) plan on doing something enjoyable with your son or daughter such as going to a movie or a sporting event.

2. Select an appropriate place and time for tutoring. It will be important for both of you to work together at a time when you are not distracted by other obligations and will not be interrupted by others in the house. Explain to family members that this is a special time that you wish to spend with this child and that you would like everyone's help in not being disturbed. Sundays tend to be especially good times.

I remember a mother of three young boys who complained that she found it impossible to find a suitable place at home to work with her son. Each time she tried to work with her son at the kitchen table, her other two sons would conspire to get her attention by spraying the garden hose through the kitchen window! The mother ended up renting a video that her other sons could watch while she tutored.

3. Use plenty of praise and encouragement. The strategy to ensure that your child profits and enjoys the tutoring sessions with you is to use praise frequently and rarely be critical. When your child is putting forth effort on learning activities, smiling, saying "That's good," and expressing other forms of encouragement will go a long way to ensure success.

4. Avoid negative comments. It is vital that your child experience the tutoring sessions as positively as possible. If you have a tendency to make negative comments rather than pointing out the positive, stick a pencil in your mouth.

5. Expect progress to be slow. Sometimes learning progresses in fits and starts. Your child may appear to be unable to remember any of the material you worked on in the previous session. At other times, he will leap ahead. Be patient.

6. Select tutoring material at an appropriate level of difficulty and interest. You should discuss with your child's teacher the material that would be suitable for you to work on with your child. Whether you are helping your child review math problems, learn new spelling words, read for meaning, or practice written expression, you should aim for ensuring that your child is getting 80 percent of the material correct.

Your child can be very helpful in selecting appropriate material. Take him to the library or educational resource store and select appropriate material together.

In selecting books, it is a good idea to select books from different reading curricula that are suited to your child's level of reading ability. Your child may feel embarrassed if it looks as though what he is learning is designed for much younger children. Be sensitive to his perception and reassure him that the practice on easier material will provide him with the necessary success in order to progress to more age-appropriate books.

7. During each session, be involved, interested, enthusiastic, and positive. There is little point in using the tutoring sessions to catch up on paperwork or daydream while your child is doing schoolwork. The more positive and enthusiastic you are, the more your child will be as well.

8. Don't be discouraged. Persist, persist, persist. During some sessions, your child may appear uninterested, apathetic, or negative. This is fairly normal and is what your child's teachers experience from time to time. Make the best of the session and show up for the next one with a cheerful and optimistic attitude.

Motivating Your Child with Encouragement and Reinforcement

No matter how much you've sweetened things for your child, she will probably not view tutoring as an old friend. After all, you will be going over material with her that she has had trouble learning and that she may continue to have difficulty in mastering. Often, children balk at actually attending a tutoring session.

You will need to have on hand external motivational methods (see chapter 4). Basically, you should consistently reinforce your child when he demonstrates that he is trying hard or has learned something from the material being covered in the session. In the first few tutoring sessions, you can afford to be very generous in your encouragement and praise. As much as possible, respond enthusiastically when you notice your child paying attention and working.

TWENTY-FIVE WAYS TO ENCOURAGE AND PRAISE YOUR CHILD

"I like the way you handled that."

"It's hard, but you will get it. I know you will."

"You have worked very hard on that. You must feel very good."

"You have worked very hard on that. I am very pleased."

"You're really improving; you didn't know this yesterday, and you know it today."

"I can see you are learning more and more each day."

"That's a hard one; don't worry about it."

"You may not feel that you have reached your goal, but look how far you've come."

"You have done a very good job."

"I am very pleased with your progress."

"Excellent answer."

"That's right."

"You are one hundred percent correct."

"You did that just right."

"Perfect."

"I couldn't have done it better myself."

"You can be proud of yourself."

"You are showing improvement."

"Outstanding effort."

"Good progress."

"Good thinking."

"We had a good day."

"I like the way you are working."

"You're working especially well."

"I knew you could do that well."

You may also elect to employ an incentive plan using token reinforcement. A formal way to use token reinforcement is the Token Game, which countless parents of elementary school children have used to motivate their children with learning problems to do their work. In this game, both you and your child decide on goals for a tutoring session. You agree to pay your child a certain number of tokens after she has achieved her goals. As a part of this game, you and your child decide on the types of privileges she can purchase for cashing in different amounts of tokens she has earned. After each reading session, you should give your child the number of tokens (buttons, marbles) she has earned. Your child can then store up tokens, and at whatever time she wishes, she can purchase any of the privileges.

An example of goals and privileges worked out for a child, as well as the specific rules for the Token Game, are presented below.

Rules for the Token Game

A. Decide on concrete goals for your child. Set token amounts so that your child can earn tokens right away. As he earns many tokens, you can readjust token amounts to make them more difficult to earn. For example:

Goal	Token Payoff
1. twenty minutes of reading with parent	3
2. thirty minutes of reading alone	3
3. reading three new sight vocabulary words on each of three consecutive nights	1 per word
4. correct spelling of new words	1 per word

B. Select a range of "expensive" and "inexpensive" privileges. For example:

Privileges	Token Amount
1. movie on weekend	20
2. staying up extra thirty minutes	7
3. favorite dessert	5
4. comic book	12
5. new bicycle	400

C. Decide goals, payoffs, and privileges at the beginning of the week. Clearly explain them to your child. Make no negotiations during the week.

D. As soon as your child earns tokens, he should immediately receive them.

E. Impose no arbitrary fines. Do not take tokens away unless this is indicated in advance as a penalty (missing a reading session).

F. When your child wants to cash tokens in, try to give him the privilege as soon as possible.

This weekly chart enables you and your child to keep track of the number of tokens he has earned during each session:

WEEKLY TOKEN GAME								
Goals	Mon.	Tues.	Wed.	Thurs.	Fri.	Sat.	Sun.
1							
2							
3							
4							
Total	___	___	___	___	___	___	___
Total for Week ___								

The Tutoring Session

The tutoring session will consist of you and your child sitting together at an appropriate time and place, working on suitable academic material. You should take care to select a time when both you and your child are free from distractions, and you should bring to the tutoring sessions the attitudes that will help both of you be successful.

The positive Habits of the Mind you should bring to tutoring include:

- Be confident in your ability to be successful.
- Have high expectations that you have the capabilities to acquire the skills necessary to tutor your child.
- Expect that some tutoring sessions will be unpleasant and hard.
- Expect that your child will make mistakes, will forget material learned yesterday, and will make very slow progress.
- Concentrate on making your tutoring sessions as enjoyable as possible for you and your child.
- Attribute your successful tutoring sessions to your own effort and persistence.

The positive Habits of the Mind to encourage in your child during the tutoring sessions are:

- I can do it.
- Just because I'm having difficulty with my work doesn't mean I'll never learn.
- Learning depends on my hard work and trying hard.
- When I learn something, it is because I tried hard to get good at it.
- Hard work may be unpleasant, but it has to be done.
- Making mistakes is a natural part of learning and does not mean I'm hopeless or stupid.

Remind your child about five minutes before you are ready that it is almost time for the tutoring session and suggest that he collect his work material. I suggest that you sit side by side with your child on your left, as this is more comfortable for right-handed people (or, if you are left-handed, have your child on your right).

During the initial tutoring sessions, I suggest that you do not try to accomplish too much. It is important that each of you enjoy the sessions as much as possible. Rather than trying to do too much specific teaching, learn to listen to your child and observe his approach to his work without jumping in too quickly. The early sessions can also be used to practice your own encouragement and reinforcement skills.

SOME REMINDERS ABOUT HOW TO LISTEN TO YOUR CHILD READ

1. When your child makes a mistake in reading a new word, you should try to help him to correct himself wherever possible. If this is not possible, clearly pronounce the word for him.
2. When your child misreads a word he knew before, you should encourage him to sound it out.
3. When your child misreads a relatively unimportant word, but pronounces it smoothly, you should ignore the mistake.
4. When your child has trouble reading a word (falters, hesitates), you should not prod or hurry him.
5. When your child makes a mistake, you should not make a negative comment or react negatively.
6. To help your child pronounce an unfamiliar word, have him pronounce the first and last sounds and then reread the unfamiliar word. Alternatively, you can encourage your child to read the other words in the sentence and then, along with pronouncing the first sound, predict what the unfamiliar word is.
7. When your child gets the right answer or reads smoothly, you should make a positive comment and react positively.

—S. Gillet & M. E. Bernard, *Reading Rescue*

It is very important for you to monitor your child's learning progress from session to session. Whether it is the number of words spelled correctly, math problems correctly computed, or questions correctly answered from silent reading, your child needs to receive feedback. Remember, you want your child to acquire as quickly as possible the belief that the harder she tries, the more she learns.

Evaluating Your Tutoring Effectiveness

One way to determine how effective you are as a tutor is to examine yourself to see whether you are using good teaching strategies. The Parent Teaching Effectiveness Self-Report Form has been employed by many parents to judge their success as tutors in the area of reading instruction. I suggest that you complete the form after your first tutoring session. You can identify areas of strength and weakness. Then, complete the form again some time later to judge your own progress as a tutor. You can modify the form to correspond with the age of your child and the area that you have chosen for tutoring.

Parent Teaching Effectiveness Self-Report Form

Directions: This form is to be filled out immediately after you have finished your teaching session. Read each statement and then circle the number that indicates your answer. Please answer all statements. Give your first impression. Do not spend too much time on any one statement. If you are not sure, make your best guess. There are no right or wrong answers.

Your name _____

Today's date _____

	Almost Never	Some-times	Often	Almost always
During the session				
1. I smiled.	1	2	3	4
2. I scowled and gave critical looks	1	2	3	4
3. I used a negative (harsh, loud) tone of voice	1	2	3	4
4. I made a negative comment.	1	2	3	4
5. I made different positive comments	1	2	3	4
6. I touched and patted my child	1	2	3	4
7. I sighed with despair.	1	2	3	4
8. I used a positive, warm tone of voice	1	2	3	4
9. I made different negative comments	1	2	3	4
10. I nodded encouragement.	1	2	3	4
11. I made a positive comment.	1	2	3	4
12. I shook my head negatively	1	2	3	4
13. I was relaxed	1	2	3	4
14. I was angry	1	2	3	4
15. I was frustrated.	1	2	3	4

Self-Report Form (continued)

	Almost Never	Sometimes	Often	Almost always
During the session				
16. I was confident	1	2	3	4
17. I was happy	1	2	3	4
18. I helped my child to correct his/her error when he/she made a mistake (or pronounced the word calmly)........	1	2	3	4
19. I rushed my child when he/she made a mistake	1	2	3	4
20. I made a positive comment when my child got the right answer	1	2	3	4
21. I ignored it when my child misread but pronounced smoothly a new word ...	1	2	3	4
22. I reacted positively (smiled, nodded) when my child got the right answer......	1	2	3	4
23. I encouraged my child to sound it out when he/she misread a word he/she knew	1	2	3	4
24. I reacted negatively (scowled, sighed, looked critical) when my child made a mistake	1	2	3	4
25. I made a negative comment when my child made a mistake	1	2	3	4

Other comments:

_____

_____

_____

PARENT REFLECTION SHEET: TUTORING YOUR CHILD

1. List all subjects that your child is studying in which you think tutoring might help boost her achievement:

   _____

   _____

   _____

   _____

2. Place a check next to the reason(s) why your child has fallen behind in that subject or is not doing as well as she could.

   __ missed school days __ child's diverse learning style

   __ child's area of academic weakness __ child doesn't try hard enough

   __ learning difficulties __ teacher does not explain material clearly

3. Who would be a suitable person to tutor your child? Why?

   possible tutor _____

   reason _____

4. Who would not be a suitable tutor? Why?

   possible tutor _____

   reason _____

5. What are some daily or weekly incentives you could provide your child, if necessary, to motivate your child to attend tutoring sessions and try hard?

   _____

   _____

6. Tutoring at home is done best if it occurs two to three times a week. What times and days would suit your child?

   _____

   _____

CHAPTER 13

HELPING YOUR CHILD TO PUT OFF PUTTING OFF SCHOOLWORK

Over the years I have met many children, especially those in the upper grades, who, despite their best of intentions, must struggle to get going in certain subjects. While they do well in subjects that they like, in subjects that fall outside of their interest and that they do not enjoy, their motivation lags and their grades drop off. What is troubling to both their parents and the students themselves is that they know that by putting off their work until the last minute they are, as a consequence, underperforming on assignments and classroom tests. Student grade point average declines, and comments from teachers in these subjects are less than generous. ("If Jamie was more conscientious in doing her work, she would be one of the better students in class.")

The World of Academic Procrastination

As students work their way up the academic ladder, researchers have noticed, there is an increase in what has been termed "academic procrastination." Procrastination is the tendency for people to delay doing things even when they see the disadvantages in the delay. Academic procrastination is in evidence when students delay or avoid doing their schoolwork even though they know that they should be doing it and that because of not doing it, they pay a price.

In thinking about your child, ask yourself how successful he is in motivating himself to do work he doesn't feel like doing. If your child dislikes history, or a foreign language, or advanced mathematics, does he put off doing his work until the very last minute (or beyond), or is he able to rise to the occasion and get the work done when it has to get done and do it well?

Early research on academic procrastination focused largely on the absence of study skills in procrastinators. More recently, research has focused on illuminating differences between high and low procrastinators in terms of their emotional states and patterns of thinking. We now know that some students who procrastinate are likely to have a fear of failure that includes anxiety about meeting the expectations of their parents, teachers, and friends, a lack of self-confidence, a lack of assertiveness skills, and low self-esteem. An even larger group of students procrastinate due to the unpleasantness of the task. That is, rather than worrying about not being able to be successful at their work, these students are turned off by the boredom and frustration they experience while working on the task. In comparison with low academic procrastinators, high academic procrastinators experience more anxiety, are more likely to attribute their success on exams to external and fleeting circumstances rather than to their own ability and effort, lack a strong belief in their ability to be successful at the task they are putting off, and appear to have less control over their emotional reactions.

What Children Have to Say About Motivation

Recently, my wife and I asked 400 students, eight through seventeen years of age, three questions concerning what motivates them and what blocks their motivation. Their answers about what turns them on or off are summarized in a few categories.

STUDENTS SPEAK

"The challenge of really doing something great with my ideas. Experimenting with different styles and ways of writing and when the results come back with a good grade, I really feel good inside." Carissa, age fourteen

"Thinking about having my work finished and the thought of relaxing without feeling guilty." Karen, age seventeen

"Seeing the good points of everything like getting good marks, self-satisfaction, and seeing the end result." Mary, age fifteen

"The thing that motivates me the most is getting a good grade." Margaret, age fifteen

"When I think about what my goal is and I know that I have to do the work to reach my goal." Paul, age fourteen

"What motivates me most is when I do something at the best of my ability and get good marks for that piece of work, I know that I understand the topic and that I will continue to be successful in that area and be successful in the future." Greg, age fourteen

"The thing that motivates me the most is the thought of failing." Jason, age sixteen

"The things that motivate me to do my work is knowing that by getting better marks, I can be proud of myself." Elisha, age thirteen

"Thinking about later years and what sort of job I would get if I didn't get my schoolwork done." Paul, age fourteen

> **STUDENTS SPEAK (CONTINUED)**
>
> "Doing all my homework in one day so I have the whole week to play with my friends. I do all my work in school so that I do not have to stay in at play time and do my work. Also, I think about my report and that I will get a better score if I finish my work and make my parents proud of me." Alexandra, age eight

Question 1: "What motivates me the most?" The students' most common answers are grouped below. The answers are ordered from most frequent to least.

1. Working toward future goals (getting into a good university, getting a good job)
2. Subjects that are fun and interesting
3. Working in order to receive a good grade
4. Self-reward after work completed (watch TV, play sport, do something fun)
5. Listening to music
6. Teachers who are fun
7. Parents and teachers who help student understand assignment
8. Time pressure of an impending deadline
9. Getting work over with
10. Pleasing parents
11. Fear of punishment

In many ways, this group of students confirmed what we predicted. Students are motivated both by extrinsic factors (grades, future) as well as intrinsic factors (teachers, work that is fun and exciting). Their answers reflect more self-interest than we predicted. That is, rather than doing their schoolwork just to please others, today's students have their

STUDENTS SPEAK

"The television and laziness." Richard, age fourteen

"The thing that stops me most is if the work is boring and the teacher is talking all the time." Carl, age fifteen

"When people annoy me or some type of interruption." Greg, age seventeen

"Other activities such as TV, motorbike riding, etc." Paul, fourteen

"Constant distractions, wanting to have fun all the time, TV and computer games." Colin, age fourteen

"In class, my friends stop me from being motivated because we just talk." Amanda, age fourteen

"Thinking of the bad points of working, like it's too hard and it will take a long time and it's not worth doing." Sharon, age sixteen

"On Saturdays, I always think 'I've always got tomorrow,' but I don't. This is very annoying and is poor time management. I want to do everything, but I procrastinate sometimes. If I have a study planner, I find that I do my homework and do it well. If I don't have a planner, I don't get motivated." Camille, age thirteen

"Extracurricular activities like sports, TV, going out, things like that." Warren, age fourteen

eye on their future and on what they have to do to be successful. And a surprisingly large number of students have learned how to reward themselves for a job well done.

Question 2: "What stops me from being motivated to do my work?" These are the most popular reasons for lack of motivation:

1. Boring work
2. Television

3. Wanting to do something else (fun activities)
4. Outside distractions (family visitors, dog, noise in house)
5. Social life (friends)
6. Tiredness
7. Other students talking in class
8. Teachers who student dislikes

The parents of these students do not appear to have a negative impact on their motivation. The prominence of television as a barrier to motivation suggests the need for parents to restrict television viewing. You will

---

STUDENTS SPEAK

"If the work is really boring, I just think of the end product, which may be a good test result or an A for an assignment." Amanda, age fourteen

"When my work is boring, I like to get it over and done with. When it is hard, I like to think of it as a challenge. When it takes a long time, I like to think of the end result of completing the work." Sharon, age fifteen

"The thing is to know that I am near the end and to prove to myself I can do the work." Ben, age fourteen

"By thinking that in the end you get rewarded. There is a saying: 'What you put into it is what you get out of it.'" Jason, age sixteen

"I concentrate hard and think how good I will feel when I finish and the grade I will get." Mike, age thirteen

"It helps me to break the work into smaller units. Thinking small, not about how dull or long it may be. The overall picture may be scary, but by taking it one step at a time, it seems less." Elly, age fifteen

> **STUDENTS SPEAK (CONTINUED)**
>
> "Wanting to get it done so I don't feel stressed out." Colin, age seventeen
>
> "Thinking about the reward I will get when I reach my goal." Paul, age fourteen
>
> "I think of what I can have when it's all done. No more homework!! (I can go out and play basketball, watch TV)." Warren, age seventeen
>
> "Listening to music for a while—it relaxes me." Paul, age fourteen
>
> "When my work gets boring or too hard I just talk to my friend for a few minutes and then try to get back to work. But if that doesn't work, I try to think of the punishment I will get if I don't finish my work." Elisha, age thirteen

want to monitor and where necessary restrict the amount of time your child spends with friends. You may also need to take steps to make sure your child gets to bed at a reasonable hour.

Question 3: "What helps me to stay motivated when the work is boring, hard, or takes a long time to finish?" These are methods that students mentioned most frequently as motivating them to do work they do not feel like doing:

1. Thinking about achieving my short-term and long-term goals (college, job)
2. Thinking about getting a good grade
3. Taking little breaks and coming back to work
4. Listening to music
5. Avoiding punishment
6. Positive thinking; thinking I can do it.

It is clear that certain coping skills help your child get through the stress of doing hard or boring work. Being able to listen to music appears to be very important, as does scheduling short breaks. Clearly, it helps if your child has a sense of the relationship of her current schoolwork to her long-term goals, and knows the consequences of academic procrastination.

Goal Setting

In chapter 7, I described in some detail the basic ideas involved in teaching your child to get in the habit of setting goals. As these students know, it is very helpful for children to have their goals clearly in mind when they are faced with frustrating, time-consuming, and boring schoolwork that they could easily put off. You may want to have your child think through her specific academic goals in all her school subjects at the beginning of each school semester.

STUDENT WORKSHEET: "TAKING CONTROL OF YOUR FUTURE: SETTING GOALS"

DIRECTIONS: In the boxes below, write down what you'd like to have achieved by the time you are thirty years of age, by the end of this school year, and by the end of today. Do this in the areas of your education, your career/work, and your personal life (the kind of person you'd like to be). Don't worry if you find this a bit hard to do; it's not supposed to be easy! Start off by writing down your goals at age thirty. Make them big!

	Education Goals	Career/Work Goals	Personal Goals	
long-term goals at thirty				These are your LONG-TERM GOALS. Now for each of these, what do you need to do in the next six months or year to help you reach these goals? Make these goals realistic.
short-term goals this year				These are your SHORT-TERM GOALS. Think of them as your stepping stones to success. Now, write down some things you can do today to help you achieve your short-term goals. Make these goals specific (e.g., how much work you'll do; the amount of time spent working; the grade you wish to receive on your assignment).
daily goals for today				These DAILY GOALS will start you on your road to success.

For older children, it is useful for them to have considered their long-term goals, short-term goals, and daily goals in the areas of their education, career, and personal life (the kind of person they would like to be). The "Taking Control of Your Future: Setting Goals" form allows a teenager to concretely consider and write down goals. You can use the form for discussion or have your child spend some time actually completing it to the best of his ability. Some children who have never spent time considering their goals will find it difficult to provide all the information requested on the form. Give your child reassurance that she only needs to fill in as much information as she can. You can work together over an extended period of time to complete it.

Ripping Up Excuses

If your child procrastinates in doing schoolwork, it is very likely that he is pretty talented at making up excuses for why he hasn't done the work. What is interesting about the tendency of procrastinators to make up excuses is that they make the excuses up for themselves so that they do not have to feel guilty about procrastinating. The excuses are, in fact, rationalizations that protect the procrastinator. Probably the most popular excuse is "I'll do it tomorrow." By making this excuse, the procrastinator can lull himself into a false sense of comfort and security that comes with imagining the task being accomplished tomorrow. Unfortunately, when tomorrow comes, the procrastinator will, if at all possible, invoke the same rationalization and will put off the work again until the following day.

STUDENT WORKSHEET: "NO EXCUSE FOR EXCUSES"

DIRECTIONS: Sometimes we make up excuses for why we put off doing our work. The excuses make it easier for us to avoid doing work that we don't feel like doing. Below is a list of common excuses. Place a check mark next to the excuses that you use when you are not motivated. If you want to get motivated and be more successful, the excuses have to go!

EXCUSES

	(check)	
	This is me	Not me
I'll do it tomorrow when I feel more motivated.	____	____
It will be easier for me to do this work when I have lots of pressure, so I'll put it off until the last minute.	____	____
I don't know how to do this work properly. I won't attempt it until I know how to do it correctly.	____	____
The world won't come to an end if I put off my work.	____	____
I'll find this work easier to do when I'm in the mood, so I'll wait for that time and do it then.	____	____
I did my work once at the very last minute and I did very well, so why not do it the same way again?	____	____
If I do this work at the last minute instead of right away, I won't have to spend too much time on it, and therefore, I will save myself a good deal of time.	____	____
I'm feeling tired. I'll rest and do my work when I'm fresh.	____	____
I cannot miss out on tonight's fun. My work can wait.	____	____
No one really cares whether I do this work or not, so I may as well keep putting it off.	____	____

Other favorite excuses:

_____

_____

_____

In order for your child to overcome academic procrastination, he will need to stop making excuses. Once he does, he can then use one or more techniques that can help him tackle his schoolwork in a timely fashion. "No Excuse for Excuses" is an activity that your child can complete and discuss with you and that will help both of you identify your child's most frequent excuses for avoiding schoolwork.

Techniques for Helping Your Child Put Off Putting Off Schoolwork

With goals in mind and excuses left behind, your child can start to learn techniques for breaking through barriers to her achievement. The techniques are easy to understand. The challenge for your child is getting in the habit of using them when she is faced with work she does not feel like doing.

Technique 1: Knock-Out Technique. The harder and more boring the work, the better it is to do it immediately just to get it out of the way. Have your child identify those different assignments at which he could apply this technique.

Technique 2: Worst-First Approach. Identify the most difficult part of an assignment and do that first. The logic of the Worst-First Approach is the same as the Knock-Out Technique. Get the most unpleasant schoolwork over with first. Sometimes, your child will procrastinate in doing even the easiest part of homework because of the anxiety associated with having to do the difficult parts. Sit down with an assignment or project that your child has been putting off. Have him describe the different things he has to do and tell you which activities he finds the hardest. Encourage your child to get onto those parts immediately.

Technique 3: Bits and Pieces Approach. Sometimes your child procrastinates because of feeling overwhelmed by the size of an assignment. This is especially a problem if your child is a perfectionist who believes that she has to know exactly what to do before starting. In using this approach, your child does anything in connection with the assignment she has to do. Gradually your child should do more and more until the assignment doesn't seem so impossible.

Technique 4. Salami Technique. Explain that just as a salami looks much more appetizing after it has been sliced into bite-sized pieces, so, too, does a large project seem more manageable after it has been broken down into simpler parts. You can use the techniques of task analysis described in chapter 7 to teach your child this method. Have your child list all the different parts he has to do to complete a project or assignment. Have him work on one part at a time until he has completed all of them.

Technique 5: Remember-Forgetting Technique. Some children who procrastinate have difficulties in organizing in their heads everything they have to do on a given day or in a particular time period. Some children's ideas appear to float in and out of their immediate consciousness. If your child seems to be disorganized and forgets important things to do in relationship to homework, teach her that whenever she remembers forgetting to do something, to do at least some of it immediately.

Technique 6: Five-Minute Plan. One of the most popular techniques for children who have difficulty getting started with an assignment is the Five-Minute Plan, which involves your child's taking something he has been putting off doing and agreeing to work on it for five minutes a day. Once he has worked on it for five minutes, he should agree to work for another five minutes and then another five minutes.

By the time he has worked for fifteen minutes, he will be well into the work, and it will not seem so bad.

Technique 7: Switching. In switching, your child learns to take the momentum she has gained from doing one activity that she really enjoys and immediately switching over to an activity she's been putting off. If your daughter loves skateboarding and hates her math homework, have her come in and start to work on her math immediately after an energetic ride.

Technique 8: Premack Procedure. As distinct from Switching, the Premack Procedure (named after a scientist who discovered it) involves your child's selecting an activity he really enjoys and not allowing himself to participate in the activity until after he has finished his homework. So, for example, your child agrees to only play computer games after he has done his homework for the night.

Technique 9: Referenting. Children who procrastinate tend to think about the advantages of not doing their work and the disadvantages of doing it. In Referenting, your child reverses this pattern of thought by writing down all the good things that will happen when she does her work and all bad things which will happen if she doesn't. Your child should then review this list regularly.

Technique 10: Establishing a Set Time. I have already mentioned that underachieving children make up their mind when they will study after they come home from school and generally when they are in the mood. This is a trap that leads to running out of study time. Encourage your child to schedule a set time to begin work ahead of time. And regardless of whether he is in the mood or not or if there are other temptations, that is when your child should begin studying.

Technique 11: Establishing Priorities. Your child needs to know which of the things he has to do are most important and which are least important. Have your child write down all the assignments that are due in the next week. Then, have him write down all the things he wants to do after school and on the weekend. Have him place a number 1 next to the most important things, a 2 next to the fairly important things, and a 3 next to the not very important things.

Technique 12: Isolation. I have shown that students perceive distractions as major impediments to doing homework. Your child needs to learn how to isolate herself from distractions when she has work to do that she doesn't feel like doing. The exception to this rule is music, which seems to relax children, keep them company, and reduce the overall unpleasant ambience surrounding certain homework tasks. Your child needs to be able to tell her friends that she has work to do just as she needs to be able to reschedule television viewing for after she has done her work.

Technique 13: Visible Reminders. Some children profit from having visual reminders about schoolwork in their room. Your child may wish to put up small signs in his room that remind him of the work he has to do: I CAN DO IT; DO IT NOW; and PUT OFF PUTTING IT OFF.

Many parents have helped their children conquer academic procrastination. It helps for a parent to understand the underlying reasons for their child's procrastination before prescribing a cure. You will want to have a sense whether your child's procrastination is caused by fear of not being able to do the work well, the inability to tolerate the frustration of homework and postponing having fun, poor time management, or hostility about having to do the work at all. The Habits of the Mind you are now equipped to teach will help you encourage your child to tackle any or all of these obstacles. In addition, the techniques presented in this final chapter will also help empower you to empower your child to develop the motivation necessary so your child can realize his potential not only in schoolwork, but in all areas of his present and future life.

You make the difference in how well your child achieves at school. By being informed, involved, firm, affectionate, and calm, you will have what it takes to provide your child with the foundation for achievement. Through your effort and persistence, you can help turn your dreams and your child's goals into reality.

REFERENCES

Chapter One

Steinberg, L., Dornbusch, S., & Brown, B. (1996). *Beyond the Classroom.* New York: Summit Books.

Stevenson, H., & Stigler, J. (1992). *The Learning Gap.* New York: Summit Books.

Chapter Four

Bernard, P. C., & Bernard, M. E. (1993). *The You Can Do It! Little Book for Parents.* North Blackburn, Victoria, Australia: Collins-Dove.

Biddulph, S. (1988). *The Secret of Happy Children.* Sydney, New South Wales, Australia: Bay Books.

Gottfried, A. E., Fleming, J. S., & Gottfried, A. W. (1994). "Role of Parental Motivational Practices in Children's Academic Intrinsic Motivation and Achievement." *Journal of Educational Psychology* 86, 104–113.

Spaulding C. L (1992). *Motivation in the Classroom.* New York: McGraw-Hill.

Woulff, N. (1983). "Involving the Family in the Treatment of the Child: A Model for Rational-Emotive Therapists." In A. Ellis and M. E. Bernard (eds.), *Rational-Emotive Approaches to the Problems of Childhood.* New York: Plenum Press.

Chapter Five

Bernard, M. E. (1996). *Teacher Guide to Boosting Student Motivation. Self-Esteem and School Achievement.* Oakleigh, Victoria, Australia: Australian Scholarships Group.

Sonna, L. A. (1990). *The Homework Solution.* Charlotte, Vermont: Williamson Publishing.

Chapter Six

Bernard, M. E., & Cartwright, R. C. (1995). *Program Achieve: A Curriculum of Lessons for Teaching Students How to Be Successful in School and Life.* Vols. 4–6. Oakleigh, Victoria, Australia: Anglo Scholarships Group.

Bernard, M. E., Linscott, J. L., & Nicholson, J. (1995). *Program Achieve: A Curriculum of Lessons for Teaching Students How to Be Successful in School and Life.* Vols. 1–3. Oakleigh, Victoria, Australia: Anglo Scholarships Group.

Chapter Seven

Bernard, M. E. (1991). *Staying Rational in an Irrational World.* New York: Carol Publishing.

———. (1994). *You Can Do It! Student Guide: Tips, Ideas and Activities for Every Student to Become Successful and Happy in School and in Life.* Tampa, Florida: You Can Do It! Education.

Ellis, A. (1994). *Reason and Emotion in Psychotherapy* (rev. ed.). New York: Carol Publishing.

McCombs, B. L., & Pope, J. E. (1994). *Motivating Hard to Reach Students.* Washington, D.C.: American Psychological Association.

Shure M. B. (1994). *Raising a Thinking Child.* New York: Henry Holt.

Chapter Eight

Holland, J. L. (1974). *SDS: Self-Directed Search.* Odessa, Florida: Psychological Assessment Resources.

———. (1992) *Making Vocational Choices: A Theory of Vocational Personalities and Work Environments.* Odessa, Florida: Psychological Assessment Resources.

———. (1994). *The Occupations Finder.* Odessa, Florida: Psychological Assessment Resources.

Rosen, D., Holmberg, K., & Holland, J. (1994). *The Educational Opportunities Finder.* Odessa, Florida: Psychological Assessment Resources.

Chapter Nine

Adderholdt-Elliott, M. (1987). *Perfectionism: What's Bad About Being Too Good?* Minneapolis, Minnesota: Free Spirit Publishing.

Chess, S., & Thomas, A. (1986). *Temperament in Clinical Practice.* New York: Guilford Press.

Coil, C. (1992). *Motivating Underachievers.* Beavercreek, Ohio: Pieces of Learning.

Mandel, H. P., & Marcus, S. I. (1988). *The Psychology of Underachievement.* New York: John Wiley.

Mandel, H. P., Marcus, S. I., & Mandel, D. E. (1992). *Helping the Non-Achievement Syndrome Student: A Clinical Training Manual.* Toronto, Canada: Institute on Achievement and Motivation.

Rimm, S. B. (1986). *Underachievement Syndrome: Causes and Cures.* Watertown, Wisconsin: Apple Publishing.

———. (1990). *How to Parent So Children Will Learn.* Watertown, Wisconsin: Apple Publishing.

Scott, S. (1986). *How to Say No and Keep Your Friends.* Amherst, Massachusetts: Human Resource Development Press.

Chapter Ten

Alvino, J. (1985). *Parents' Guide to Raising a Gifted Child.* New York: Ballantine Books.

Bain, L. J. (1991). *A Parent Guide to Attention Deficit Disorders.* New York: Dell Books.

Cogen, V. (1990). *Boosting the Underachiever.* New York: Plenum Press.

Farnham-Diggory, S. (1978). *Learning Disabilities.* London, U.K.: Fontana/Open Books.

Fuller, C. (1994). *Unlocking Your Child's Learning Potential.* Colorado Springs, Colorado: Navpress.

Healy, J. M. (1994). *Your Child's Growing Mind.* New York: Doubleday.

Smith, S. (1980). *No Easy Answers: The Learning Disabled Child at Home and at School.* New York: Bantam Books.

Torrance, E. P. (1962). *Guiding Creative Talent.* Englewood Cliffs, New Jersey: Prentice-Hall.

Umansky, W., & Smalley, B. S. (1994). *ADD: Helping Your Child.* New York: Warner Books.

Weill, M. (1995). "Helping Students with Attention Problems: Strategies for Parents." Washington, D.C.: National Association for School Psychologists.

Chapter Eleven

Bernard, M. E., & Hajzler, D. J. (1987). *You Can Do It! What Every Student (and Parent) Should Know About Success in School and Life.* North Blackburn, Victoria, Australia: Collins-Dove.

Canter, L., & Hausner, L. (1987). *Homework Without Tears.* New York: Harper & Row.

Costa, R. L., & Garmston, R. J. (1994). *Cognitive Coaching: A Foundation for Renaissance Schools.* Norwood, California: Christopher-Gordon.

Evered, R., & Selman, J. (1989). "Coaching and the Art of Management." *Organizational Dynamics* 18, 16–32.

Olympia, D. E., et al. (1992). "Training Parents to Facilitate Homework Completion." In S. L. Christenson & J. C. Conoley (eds.), *Home-School Collaboration: Enhancing Children's Academic and Social Competence.* Silver Spring, Maryland: National Association of School Psychologists.

———. (1994). "Homework: A Natural Means of Home-School Collaboration." *School Psychology Quarterly* 9, 60–80.

Rosemond, J. (1990). *Ending the Homework Hassle.* Kansas City, Kansas: Andrews and McMeel.

Chapter Twelve

Gillet, S., & Bernard, M. E. (1989). *Reading Rescue: A Parents' Guide.* Hawthorn, Victoria, Australia: Australian Council for Educational Research.

Chapter Thirteen

Bernard, M. E. (1991). *Procrastinate Later!* Melbourne, Victoria, Australia: Schwartz-Wilkinson.

Rothblum, E. D., Solomon, L. J., & Murakami, J. (1986). "Affective, Cognitive and Behavioral Differences Between Low and High Procrastinators." *Journal of Counseling Psychology* 33, 388–394.

Solomon, L. J., & Rothblum, E. D. (1984). "Academic Procrastination: Frequency and Cognitive-Behavioral Correlates." *Journal of Counseling Psychology* 31, 503–509.

Additional Resources Developed by Michael E. Bernard

Student Development Programs

You Can Do It! A Motivational and Personal Development Program to Increase Children's Achievement and Happiness in School and Life (12 yrs. old+). Tampa, Florida: You Can Do It! Education. (Sixty-minute video, Leader's Guide, Student Guide.)

The You Can Do It! Audio-Cassette Student Motivational Program (12 yrs. old+). (Four audiocassettes.)

Program Achieve: A Curriculum of Lessons for Teaching Students How to Be Successful in School and Life. Vol. 1 (grades 1–2). Vol. 2 (grades 3–4), Vol. 3 (grades 5–6), Vol. 4 (grades 7–8), Vol. 5 (grades 9–10), Vol 6. (grades 11–12+).

School Professional Development Programs

The You Can Do It! Professional Development Program: Improving Student Motivation and School Achievement: A Professional Development for Teachers, Special Educators, School Administrators and Student Service Personnel. (Over 300 pages including 150 overheads/handouts.) Designed for use in in-service days and other professional development activities.

- Module 1: Educational Under-Achievement and Student Motivation
- Module 2: Habits of the Mind
- Module 3: Best Practices in Student Achievement and Motivation
- Module 4: Best Practices in Working with Individual Students

Parent Education Programs

The You Can Do It! Parent Education Program: What Parents Need to Know (and Do) to Boost Their Children's Motivation and Achievement. (Over 600 pages including 200 overheads/handouts.) Thirteen modules (23 sessions) designed for use in parent information nights, parent education classes, and parent communication.

Interested individuals and organizations wishing to learn more about You Can Do It! Education or to receive a catalogue of resources should contact You Can Do It! Education:
P.O. Box 4496
Laguna Beach, CA 92651-2033
Toll Free: 1-888-808-DOIT
Fax: 714-497-1920

In Canada, contact:
Hindle & Associates
125 Hard Island Road
RR #4, Athens, Ont., Canada K0E 1B0
Toll Free: 1-800-815-1594
Fax: 613-924-1388

About the Author

Michael E. Bernard, Ph.D., is a recognized international authority in the area of children's learning, motivation, and achievement. After graduating from the University of Wisconsin, Madison, in 1975, with a Ph.D. in educational psychology, he took a position in the Faculty of Education, University of Melbourne, Australia. Dr. Bernard spent the following eighteen years as a professor and, eventually, director of the Master of Educational Psychology program, which trains psychologists to work in educational settings. In 1983, he became a co-director of the Australian Institute for Rational-Emotive Behavior Therapy. In 1990, he founded You Can Do It! Education, an approach to parenting and teaching designed to help all children realize their potential at school and in other areas of their lives.

While in Australia Michael Bernard had extensive experience in working as a counselor and psychologist with children and their families in order to provide new ways to help children be successful at school.

Michael Bernard is the author of many professional articles, chapters of books, and over twenty books, including *You Can Do It! What Every Student (and Parent) Should Know About Success in School and Life; Reading Rescue: A Parents' Guide; Taking the Stress Out of Teaching; The Teacher Guide to Boosting Student Motivation, Self-Esteem and School Achievement; Rational-Emotive Therapy with Children and Adolescents; Procrastinate Later!: How to Motivate Yourself to Do It Now;* and *Staying Rational in an Irrational World.*

Michael Bernard is currently associate professor in the College of Education at California State University, Long Beach. He is happily married to Patricia Bernard and is the proud father of two children, Jonathon and Alexandra.